LAN
ACQU
BY EYE

LANGUAGE ACQUISITION BY EYE

Edited by

Charlene Chamberlain
McGill University

Jill P. Morford
University of New Mexico

Rachel I. Mayberry
McGill University

Psychology Press
Taylor & Francis Group

New York   London

First Published by Lawrence Erlbaum Associates, Inc., Publishers

Published 2009 by Psychology Press
711 Third Avenue, New York, NY 10017
27 Church Road, Hove, East Sussex BN3 2FA, UK

First issued in paperback 2014

Psychology Press is an imprint of the Taylor and Francis Group, an informa business

Lawrence Erlbaum Associates, Inc., Publishers
10 Industrial Avenue
Mahwah, New Jersey 07430

Cover design by Kathryn Houghtaling Lacey

Library of Congress Cataloging-in-Publication Data

Language acquisition by eye / edited by Charlene Chamberlain, Jill P.
Morford, Rachel I. Mayberry.
    P. cm.
    Includes bibliographical references (p.) and indexes
    ISBN 0-8058-2937-7   (cloth : alk. paper)
    1. Sign language. 2. Language acquisition.   I. Chamberlain,
Charlene. II. Morford, Jill Patterson, 1963- . III. Mayberry,
Rachel I.
HV2474.L33   1999
419--dc21   99-30894
                                                    CIP

ISBN 13: 978-0-8058-2937-2 (hbk)
ISBN 13: 978-1-138-00307-1 (pbk)

Contributors

Charlene Chamberlain	*McGill University*
Jane A. Coerts	*University of Amsterdam*
Kimberly E. Conlin	*Texas School for the Blind*
Robert J. Hoffmeister	*Boston University*
Nini Hoiting	*University of Amsterdam*
Amanda S. Holzrichter	*University of Texas at Austin*
Nobuo Masataka	*Kyoto University*
Paula F. Marentette	*Augustana University College*
Susan M. Mather	*Gallaudet University*
Claude Mauk	*University of Texas at Austin*
Rachel I. Mayberry	*McGill University*
Richard P. Meier	*University of Texas at Austin*
Gene R. Mirus	*University of Texas at Austin*
Jill P. Morford	*University of New Mexico*
Carol Padden	*University of California, San Diego*
Laura Ann Petitto	*McGill University*
Philip Prinz	*San Francisco State University*
Claire Ramsey	*University of Nebraska, Lincoln*
Dan I. Slobin	*University of California, Berkeley*
Michael Strong	*University of California, Santa Cruz*
André Thibeault	*Gallaudet University*

For grandma Joyce (1906–1998), who without knowing anything about science or scholarship taught me all the basics: persistence, a systematic eye for detail, and above all else, patience, patience, patience.

C. C.

Contents

Preface

The primary goal of this book is to encourage the reader to consider the young child's signed language acquisition and subsequent reading development. Our primary proposition is that theories of language acquisition and reading development must account for signed languages in order to understand the universal, modality-specific, and language-specific characteristics of language acquisition and the learning mechanisms that account for reading. Theories of language acquisition and reading have traditionally been derived from studies of spoken language and unintentionally excluded signed languages—primary languages perceived solely by eye. This exclusive focus on spoken languages has often produced theoretical principles based on the psycholinguistic mechanisms related to hearing and the articulation of speech, principles that do not necessarily apply to seeing and the gesticulation of signs. Our second goal for the book is thus to advance language research and theory by presenting a new set of signed language studies for consideration.

The initial chapters represent the first collection of research papers investigating signed language acquisition by native learners exclusively, that is, children who are exposed to a signed language from birth at home. Exposure to spoken languages from birth at home is the norm for children who are hearing and constitutes the data set from which current theories of language acquisition are derived. Early exposure to signed languages is the exception rather than the rule for children who are born deaf, due to the cultural and sociological circumstances of deaf children born into families where everyone listens and speaks language rather than watches and signs it.

Accumulating evidence shows that early exposure to signed languages results in a very different developmental outcome as compared to later exposure at older ages beyond early childhood. Past research has not always distinguished between these two types of language acquisition by eye so that the resulting picture of the acquisition landscape has been unclear at best, and misleading at worst. Only studies of the signed language acquisition of children acquiring it from birth at home in rich linguistic environments parallels the spoken language data on which acquisition theories are based. Making the distinction between these two circumstances of signed language acquisition is essential if we are to chart and understand the path of signed language acquisition. To this end, the chapters of the first half of the book all ask the same question: What does the acquisition of signed language look like at its earliest stages? These chapters also represent the first collection of cross-linguistic studies of young children's native acquisition of signed languages, including American Sign Language (ASL), Japanese Sign Language (JSL), Sign Language of the Netherlands (SLN), and Langue des Signes Québecoise (LSQ).

Although there is increasing recognition that linguistic theory must encompass signed languages, the inclusion of signed language data in theoretical explanations of reading development is nearly nonexistent. Despite the fact that a majority of deaf children use signed languages as primary languages, we know very little about whether and how they use knowledge of signed languages to learn to read. The prevailing theoretical view of reading development is that a lack of experience with speech sounds coupled with the development of a signed language make for an insurmountable barrier to reading development in deaf children. Theories of reading development, even more so than theories of language acquisition, are derived from investigations of spoken languages alone. Although many theorists are willing to accept the proposition that primary languages can be perceived solely by eye, other theorists believe that a primary signed language cannot form the foundation for learning to read. The third goal of this book is thus to broaden our understanding of how the child can learn more than one system of linguistic representation by eye.

The chapters of the second half of the book all investigate the relation between reading and the acquisition of signed language and, as such, represent a significant step in tackling this complex question. Just as it is important in acquisition research to distinguish between the two different types of circumstances of signed language acquisition, it is equally important to make the distinction in reading research. To answer the question of whether the acquisition of signed language is related to reading development, it is first necessary to measure skill in signed language. Each of these chapters measures skill in signed language in a different way and arrives at the same result. Contrary to theoretical predictions, the acquisition of signed language is positively related to reading development. The chapters in the second half of the book represent an important breakthrough in answering the question of whether and how the acquisition of signed languages is related to reading development.

Most of these chapters were originally presented at the Fifth International Conference on Theoretical Issues in Sign Language Research (TISLR) held in Montreal in September of 1996, but were considerably expanded and edited for this book. The TISLR meeting was a success due to the work of many individuals, but we would especially like to recognize the organizing committee, which included Denis Bouchard, Chris Miller, and Astrid Vercaingne-Ménard from the Université du Québec à Montréal; and Patrick Boudreault, James MacDougall, and ourselves from McGill University. This book, however, is not intended to be representative of the TISLR conference as a whole, and a host of excellent papers from the conference are not included in this volume.

One of the main challenges of the organizing committee was finding funds to support two interpreting teams, one for ASL–English and another for ASL–LSQ–French. That goal was met through the generosity of a number of organizations, including the Department of Linguistics and Décanat des études avancées et de la recherche at the Université du Québec à Montréal, the Canadian Deafness Research and Training Institute, the Office des personnes handicapées du Québec, the Mackay Center, and from McGill University from the School of Communication Sciences and Disorders, the Psychology Department, the Faculty of Science, and the Faculty of Medicine.

Our singular focus on acquisition and reading development in this book comes from the primary funding source for the TISLR conference, a grant from the Social Sciences and Humanities Research Council of Canada (SSHRC 646-95-1025) awarded to the editors. One of the mandates of the SSHRC is to promote research in literacy development, and this book is an attempt to meet that goal. Our understanding of signed language acquisition and reading development is sparse in comparison to our understanding of the linguistic structures of signed languages and how they compare to spoken languages. Our hope is that this book will help fill this knowledge gap.

Rachel I. Mayberry
Jill P. Morford
Charlene Chamberlain

Foreword

Nini Hoiting
University of Amsterdam

Dan I. Slobin
University of California, Berkeley

> *American Sign Language turned out to be in fact a complexly structured language with a highly articulated grammar, a language that exhibits many of the fundamental properties linguists have posited for all languages. But the special forms in which such properties are manifested turn out to be primarily a function of the visual-gestural mode.*

> —Edward S. Klima and Ursula Bellugi (1979, p. vi)

The insights that Klima and Bellugi arrived at two decades ago have proven stable, and are applicable—again and again—to the study of sign languages beyond ASL. This collection of chapters is part of a continuing international endeavor to more deeply understand the structure and fuctions of such languages. The focus here is on acquisition, and the authors deal with features of sign languages that are common to all human languages, as well as features that are specific to the modality of hand and eye. We have passed the historical period in which it was necessary to demonstrate that the natural lanaguages of the Deaf are full human languages, and now the "special forms in which [linguistic] properties are manifested" can be approached as linguistic domains in themselves. Indeed, the issue of modality gains in importance as we learn more about the nature of various sing languages.

Part I of this volume deals with the role of hand and eye in the signing of mothers and the perception and early acquisition of such signs by their babies. Part II takes us ahead to the time when signing children are faced with the task of acquiring another visual symbolic system—that is, the mastery of literacy in the national language of the country. Both of these tasks of acquisition require coordination of hand and eye, though in quite

different ways. It is clear from the chapters in both parts of the book that
early exposure to the visual-manual system of signing plays a critical role
in later mastery of the visual-manual systems of reading and writing.
However, we are far from understanding the details of either course of
acquisition, let alone their interaction.

These chapters were originally presented at the Fifth International
Conference on Theoretical Issues of Sign Language Research, held in
Montreal in 1996. At that conference it became evident that we have
reached an important turning point in sign language linguistics. An earlier
era of close modeling of the linguistics of spoken languages is being
replaced by an era of sign language linguistics as a field in its own right.

A central issue in this reformulation is the role of modality in shaping a
number of the crosslinguistic similarities between sign languages, pointing
to special uses of space and movement in such languages. Chapters here
explore particular uses of space and movement in the child-directed signing
of American and Japanese mothers, along with the roles of modality-
specific anatomy in the first signs used by children. These are clearly
modality-specific issues. And, at the same time, the chapters point to
dimensions of rhythm in sign that are comparable to the prosody of speech.
Most notable, thus far, are studies of manual and vocal babbling. It is
evident that we need more detailed analyses of such dimensions in signed
languages, as well as a developmental account that takes us beyond the
initial phases presented here.

Rapid advances in neurolinguistics make it possible to pose new
questions about the involvement of the brain in acquiring spoken, signed,
and written forms of language. The chapters in Part II of this book all
point to problems of facilitation or transfer from signing skills to literacy.
All of the authors stress the advantages of early exposure to signing,
although it is not yet clear where the advantage lies: in communication, in
mastery of structured language per se, in metalinguistic skills, in
sociocultural uses of language—perhaps all of these. In order to sort out
these issues we will need models that include several types of interacting
factors.

In any event, the findings of these chapters underline the importance
of the involvement of Deaf teachers and researchers in child development.
Some of the chapters presented here have Deaf authors. Others show the
importance of the communicative skills of native signers in facilitating
the acquisition of both sign language and literacy in school settings. An
overarching theme is the interplay between communicative practices and
the acquisition of language—both signed and written. For all of these issues
of research and practice, the participation of native signers will be critical.

The two parts of the book are anchored in the toddler phase and the school pupil phase. There is a long developmental path between these two phases, and we hope that these spotlights on the anchor points will stimulate readers to begin to trace out the routes that Deaf children follow from one to the other. Along the way, there are many critical landmarks—achievements of morphological, syntactic, and pragmatic mastery—all in the framework of the manual–visual modality and the special typological characteristics of sign languages. With regard to typology, it is clear that sign languages as a group have far more in common than one would expect of a collection of languages drawn from around the world. Returning to the theme of modality, it seems reasonable to expect that sign languages fall into a specific typological category (Slobin & Hoiting, 1994). Only by understanding the ontogenetic development and linguistic typology of sign languages, can we evaluate the intriguing theoretical claims about the human language capacity raised here: the roles of modality and species-universal biological factors, the roles of signing in the acquisition of literacy, and the roles of society and culture in providing the frameworks for these human achievements. We are grateful to the editors and authors for lighting the way in this search for language acquisition by eye.

REFERENCES

Klima, E. S., & Bellugi, U. (1979). *The signs of language.* Cambridge, MA: Harvard University Press.
Slobin, D. I., & Hoiting, N. (1994). Reference to movement in spoken and signed languages: Typological considerations. *Proceedings of the 20th Annual Meeting of the Berkeley Linguistics society* (pp. 487-505). Berkeley, CA: Berkeley Linguistics Society.

Part I

EARLY LANGUAGE ACQUISITION

The Role of Modality and Input in the Earliest Stage of Language Acquisition: Studies of Japanese Sign Language

Nobuo Masataka
Kyoto University

There is no single route to the acquisition of language, and children, particularly in early childhood, show a large range of individual variation both in their speed of development and in the strategies they employ. Their progress through early language might be thought of as a journey through an epigenetic landscape rather than a passage through a linear succession of stages. This notion is most convincingly demonstrated along studies that compared the language development of deaf children with that of hearing children. Recent studies of signed language development in children growing up in a signing environment from birth reported that the language is acquired by much the same route as spoken language (Caselli, 1983, 1987; Volterra, 1981; Volterra & Caselli, 1985). First signs appear at a similar time to first words. When deaf children first use signs, they do so to refer to objects, individuals, and events with which they become familiar within the social-interactional context, just as hearing children initially use words. The learning of early sign combinations is also comparable to the learning of early word combinations as is the mastery of syntax.

However, as to how this is accomplished, little is known yet, and this is particularly the case during early infancy. Thus, I devote this chapter to consider the role of both modality (speech vs. sign) and input (deaf vs. hearing) in the earliest stage of language acquisition. This chapter actually consists of two major sections, motherese and babbling. First, the perception of linguistic input typically characteristic during early infancy is com-

pared between deaf and hearing infants, and then the effects of the presence or absence of such input are examined.

PREVIOUS FINDINGS ABOUT MOTHERESE

It is a commonplace observation that adults tend to modify their speech
in an unusual and characteristic fashion when they address infants and
young children. Charles Ferguson (1964) first offered a coherent description of the linguistic features of this modified speech known as *motherese.*
Since that study, our knowledge about paralinguistic or prosodic features
of parental speech to infants has been accumulating (Garnica, 1977; Newport, Gleitman, & Gleitman, 1977; Papousek, Papousek, & Bornstein,
1985). The linguistic modifications of motherese include fewer words per
utterance, more repetitions and expansion, better articulation, and de-
creased structural complexity (Ratner & Pye, 1984; Snow, 1977). Prosodic
features include higher overall pitch, wider pitch excursions, more distinctive pitch contours, slower tempo, longer pauses, and increased emphatic
stress (Garnica, 1977; Masataka, 1992a). Cross-linguistic research has documented common patterns of such exaggerated features in parental speech
to infants younger than 8 months of age across a number of European
languages and Japanese (Fernald et al., 1989; Masataka, 1992b) and in
maternal speech in Mandarin Chinese (Grieser & Kuhl, 1988). The various
earlier studies suggest that motherese may have universal linguistic and
prosodic features.

Interest in the structure and function of motherese stems from the
possibility that such speech may enhance the young child's language learning. Indeed, several experimental studies investigated the salience of
motherese for young children and, up to now, the features were assumed
to serve three functions, all of which are related to spoken language development. First, the enhanced acoustic features of motherese may differentially elicit and, perhaps, maintain the infant's attention. Three- to 4-
month-old infants are more likely to pay attention to motherese than
adult-directed speech. Fernald (1985) demonstrated that infants turned
their heads more frequently in the direction necessary to activate a recording of female infant-directed speech than female adult-directed speech,
using a conditioned head-turning procedure. A more recent study by Cooper and Aslin (1990) showed that infants' preference for exaggerated
prosodic features was present when tested at the age of 2 days. Second, a
possible affective role of motherese has been reported. The linguistic rele-
vance of affect in spoken language acquisition is demonstrated by findings
that 4- to 9-month-old infants are responsive to meaning conveyed by
prosodic contours long before they respond to the segmental content of

utterances by adults (Papousek et al., 1985; Sullivan & Horowitz, 1983). The infants' direct and affective responding to the prosodic features of the vocalizations around this age does not require linguistic comprehension because the phonetic form becomes gradually decontextualized from its typical prosodic pattern at a later point of development. Rather, the earliest signs of comprehension of speech are mainly mediated by affect. This interpretation is supported by the finding that 4- to 5-month-old and 7- to 9-month-old infants who watched videotapes of a woman talking to an infant or talking to an adult demonstrated more positive affect while watching the infant-directed tape (Werker & McLeod, 1989). Furthermore, the magnitude of this effect was greater in the case of younger infants. These results indicate that infants find infant-directed speech less affectively ambiguous than adult-directed speech. They appear to show more readiness for social engagement when listening to motherese than when listening to adult-directed speech, and this tendency is more robust in younger infants. Finally, a potential linguistic benefit of motherese may exist. Motherese facilitates the infant's detection and discrimination of major linguistic boundaries. Certain characteristics of motherese make these boundaries more noticeable, thereby "instructing" infants about language (Karzon, 1985). No doubt, not all of these three functions are necessarily active at the same time. The particular function such input serves could change with the developmental status of the infant and, probably, the attention-getting properties and the affective roles of motherese are mainly called for before the infant is old enough to process the syntactic form of the speech directed toward him or her.

Taken together, the available data indicate that motherese is a prevalent form of language input to infants, at least in speech, and that the salience of motherese for the preverbal infant results both from the infant's attentional responsiveness to certain sounds more readily than others and from the infant's affective responsiveness to certain attributes of the auditory signal. In this chapter, I describe the results of a series of experiments in which I have attempted to identify these characteristics of motherese in mother–infant communication in Japanese Sign Language (JSL). The results reveal that a phenomenon quite analogous to motherese in maternal speech is present in the signing behavior of deaf mothers when communicating with their deaf infants. Although humans apparently possess some innately specified capacity for language (e.g., Chomsky, 1975), flexibility exists with respect to the modality in which the capacity is realized in each individual. This leads to the possibility that the specifically patterned linguistic input that is expressed as motherese might enhance infants' acquisition of the basic forms of the language equally in either the signed or spoken modalities. This is indeed the case as revealed by the studies I describe.

SIGN CHARACTERISTICS OF DEAF MOTHERS
INTERACTING WITH THEIR DEAF INFANTS

An important characteristic of motherese is that mothers substantially alter
the acoustic characteristics of their speech when they address their infants.
Therefore, as a first step in my studies of the sign motherese phenomenon,
I examined the possibility that a similar phenomenon might occur in a
signed language by comparing the movements associated with each sign
when deaf mothers were interacting with their deaf infants and when they
were interacting with their adult deaf friends.

Preliminary evidence suggesting the existence of motherese in signed
languages was previously found by Erting, Prezioso, and O'Grady-Hynes
(1990). They focused on the sign for MOTHER produced by two deaf
mothers, who had acquired American Sign Language (ASL) as their first
language, during interaction with their deaf infants when the infants were
between 5 and 23 weeks of age as well as during interaction with their
adult friends. When a total of 27 MOTHER signs directed to the infants
were compared with the same number of the signs directed to the adults,
the mothers were found to (a) place the sign closer to the infant, perhaps
the optimal signing distance for visual processing, and (b) orient the hand
so that the full handshape was visible to the infant. Moreover, (c) the
mother's face was fully visible to the infant, (d) eye gaze was directed at
the infants, and (e) the sign was lengthened by repeating the same movement. These results appear to support the claim that parents use special
articulatory features when communicating with infants, including parents
from a visual culture whose primary means of communication is visual-gestural rather than auditory-vocal.

In a series of experiments investigating sign motherese, I attempted to
replicate the finding with a larger sample of participants who live in a
different cultural background from those studied by Erting et al. (1990)
with a more extensive methodology for analysis of signs. The mothers I
studied had all acquired JSL as a first language. In all, 14 mothers participated in the recordings. Eight of them were observed when freely interacting with their deaf infants and when interacting with their deaf adult
friends (Masataka, 1992a). The remaining 5 were instructed to recite seven
prepared sentences either toward their infants or toward their adult friends
(Masataka, 1996). Recordings were made with each mother and her infant
or friend seated in a chair in a face-to-face position. The height of each
chair was adjusted such that eyes of the mother, her infant, and her friends
were about 95 cm above the floor. The infant's body was fastened to the
seat by a seat belt. The mother's behavior was monitored with two video
cameras. One of the two provided the frontal view and the other captured
the profile. At the beginning of each recording session, the mother was

instructed to interact with her infant or friend as she normally might when they were alone together. She was also told not to move her head during the session. Nearly all signed languages studied to date, including ASL, are known to use head movement as well as facial expression for linguistic as well as affective purposes. However the role of such cues from a grammatical perspective is not fully understood in JSL at this time.

For each recognizable sign recorded on the tape, the following four measurements were performed: (a) duration (number of frames), (b) average angle subtended by the right hand with respect to the sagittal plane of the mother, (c) average angle subtended by the right elbow with respect to the body axis of the mother, and (d) whether the mother repeated the same sign consecutively or not. For measuring the positions of the hand and the elbow, each of the frames was projected by a movie projector onto a digitizer, which was connected to a minicomputer. By plotting the position of the hand and the head or the position of the elbow and the body axis on the digitizer with a light pen, the computer measured the angle between them with an accuracy of 0.5° (see Fig. 1.1). Subsequently, measured values were averaged for each sign by the mother. These measurements were calculated to analyze the degree of exaggeration of signing by the mother. Whereas spoken languages are processed by hearing infants mainly by the auditory mode, signed languages are processed by deaf infants in the visual mode. Thus, it was hypothesized that the degree of exaggeration of signing should be elucidated by measuring the position of the hand and the elbow; that is, when exaggeration

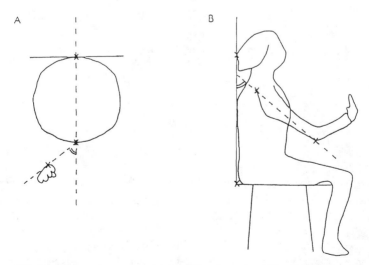

FIG. 1.1. Schematic representation of the plane view (A) and the side view (B) of the mothers as recorded on film. The points marked by a light pen on the digitizer are indicated by an X (from Masataka, 1992a).

occurred in making the signing gestures, it was expected to become most robust in the pattern of movements of hands and arms.

As shown by Table 1.1, striking differences were found with regard to all four of the parameters measured. All the differences were statistically significant. For analysis of the duration of signs, values were averaged across participants for each condition. The duration was longer in the case of signs directed to infants than in the case of signs directed to adult friends. When the angle of the hand and elbow subtended to the sagittal plane or body axis was calculated across participants for each condition, the same tendency was apparent. Mean scores for maximum values of angles for each sign directed to infants significantly exceeded those for signs directed to adults with respect to both the hand and the elbow. Similarly, mean scores of averaged values of angles for each sign directed to infants significantly exceeded those for signs directed to adults. With regard to all three of these parameters, post hoc comparisons revealed that each participant demonstrated a significant increase in these scores when she interacted with her infant. Comparison of the rates of repetition for infant-directed and adult-directed signs also indicated that the mean repetition rate for the 13 mothers was greater when they interacted with their infants than when they interacted with their adult friends, and that each individual mother demonstrated a significant increase in repetitions when she interacted with her infant.

Overall, the results indicate the presence of striking differences between the signed language used by Japanese deaf mothers when they interact with their infants and when they interact with their adult friends. When interacting with their infants, they use signs at a relatively slower tempo

TABLE 1 1

Average Duration, Size (by Angle Degree), and Repetition Rates for Infant Directed and Adult-Directed Signs

| | Duration (no. of frames) | | Angle (in degrees) | | | | | |
| | | | Hand-sagittal plane | | Elbow-body axis | | Repetition rate (%) | |
Condition	Infant	Adult	Infant	Adult	Infant	Adult	Infant	Adult
Interacting freely (n = 8)	39.1	32.8	23.6	17.9	16 4	11.5	6.6	2 9
Reciting prepared script (n = 5)	41.2	31 0	26.5	20.4	18.9	15.5	5.9	2.5

and are more likely to repeat the same sign. The movements used to make the signs are exaggerated. The outcome of this experiment reveals a phenomenon that is analogous to motherese in maternal speech. It is well-known that signed languages are organized in an identical fashion to spoken languages with regard to most linguistic aspects (Klima & Bellugi, 1979). When adults produce manual activities that are part of the phonetic inventory of signed languages in communicating with young deaf children, who have only rudimentary knowledge of language, one would predict that the social interaction should have as unusual a quality as when adults speak to young hearing children. That is, if the communicative interaction is to be established and maintained, adults must use special constraints in their communications to produce signals, in either the signed or spoken modalities, in a somewhat modified manner to fit the infant's level of attention and comprehension. This explanation is strongly supported by the results of my experiments just described.

It is particularly important to note that the mothers manipulated the duration, scope (angle), and word repetition rate of their sign productions when signing to their infants as contrasted to their adult friends. This "sign motherese" is thus parallel to "speech motherese" in manipulating or varying the prosodic patterns of the signal because duration, scope, and repetition rate are all dimensions of prosody in sign, roughly analogous to duration, pitch, and repetition in speech. The fact that the mothers involved in the experiments clearly manipulated or changed these dimensions of sign production indicates that they were doing something in addition to and presumably apart from their manipulation of affective dimensions of sign production. In the case of speech, motherese is known to be frequently accompanied by pronounced modifications in facial expression (i.e., more frequent and more exaggerated smiling, arched eyebrows, and rhythmical head movement; Gusella, Roman, & Muir, 1986; Sullivan & Horowitz, 1983). Nevertheless these components all can be regarded as paralinguistic in speech, and also in JSL; their occurrence, if they do occur, does not influence mother-infant communication from a grammatical perspective, as described earlier. Thus, it can be concluded that the phenomenon of motherese occurs equally in the manual mode and in the vocal mode, at least with regard to prosodic dimensions.

INFANT PERCEPTION OF SIGN MOTHERESE

We have identified a phenomenon quite analogous to spoken motherese in signed language. However, although in the spoken modality the available data indicate motherese is certainly a prevalent form of language input to infants, it is still unclear whether the same is the case for sign motherese.

Certainly in the studies described earlier, the experimenters were able to tell the difference between the form of infant-directed signing and that of adult-directed signing on behavioral and physical grounds. However, the question of whether deaf infants can perceive the difference remains unanswered. Deaf mothers might modify various features of their signing so as to maintain the degree of the infants' responsiveness at an optimal level by continually monitoring the infants' degree of attention and understanding. Does sign motherese enhance the infant's acquisition of the basic units of signed language? In order to test this hypothesis, I undertook the following perception study of sign motherese.

The experiment consisted of two parts: Part one involved congenitally deaf infants of deaf mothers and part two involved hearing infants of hearing mothers. In the first experiment, 7 deaf infants at 6 months of age were presented with a stimulus videotape that comprised excerpts of the infant- and adult-directed sign produced by the 5 deaf mothers described previously. All of the deaf mothers of the infants, whose husbands were also deaf, were signers of JSL as their first language. In the stimulus tape, the following seven sentences were recited toward infants or toward adults: "Good morning. How are you today? Get up. Come on now. If you get up right away, we have a whole hour to go for a walk. What do you want to do? Let's go for a walk."

Obviously, the question being asked in this study is whether deaf infants will attend to and prefer infant-directed signing over adult-directed signing. Therefore, the infant's reactions to the stimulus presentations were videotaped and later scored in terms of attentional and affective responsiveness to different video presentations. The stimulus presentation and recording took place in a black booth. Throughout the experiment, each of the 12 infants was presented the stimulus tape only once. During each session, a mother stood with her back to the video monitor and held the infant over her shoulder so as to allow the infant to face the video display at a distance of approximately 60 cm. The session was conducted only when the infant was quiet and alert. During the session, the mother was told to wear a music-delivering headphone and to direct her gaze to a picture on the wall, 90° to her right. Although deaf, the mother was asked to wear the headphone so that hearing mother–infant dyads with no exposure to a signed language could be comparatively investigated, as described later.

The infant's reactions were evaluated by four raters, two for attentional responsiveness and the other two for affective responsiveness. The percentage of the total video display time the infant spent looking at the video screen, averaged between the two raters, was measured as an indicator of attentional responsiveness. For this measurement, the two raters watched the infant on the screen independently and pushed a button whenever the infant's gaze fixated on the video display. These button presses were

counted and timed by a computer. In order to measure affective responsiveness, each of the other two observers independently attended to facial
features as well as vocalizations of the infant. They rated the infant's affective responsiveness on a 9-point scale on the following three dimensions:
Communicative Intent ("How much do you think the infant was trying to
communicate?"), Social Favorability ("How interested do you feel the infant
was?"), and Emotionality ("What is your feeling about the infant's emotional state?"). Each of these 9-point scales had specific anchor points. For
the first two questions, the scale ranged from 1 (*not at all*) to and 9 (*totally*);
for question 3, it ranged from 1 (*experiencing negative or unpleasant feeling*)
to 9 (*experiencing positive or pleasant feelings*). The scales were those originally
used by Werker and McLeod (1989). The three dimensions were treated
as indices of a single underlying factor, and one cumulative score of affective responsiveness was created for each infant by summing ratings on
the three dimensions for each rater and then taking the average of the
two raters. Thus, the maximum and the minimum cumulative scores were
27 and 3, respectively, for each infant for each stimulus condition. The
higher the score received by the infants on the dimensions, the more
positive emotions they were judged to be experiencing.

Figure 1.2 summarizes the results of the experiment. When the actual
amount of time each infant fixated on the videotape during depictions of
infant-directed signing versus adult-directed signing was analyzed statistically, a significant difference was found. Overall mean proportion of time
each infant fixated on the videotape was 90.4 % (*SD* = 6.3) for infant-directed signing and 69.8 % (*SD* = 14.7) for adult-directed signing. The
infants looked at the videotape segment of infant-directed signing longer

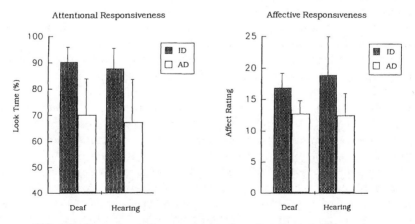

FIG. 1.2. Comparison of responsiveness for infant-directed (ID) signing
versus adult-directed (AD) signing between hearing infants and deaf infants.
Error bars represent standard deviations (from Masataka, 1998).

than the segment of adult-directed signing. With respect to affective responsiveness, every infant received higher scores for the segment of infant-directed signing than for the segment of adult-directed signing. Overall mean score was 16.9 ($SD = 2.5$) for infant-directed signing and 12.8 ($SD = 2.1$) for adult-directed signing. The infants were affectively more responsive to infant-directed signing than to adult-directed signing. The results of this experiment reveal that sign motherese evoked more robust responsiveness than adult-directed signing did from the deaf infants. This offers the long-term prospect of identifying features of motherese that are not specific to a particular language modality.

No doubt, in order to answer the question of whether sensitivity to a particular modality must be triggered by some amount of experience or not, we must examine the response to these patterns in those infants who have not had substantive experience (linguistic exposure) in the modality. Indeed, with respect to speech motherese, several researchers have addressed this question. Cooper and Aslin (1990), among others, showed that infant's preference for exaggerated prosodic features is present as young as 2 days of age. These results suggest that postnatal experience with language does not have to be extensive for infants to learn about the prosodic features of their native language. It has been shown that newborns show a preference for the intonational contour, temporal patterning, or both, of a prenatally experienced melody (Panneton, 1985). Both prenatal and postnatal auditory experience affect the relative salience of prosodic cues for young infants. In a subsequent study, 4- and 9-month-old English-learning infants were reported to show a robust attentional and affective preference for infant-directed speech over adult-directed speech in Cantonese, although the language was completely "foreign" for them (Werker, Pegg, & McLeod, 1994), but these infants had heard speech before. No convincing evidence has ever been presented to support the hypothesis that infants will prefer infant-directed communication in a modality in which they have had no prior linguistic exposure. Rather, it can be said that as long as hearing infants are investigated, it is extremely difficult, if not impossible, to address the question of whether exposure to any language is necessary for the infant to be able to react to the motherese form of the language.

Therefore I conducted the next experiment to determine whether hearing infants with no exposure to signed language also prefer sign motherese. If such a preference exists, this would be the first demonstration that human infants lock onto particular kinds of patterned input in a language modality completely independent of prior experience. Participants were 45 sets of hearing mothers and their first born, full-term, hearing infants with no exposure to a signed language (21 boys and 24 girls). All of the infants were 6 months old. Their mothers were all monolingual women who spoke only Japanese, were between 22 and 29 years old, and were middle class. The stimulus tape shown to each of the 45 infants was the same videotape used in the experiment on deaf infants. The protocol of stimulus presentations and that of scoring the infant's reactions to the stimulus presentations were also the same as in the previous experiment.

The analysis of the data obtained from the 45 infants revealed that there was a significant main effect for stimulus type with respect to their attentional responsiveness. The hearing infants looked at the videotape of infant-directed signing longer than at the tape of adult-directed signing. The overall mean proportion of time that the infants fixated on the stimulus tape was 87.5% ($SD = 8.2$) for infant-directed signing and 66.0% ($SD = 17.3$) for adult-directed signing. Moreover, when comparing responsiveness for infant-directed signing versus adult-directed signing of the hearing infants with that of the deaf infants involved in the experiment just described, no significant difference in the scores between the two groups was found (see Fig. 1.2). Concerning affective responsiveness, a similar tendency was also found. For the 45 hearing infants, overall mean scores were 18.9 ($SD = 6.1$) for infant-directed signing and 12.6 ($SD = 3.4$) for adult-directed signing. A statistically significant difference was found between the two stimulus conditions. Comparing these scores with those of the deaf infants, no significant difference was found between the two participant groups.

Clearly, hearing infants who have had no exposure to any form of signed language are attracted to motherese in JSL in a manner strikingly similar to that of deaf infants who have been exposed to the language from birth. Infants are attracted to sign motherese, regardless of whether they have ever seen sign language. Space and movement are known to be the means for transmitting morphological and syntactic information in signed languages. The continuous, analogue properties of space and movement are used in systematic, rule-governed ways in most signed languages that have been investigated so far (Armstrong, Stokoe, & Wilcox, 1995; Newport, 1981). JSL is not an exception to this finding. The abstract spatial and movement units are analogous in function to discrete morphemes found in spoken languages. The grand sweeps in changes in fundamental frequency (dynamic peak-to-peak changes) are hypothesized to attract hearing infants to spoken motherese (Fernald, 1989; Fernald & Simon, 1984). It is likely to be the sweeps of peak visual movement in sign motherese that attract deaf infants and is a visual analogue to such acoustic features. These special properties evident in infant-directed communication may have universal attentional and affective significance. Human infants appear to be predisposed to attend to these properties even if they have had no exposure to them before.

A COMPARISON OF EARLY VOCAL DEVELOPMENT
IN DEAF AND HEARING INFANTS

These findings led me to consider as a next step of my research how the presence or absence of such linguistic input affects the linguistic behavior infants acquire. Many studies indicate that auditory perception influences the production of speech as early as in the first year of life. At the babbling stage, the quality of the utterances has been anecdotally known to differ according to the linguistic input to which infants are exposed. Nevertheless, until recently, no systematic comparisons had been attempted between developmental processes of vocal behavior in deaf infants and that in hearing infants within the first year of their lives. After the mid-1990s, several studies were published on this topic and the reported findings were quite consistent with one another (Clement & Koopmans-van Beinum, 1995, 1996; Eilers, 1996; Locke, 1993). Using terms and definitions that Oller (1980) developed to account for the vocal development through which preverbal infants pass, no significant differences have been found between vocal behavior of deaf infants and that of hearing infants during the phonation stage (0–1 month), the GOO stage (2–3 months), and the expansion stage (4–6 months). Thereafter, hearing infants proceed to the next stage, the reduplicated babbling stage (7–10 months), whereas deaf infants rarely proceed. Reduplicated consonant–vowel syllables (e.g., *dadada*) are commonly referred to as *canonical babbling*, but their production is usually preceded chronologically by another rhythmic speech-like vocal activity that is known as *marginal babbling*.

Marginal babbling, like canonical babbling, is characterized by a well-formed margin (consonant) and nucleus (vowel), but can be distinguished from canonical babbling by a slow (usually > 120 ms) formant transition. On the other hand, canonical babbling is characterized by a relatively rapid (usually < 70 ms) formant transition (Eilers et al., 1993). Developmentally, this marginal babbling is produced by deaf infants as well as by hearing infants. However, deaf infants rarely come to utter canonical babbling. Clement and Koopmans-van Beinum (1996) observed the vocal ontogeny of 6 congenitally deaf infants longitudinally between 2 or 3 months and 12 months of age, and reported that among the 6 children, canonical babbling was recorded from only 1 of the deaf children whereas marginal babbling was recorded from all of them at the age of 6 to 7 months. Overall, vocal activity in the other 5 infants showed a dramatic decrease during the period that would normally correspond to the reduplicated babbling stage. Even marginal babbling, once emerged, disappears soon unless canonical babbling develops. The results indicate that the lack of auditory feedback crucially affects the vocal ontogeny of deaf infants when acquiring the ability to produce reduplicated consonant–vowel syllables.

The onset of canonical babbling is known to be quite abrupt, typically beginning some time after the age of 6 to 7 months no matter what languages infants are exposed to. As a result, the onset was previously speculated to be a deeply biological phenomenon, geared predominantly by maturation and virtually invulnerable to the effects of auditory experience or other environmental factors (Lenneberg, 1967). The findings presented previously apparently contradict this argument. In addition, a longitudinal investigation by Eilers et al. (1993) revealed that, on the basis of the recording of babbling and other motor milestones in full-term and preterm infants of middle and low socioeconomic status, neither preterm infants whose ages were corrected for gestational age nor infants of low socioeconomic status were delayed in the onset of canonical babbling. They also reported that hand banging was the only important indicator of a certain kind of readiness to produce reduplicated consonant–vowel syllables, and that other motor milestones showed neither delay nor acceleration of onset in the same infants. The greater auditory experience of the preterm infants might account for the relatively early appearance of babbling as well as hand banging in the infants.

Locke (1993) also noticed that the onset of repetitive motor action involving the hands is chronologically related to the onset of canonical babbling. Based on this fact as well as the preference of hearing infants for noisemakers around this age, Locke assumed that both the motor action and babbling emerge together because the two are commonly motivated or sustained by their audibility. He presented this argument to explain the co-occurrence of babbling and rhythmic motor action, pointing out the possibility that the strong "sound" motivation could be present in infants before the onset of canonical babbling. The sound motivation hypothesis assumes an auditory preference for rhythmic sounds, namely, infants babble because they like sounds of this sort. This preference is proposed to emerge in the infants to self-reinforce babbling behavior. As evidence supporting this notion, Locke mentioned the culturally, universal attractiveness of noisemakers and noisy toys to hearing infants around 6 to 7 months of age.

A graduate student, Keiko Ejiri, and I pursued this issue further. Ejiri (1998) observed 4 healthy hearing infants between the ages of 4 to 5 months and 11 months longitudinally. For each infant, a total of 12 to 20 hours of videotaping was done monthly. Vocalizations of the infant were tape-recorded simultaneously. Each videotaped motor activity was categorized and the temporal relation of the action to the occurrence of cooing, marginal babbling, canonical babbling, and other vocalizations was noted. Rhythmic manual action was found to co-occur primarily with a specific type of vocal activity, marginal babbling. On average, 40% of rhythmic manual activity co-occurred with marginal babbling, whereas less than 5% of rhythmic manual activity co-occurred with other categories of vocalization. Further, more than 75% of all marginal babbling was accompanied by rhythmic manual activity.

Moreover, the co-occurrence between marginal babbling and rhythmic manual action most frequent during a specific and relatively brief period in each infant was during the period between the onset of marginal babbling and the onset of canonical babbling. As already noted, the onset of marginal babbling precedes that of canonical babbling. However, after the onset of canonical babbling, marginal babbling is not totally replaced by canonical babbling. Although frequencies tend to decline, marginal babbling still occurs even after the onset of canonical babbling. In the case of the 4 infants Ejiri (1998) investigated, marginal babbling first emerged 1 to 2 months earlier than canonical babbling. The number of occurrences of marginal babbling recorded after the onset of canonical babbling was approximately half as many as those recorded before its onset, but it still occurred rather abundantly. Nevertheless, the average rate of marginal babbling that co-occurred with rhythmic manual action was roughly 60% before the onset of canonical babbling and less than 10% during the next 1-month period. The cooccurrence takes place immediately after the onset of marginal babbling with the highest frequency, which then shows a dramatic decrease once canonical babbling emerges in hearing infants.

Ejiri (in press) made a longitudinal observation of the vocal production and motor activity in a congenitally deaf infant between the ages of 4 and 11 months, and found marginal babbling was produced by the infant although its frequency was lower when compared with hearing infants. The deaf infant's marginal babbling was also likely to co-occur with rhythmic manual action. However, canonical babbling did not emerge and marginal babbling did not continue long.

Ramsay (1984) had previously found that 8 hearing infants he had observed from 5 months of age through 8 weeks after the onset of reduplicated consonant–vowel syllables performed rhythmic action frequently before the onset of the syllables, but that the rhythmic action was replaced by unimanual manipulative action after their onset. He interpreted the finding in terms of developmental change in hemispheric specialization at some subcortical level or levels and assumed some sort of brain reorganization was occurring. In fact, the Supplementary Motor Area, which is located on the medial surface of the superior frontal gyrus, has been known to serve as a basis of control over various rhythmic action patterns (Brickner, 1940). Electrical stimulation of this area evokes involuntary body movements as well as involuntary iterative vocalizations. Penfield and Welch's (1951) classic experiment revealed that stimulation of the area evoked stepping movements, waving of the hand, and complex movements of the hand involving successive flexion and extension of the fingers and wrist. The motor patterns were repeated during continued stimulation.

Stimulation of the Supplementary Motor Area caused a patient to suddenly utter "err" sounds that were rhythmically repeated.

On the basis of these facts, a theory about the production of babbling (Davis & MacNeilage, 1995; MacNeilage & Davis, 1990) proposed that the early production of babbling is mechanically controlled by repetitive opening and closing of the jaw. The movement was a syllable frame, which was proposed to be generated by the Supplementary Motor Area. These syllable frames are determined only by the immature motor capabilities of infants. As a consequence, the acoustic quality or content of the syllable during this period should be under involuntary control. For infants to acquire motor control over their vocal production, further development is needed. Individual segments become voluntarily well-articulated and are inserted into syllable frames. This happens during the period that was referred to by Oller (1980) as the reduplicated babbling stage. At this point in development, whether the infants are hearing or deaf becomes critical for their subsequent ontogeny of vocal activity.

There is also evidence indicating that the co-occurrence of early marginal babbling with rhythmic manual activity is not merely an incidental concordance due to sharing the same underlying physiological mechanism controlling each of the behaviors. Ejiri and Masataka (1999) undertook meticulous sound spectrographic analyses on marginal as well as canonical babbling recorded from the infants that Ejiri (1998) had observed during 4 to 5 and 11 months of age and found that, before the onset of canonical babbling, the average syllable length of the marginal babbling that did *not* co-occur with motor action was significantly longer than the marginal babbling that did co-occur with motor action during the same period. However, after the onset of canonical babbling, the syllable length of marginal babbling, although no longer co-occurring with motor action, was as short as that of the marginal babbling that co-occurred with motor action before the onset of canonical babbling.

Similarly, before the onset of canonical babbling, the average formant frequency transition duration of the marginal babbling that did not co-occur with motor action was significantly longer than that of marginal babbling that co-occurred with motor action during the same period. However, the value of this parameter after the onset of canonical babbling, although measured in marginal babbling that did not co-occur with motor action, was as short as that of the marginal babbling that did co-occur with motor action before the onset of canonical babbling. The value close to the value of the parameter of canonical babbling that was produced during the same period.

The results of these analyses indicate that some acoustic modifications in marginal babbling take place only when co-occurring with rhythmic manual action. The modifications would appear to facilitate hearing infants' acquisition of the ability to produce canonical babbling. Indeed, the parameters that were modified when they co-occurred with motor activity concern those that essentially distinguish canonical babbling from earlier speech-like vocalizations. For instance, a vocalization that can be transcribed as /ta/ would be deemed canonical if articulated with a rapid transition duration in a relatively short syllable, but would be deemed noncanonical if articulated slowly. In the latter case, those syllables have been conventionally called marginal babbling (Oller, 1986).

THE EMERGENCE OF MANUAL BABBLING

Interestingly, the onset period of canonical babbling in hearing infants exactly coincides with the onset period of manual babbling, which was proposed to occur in deaf infants as well as in hearing infants by Petitto and Marentette (1991). In the course of conducting research on signing infants' transition from prelinguistic gesturing to first signs, they performed a close analysis of the physical variables (analogous to the acoustic level of sound analyses) as well as the articulatory variables (analogous to the phonetic level) of all manual activity produced by deaf infants of ASL-signing deaf parents from the age of 6 months. During the investigation, they noticed the presence of a class of manual activity that was unlike anything else that had been reported so far in previous literature. These manual behaviors included linguistically relevant units but were produced in entirely meaningless ways, and were wholly distinct in their pattern from all other manual activity, that is, general motor activity, communicative gestures, and signs. The infants produced these units between 9 and 12 months of age, the period corresponding to the canonical babbling stage for hearing infants acquiring speech. Indeed, subsequent analyses revealed that this class of manual activity was characterized by the identical timing, patterning, structure, and use as the vocal behavior of hearing infants that is universally identified as babbling. As a result, it was termed *manual babbling*. Further comparison of the ontogeny of manual action of hearing infants who were acquiring spoken language with no exposure to a signed language and deaf infants who were acquiring ASL as their first language revealed that both of them produced a roughly equal proportion of communicative gestures (e.g., arms raised to request being picked up) at approximately 8 to 14 months of age. Nevertheless, the deaf infants produced far more manual babbling forms (e.g., handshape-movement combinations exhibiting the phonological structure of forml signed language) than did the hearing infants, and manual babbling accounted for approximately 40% of manual activity in deaf infants and less than 10% of the manual activity of hearing infants.

In spite of this quantitative difference, however, it is noteworthy that even hearing infants, with no exposure to a signed language, did produce manual babbling (Petitto & Marentette, 1991). Given the fact that manual babbling progresses through the same stages as vocal babbling, language capacity appears to manifest itself in human infants equally as speech or sign. In hearing infants, the vocal and gestural modalities can develop language simultaneously and in a similar manner, at least during the pre-verbal period. In fact, some infants come to produce almost equal amounts of first words both in speech and gesture around the same period (Good-wyn & Acredolo, 1993). In the case of deaf infants, the progression of spoken language acquisition is hindered earlier because childhood deaf-ness profoundly affects both their speech output and their comprehension of spoken language. As a consequence, they are obliged to rely exclusively on the manual mode to realize their linguistic capacity. This fact could partly account for a richer repertoire of manual babbling by the sign-exposed infants in Petitto and Marentette (1991). But it is not the only variable determining the difference.

I myself (Masataka, in preparation) recently observed the ontogeny of manual activity of three preverbal deaf infants of hearing parents with no exposure to a signed language, and found that although the infants did perform manual babbling, and although the amount of the behavior was greater than that produced by hearing infants, it was much smaller than that exhibited by deaf infants with exposure to JSL. In this study, I made a comparison of the pattern of development of manual activity between the ages of 8 months and 12 months in three groups of infants: (a) 3 deaf infants of deaf parents with exposure to JSL, (b) 3 deaf infants of hearing parents with no exposure to any signed language, and (c) 2 hearing infants of hearing parents with no exposure to any signed language. When all of the infants' manual activities were transcribed in an identical manner, they were found to be of two types in each infant: syllabic manual babbling and gesture. All the infants in the three groups produced similar types and quantities of gestures during the study period. However, they differed in their production of manual babbling. Babbling accounted for 25% to 56% of manual activity in deaf infants with exposure to JSL and a mere 2% to 6% of the manual activity of the hearing infants. Manual babbling as a percentage of manual activity [manual babbling/(manual babbling + gesture)] showed a significant increase as the deaf infants developed but did not exhibit such change in the hearing infants. The deaf infants with no exposure to any signed language produced an intermediate amount of manual babbling, between 10% and 15%. Interestingly, the rate of babbling was greatest at the age of 8 months in all the infants in each of the three groups and showed a significant decrease as they developed.

POSSIBLE LINGUISTIC BENEFITS OF SIGN
MOTHERESE FOR SIGNED LANGUAGE ACQUISITION

Taken together, my research on motherese and babbling reveals that concerning the aspect of linguistic input, human infants are prepared to detect motherese characteristics equally in the manual mode and in the vocal mode. If infants with little or no auditory feedback from their own vocalizations are exposed to sign motherese, the manual articulator is to develop in them, instead of the oral articulator. The time course of such manual babbling appears to be quite similar to that of vocal babbling. This commonality could be due to properties of motor organization that are shared by the systems controlling the manual articulator and that controlling the oral articulator. It is known that deaf children whose access to usable conventional linguistic input is severely restricted nevertheless use gesture to communicate (Fant, 1972). These gestures are known to show a strong similarity to natural language in that they are structured at the level of sentence and word. Infants' tendency to use gesture for communication may partly be accounted for by the fact that the deaf children's hearing parents, like all speakers, use gesture abundantly as they talk. But the children themselves are also responsible for introducing language-like structure into their gestures (Goldin-Meadow & Mylander, 1983). Recent observation of 2- to 5-year-old deaf children in two different cultures (Goldin-Meadow & Mylander, 1998) revealed the presence of a number of surprising structural similarities shared by the spontaneous "home sign" systems developed in each of the cultures. Manual babbling may lead to home sign, developmentally. This is quite different from what happens in the vocal babbling because deaf infants do not produce canonical babbling, acquire words, or create spoken sentences without input. The difference may be accounted for by the fact that, unlike deaf infants who do not receive auditory feedback from their own vocalizations, sighted children receive visual feedback from their own gesturing.

If infants are exposed to structured patterned linguistic input, the development of their predispositional tendency toward language production is enhanced so that the produced pattern is linguistically in line with that of the input. To accomplish this, young infants already possess many of the language perception capacities required for language learning. With regard to this issue, previous work has mostly been conducted in the domain of spoken languages. Typically, infants younger than 6 months distinguish a wide range of speech contrasts and have some capacity to compensate for differences in voices and speaking rates. After 6 months of age, infants demonstrate some recognition of the particular phonetic and prosodic characteristics of their native language. Moreover, 7.5-month-old infants acquire the ability to segment fluent speech into word-sized units. These studies strongly indicate that infants are innately predisposed to discover the particular patterned input of phonetic and syllabic units, that is, the particular patterns in the input signal that correspond to the temporal and hierarchical grouping and rhythmical characteristics in natural spoken language phonology (see Jusczyk, 1982; Jusczyk & Hohne, 1997; Mehler et al., 1988, for review). There is also evidence supporting the possibility that speech motherese facilitates the infant's detection and discrimination of segmental contrasts. Karzon (1985) reported that 1- to 4-month-old infants were able to discriminate a change in the second syllable of a three-syllable word only when the phonetic contrast was accompanied by increases in fundamental frequency, intensity, and duration, the same prosodic features that co-occur in speech motherese. Interestingly, Karzon also demonstrated that it was not the general presence of these exaggerated prosodic cues that enhanced phonetic discrimination. When the same cues accompanied the initial (but not the target) syllable, no discriminatory advantage was see. Kemler-Nelson, Hirsh-Pasek, Jusczyk, and Wright-Cassidy (1989) found that 7- to 9-month-old infants preferred to listen to speech that preserved natural clausal structure as long as the speech was characterized by motherese properties. However, no preference for natural clausal structure was found with nonmotherese speech. In a nonspeech context, Aslin (1989) demonstrated that 8-month-old infants' ability to detect the presence of a frequency sweep (a phonetically relevant portion of the signal) was improved for long sweep duration. If the slower tempo of motherese speech results in similar elongations, then infant-directed speech may enhance a variety of phonetic discriminations. Jusczyk and Hohne (1997) exposed 8-month-old infants to recordings of three children's stories for 10 days during a 2-week-period and explored the infants' long-term retention of the sound patterns of words. They found that the infants listened significantly longer to the list of words that occurred often in the stories as compared to the list of words that did not occur in the stories. These findings suggest the possibility of long-term storage of words that occur frequently in speech directed to infants. This is obviously an important prerequisite for learning language. Under such circumstances, the difficulty language-learning infants face is the segmentation of fluent speech into words. Thus, the possibility is highly plausible that the process of lexical storage may be improved if they are exposed to words that occur in infant-directed speech.

Although signed languages have been regarded as lacking most properties shared by the grammar of oral languages, recent research concluded that such privileged speech–language association is misleading and that signed languages are also highly constrained, following general restrictions on structure and organization comparable to those proposed for oral languages (Armstrong et al., 1995; Padden, 1988). Given the fact that mother-

22   MASATAKA

ese is a phenomenon concerning an amodal language capacity, patterned input with phonetic and syllabic organization could serve as the vehicle for development of language in the signed modality as well as in the spoken modality. Thus, the production of motherese in the manual mode could help deaf infants identify visually the finite inventory of basic units, from which a signed language is constructed. When a particular patterned input is expressed as motherese, it may play an important role in enhancing infants' acquisition of the basic forms of signed language.

REFERENCES

Armstrong, D. F., Stokoe, W. C., & Wilcox, S. E. (1995). *Gesture and the nature of language.* Cambridge, England: Cambridge University Press.

Aslin, R. N. (1989). Discrimination of frequency transitions by human infants. *Journal of the Acoustical Society of America, 86,* 582–590.

Brickner, R. (1940). A human cortical area producing repetitive phenomena when stimulated. *Journal of Neurophysiology, 3,* 128–130.

Caselli, M. C. (1983). Communication to language: Deaf children's and hearing children's development compared. *Sign Language Studies, 39,* 113–114.

Caselli, M. C. (1987). Language acquisition in Italian deaf children. In J. K. Kyle (Ed.), *Sign and school· Using sign in deaf children's development* (pp. 34–78) Clevedon, England: Multilingual Matters.

Chomsky, N. (1975). *The logical structure of linguistic theory.* New York: Plenum.

Clement, C. J., & Koopmans-van Beinum, F. J. (1995). Influence of lack of auditory feedback: Vocalizations of deaf and hearing infants compared. *Proceedings of the Institute of Phonetic Sciences, University of Amsterdam, Proceedings, 19,* 25–37.

Clement, C. J., & Koopmans-van Beinum, F. J. (1996, April). *Influence of lack of auditory feedback on infant vocalization in the first year.* Abstract of the European Conference "The development of sensory, motor and cognitive abilities in early infancy: Antecedents of language and symbolic function" (p. 24). San Feliu de Guixols, Spain.

Cooper, R. P., & Aslin, R. N. (1990). Preference for infant-directed speech in the first month after birth. *Child Development, 61,* 1584–1595.

Davis, B. L., & MacNeilage, P. F (1995). The articulatory basis of babbling. *Journal of Speech and Hearing Research, 38,* 1199–1211.

Eilers, R. E. (1996, September). *Correlates of the late onset canonical babbling in infancy.* Paper presented at the symposium "The emergence of human cognition and language," Tokyo.

Eilers, R. E , Oller, D K., Levine, S , Basinger, D., Lynch, M. P., & Urbano, R. (1993). The role of prematurity and socioeconomic status in the onset of canonical babbling in infants. *Infant Behavior and Development, 16,* 297–315.

Ejiri, K. (1998). Synchronization between preverbal vocal behavior and motor action in early infancy. I. Its developmental change. *Japanese Journal of Psychology, 68,* 433–440.

Ejiri, K. (in press). Comparison of synchronization between vocal behavior and motor action between deaf and hearing infants. *Japanese Journal of Educational Psychology*

Ejiri, K., & Masataka, N. (1999). Synchronization between preverbal vocal behavior and motor action in early infancy. II. An acoustical examination of the functional significance of the synchronization. *Japanese Journal of Psychology, 69,* 433–440.

Erting, C. J., Prezioso, C., & O'Grady-Hynes, M. (1990). The interactional context of deaf mother-infant communication. In V. Volterra & C. J. Erting (Eds.), *From gesture to language in hearing and deaf children* (pp. 97–106). Berlin, Germany: Springer.

Fant, L. (1972). *Ameslan.* Silver Spring, MD: National Association of the Deaf.

Ferguson, C. A. (1964). Baby talk in six languages. *American Anthropologist, 66,* 103–114.

Fernald, A. (1985). Four-month-old infants prefer to listen to motherese. *Infant Behavior and Development, 8,* 181–195.

Fernald, A. (1989). Intonation and communicative intent in mother's speech to infants: Is the melody the message? *Child Development, 60,* 1497–1510.

Fernald, A, & Simon, T. (1984) Expanded intonation contours in mother's speech to newborns. *Developmental Psychology, 20,* 104–113.

Fernald, A., Taeschner, T., Dunn, J., Papousek, M., Boysson-Bardies, B. de, & Fukui, I. (1989). A cross-linguistic study of prosodic modification in mothers' and fathers' speech to preverbal infants. *Journal of Child Language, 16,* 477–501.

Garnica, O. (1977). Some prosodic and paralinguistic features of speech to young children. In C. E. Snow & C. A. Ferguson (Eds.), *Talking to children: Language input and acquisition* (pp. 104–123). Cambridge, England: Cambridge University Press.

Goodwyn, S. W., & Acredolo, L. P. (1993). Symbolic gesture versus word: Is there a modality advantage for onset of symbol use? *Child Development, 64,* 688–701.

Goldin-Meadow, S., & Mylander, C. (1983) Gestural communication in deaf children: The non-effects of parental input on language development. *Science, 221,* 372–374.

Goldin-Meadow, S., & Mylander, C. (1998). Spontaneous sign systems created by deaf children in two cultures. *Nature, 391,* 279–281.

Grieser, D. L., & Kuhl, P. (1988). Maternal speech to infants in a tonal language: Support for universal prosodic features in motherese. *Developmental Psychology, 24,* 14–20.

Gusella, J., Roman, M., & Muir, D. (1986, September). *Experimental manipulation of mother-infant actions.* Paper presented at the International Conference of Infant Studies, Los Angeles.

Jusczyk, P. W. (1982). Auditory versus phonetic coding of speech signals during infancy. In J. Mehler, M. Garrett, & E. Walker (Eds.), *Perspectives in mental representation: Experimental and theoretical studies of cognitive processes and capacities* (pp. 145–197). Hillsdale, NJ: Lawrence Erlbaum Associates.

Jusczyk, P. W., & Hohne, E. A. (1997). Infants' memory for spoken words. *Science, 277,* 1984–1986.

Karzon, R G. (1985). Discrimination of polysyllabic sequences by one- to four-month-old infants. *Journal of Experimental Child Psychology, 39,* 326–342.

Kemler-Nelson, D. G., Hirsh-Pasek, K., Jusczyk, P. W., & Wright-Cassidy, K. (1989). How the prosodic cues in motherese might assist language learning. *Journal of Child Language, 16,* 53–68.

Klima, E. S., & Bellugi, U. (1979). *The signs of language.* Cambridge, MA: Harvard University Press

Lenneberg, E H. (1967). *Biological foundations of language.* New York: Wiley.

Locke, J. L (1993). *The child's path to spoken language.* Cambridge, MA: Harvard University Press.

MacNeilage, P. F., & Davis, B. L. (1990). Acquisition of speech production: The architect of segmental independence. In W. J. Hardcastle & A. Marchal (Eds.), *Speech production and speech modeling* (pp. 55–68). Dordrecht, Netherlands: Kluwer.

Masataka, N. (1992a). Motherese in a signed language. *Infant Behavior and Development, 15,* 453–460.

Masataka, N. (1992b). Pitch characteristics of Japanese maternal speech to infants. *Journal of Child Language, 19,* 213–223.

Masataka, N. (1996). Perception of motherese in a signed language by 6-month-old deaf infants. *Developmental Psychology, 32,* 874–879.

Masataka, N. (1998). Perception of motherese in Japanese Sign Language by 6-month-old hearing infants. *Developmental Psychology, 34,* 241–246.

Masataka, N. (in preparation). *Early ontogeny of manual activity in deaf infants.*

Mehler, J , Jusczyk, P. W., Lambertz, G., Halsted, N., Bertoncini, J., & Amiel-Tilson, C. (1988). A precursor of language acquisition in young infants. *Cognition, 29,* 143–178.

Newport, E. (1981). Constraints on structure: Evidence from ASL and language learning. In W. Collins (Ed.), *Minnesota symposia on child psychology* (Vol. 14, pp. 65–128). Hillsdale, NJ: Lawrence Erlbaum Associates.

Newport, E. L., Gleitman, H., & Gleitman, L. R. (1977). Mother, I'd rather do it myself: Some effects and non-effects of maternal speech style. In C. E. Snow & C. A. Ferguson (Eds.), *Talking to children. Language input and acquisition* (pp. 165–207). Cambridge, England: Cambridge University Press.

Oller, D. K. (1980). The emergence of the sounds of speech in infancy In G. Yeni-Komshian, J. Kavanagh, & C. Ferguson (Eds.), *Child phonology Vol. 1 Production* (pp. 93–112). New York: Academic Press.

Oller, D. K. (1986). Metaphonology and infant vocalizations. In B. Lindblom & R. Zetterstrom (Eds.), *Precursors of early speech* (pp. 21–35). New York: Stockton.

Padden, C. A. (1988). Grammatical theory and signed languages. In F. Newmeyer (Ed.), *Linguistics: The Cambridge survey* (Vol. 2, pp. 250–266). Cambridge, England: Cambridge University Press.

Panneton, R. K. (1985). *Prenatal experience with melodies: Effect on postnatal auditory preference in human newborns.* Unpublished doctoral dissertation, University of North Carolina at Greensboro.

Papousek, M., Papousek, H., & Bornstein, M. (1985). The naturalistic vocal environment of young infants: On the significance of homogeneity and variability in parental speech. In T. M. Field & N. A. Fox (Eds.), *Social perception in infants* (pp. 56–84). Norwood, NJ: Ablex.

Penfield, W., & Welch, K. (1951). The supplementary motor area of the cerebral cortex. *Archives of Neurology and Psychiatry, 66,* 289–317.

Petitto, L. A., & Marentette, P. F. (1991). Babbling in the manual mode: Evidence for the ontogeny of language. *Science, 251,* 1493–1496

Ramsay, D. S. (1984). Onset of duplicated syllable babbling and unimanual handedness in infancy: Evidence for developmental change in hemispheric specialization? *Developmental Psychology, 20,* 64–71.

Ratner, N. B., & Pye, C. (1984). Higher pitch in BT is not universal: Acoustic evidence from Quiche Mayan. *Journal of Child Language, 11,* 512–522.

Snow, C. E. (1977). The development of conversation between mothers and babies. *Journal of Child Language, 4,* 1–22.

Sullivan, J. W., & Horowitz, F. D. (1983). Infant intermodal perception and maternal multimodal stimulation: Implication for language development. In L. P. Lipsitt & C. K. Rovee-Collier (Eds.), *Advances in infancy research* (Vol. 2, pp. 184–239). Norwood, NJ: Ablex.

Volterra, V. (1981). Gestures, signs and words at two years· When does communication become language? *Sign Language Studies, 33,* 351–362.

Volterra, V., & Caselli, M.C. (1985). From gestures and vocalisations to signs and words. In W. Stokoe & V. Volterra (Eds.), *SLR '83* (pp. 154–180). Silver Spring, MD: Linstok.

Werker, J. F., & McLeod, P. J. (1989) Infant preference for both male and female infant-directed talk: A developmental study of attentional and affective responsiveness. *Canadian Journal of Psychology, 43,* 230–246.

Werker, J. F., Pegg, J. E., & McLeod, P. J. (1994). A cross-language investigation of infant preference for infant-directed communication. *Infant Behavior and Development, 17,* 323–333.

Chapter 2

Child-Directed Signing
in American Sign Language

Amanda S. Holzrichter
Richard P. Meier
University of Texas at Austin

Child-directed language has been the subject of much research since the 1970s. Although recent cross-linguistic studies show the need for caution in assuming the universality of *motherese* in parent–child interactions (Heath, 1983; Ratner & Pye, 1984; Schieffelin, 1990), a number of common characteristics are reported in studies of child-directed speech in English and many other spoken languages (see Gallaway & Richards, 1994; Snow, 1977, for an overview). Moreover, researchers have found that child-directed speech is highly attractive to infants and that it contains clues to segmentation that might be of use to the early language learner. For instance, even very young infants have shown a preference for child-directed prosody (Cooper & Aslin, 1990; Fernald, 1985). Clause boundaries are also more reliably marked in child-directed than in adult-directed speech (e.g., Garnica, 1977), and infants seem to prefer to listen to speech in which pauses coincide with clause boundaries than speech in which they do not (Hirsh-Pasek, Kemler-Nelson, Jusczyk, Wright, & Druss, 1987; Kemler-Nelson, Hirsh-Pasek, Jusczyk, & Wright-Cassidy, 1989).

Although the existence of motherese has been documented in many languages, whether characteristics of child-directed language actually promote language acquisition continues to be the subject of much debate. Attempts to link children's language development to specific features of their caregiver's language have been frequent but largely unsuccessful (but see Newport, Gleitman, & Gleitman, 1977). There is some evidence, however, that quantity of input is a good predictor of children's early vocabulary growth (Huttenlocher, Haight, Bryk, Seltzer, & Lyons, 1991). Of course, for a caregiver's language to become input to the acquisition process, children must first perceive and process that language through one of their senses (i.e., audition, vision, and/or touch). Here then is a possible role for motherese. It has been suggested in several studies (Fernald, 1984, 1992; Gottlieb, 1985) that one of the primary functions of motherese prosody is to attract and maintain infants' attention. Indeed, even if child-directed language does nothing to directly facilitate language acquisition, it may still assist the acquisition process by creating opportunities for children to receive linguistic input. Parents' use of distinctive child-directed language might therefore vary as a function of the child's focus of attention. On this hypothesis, an inattentive child elicits the use of motherese.

Studies of signed communication between parents and children provide a unique opportunity to examine children's attention. The fact that children who are learning a signed language must attend visually might be expected to limit the quantity of input that a signing child receives. Unlike hearing children acquiring a spoken language, deaf children acquiring a signed language can choose not to attend—and thus control when they receive input.[1] Mothers of deaf children must therefore monitor their children's attention more closely than (speaking) mothers of hearing children. However, the constraints of the visuo-gestural modality also make the input process more observable. That is, because it is fairly easy to determine a child's eye gaze, an observer can more reliably monitor a child's attention to signed language than to spoken language. While there may be no visible indication that a hearing child is attending, the mother of that child can reasonably expect that the child will hear her. For a hearing mother accustomed to speaking without always waiting for visual attention, it is sometimes difficult to adjust to the visual needs of a deaf child. Studies suggest that deaf mothers are more successful than hearing mothers at engaging deaf children in interactions (Jamieson, 1994; Spencer & Gutfreund, 1990; Swisher, 1992).

To date, there have been relatively few studies of deaf parents' child-directed signing. As our brief review of the speech literature indicates, we cannot assume the existence of motherese in signed languages. Moreover, we might ask what form motherese might take in signed language: For instance, is there an equivalent of motherese "prosody" in the visuo-gestural modality? Clearly, the existence and form of motherese in American Sign Language (ASL) cannot merely be taken for granted. Nonetheless, characteristics such as slower signing, larger sign size, repetitiousness, and signing on the child's body have been reported for ASL (Erting, Prezioso, & Hynes, 1990; Holzrichter, 1995; Kantor, 1982; Launer, 1982; Maestas y

---

[1]Hearing children can choose not to attend, but they cannot choose not to hear.

Moores, 1980) and British Sign Language (Harris, Clibbens, Chasen, & Tibbitts, 1987; Kyle & Ackerman, 1987). Baker and Bogaerde (1996) reported that deaf mothers who are signers of the Sign Language of the Netherlands sometimes displace signs from their expected place of articulation, either by moving them into their child's visual field or by producing them on the child's body. Masataka (1992, 1996, chap. 1, this volume) compared child- and adult-directed signs in Japanese Sign Language and found that child-directed signs were measurably larger, slower, and more repetitious than adult-directed signs. Thus, in at least some signed languages, there is a motherese register similar to that found in many spoken languages. More research is needed to understand children's perception of child-directed versus adult-directed signing in ASL and other sign languages. However, Masataka's (1996) study suggested that child-directed signing, like child-directed speech, is especially attractive to infants.

In this study, we examine modifications in signs addressed to deaf infants by their deaf parents. Our analysis focuses on four properties of child-directed signing: cyclicity, duration, location in space, and size. Because of the hypothesized attention-getting function of child-directed language, we are interested in the possible influence of parent–child eye contact on parents' signing. We therefore analyze the relation between eye gaze and modifications in the cyclicity, duration, location, and size of signs in child-directed signing.

Also, because signs differ in interesting phonological ways, we hypothesized that signs of different types might be differentially modified in child-directed signing. Evidence suggests that in ASL the "canonical" sign shape is one with path movement. Signs without path movement regularly gain path movement under certain aspectual markings in ASL. For instance, the sign SILLY is produced with a Y-handshape and shaking movement (forearm rotation) near the nose. The related sign FOOLISH (i.e., "characteristically silly") is created by adding reduplicated path movement to the sign SILLY (Klima & Bellugi, 1979). Evidence from modifications made to stressed signs also suggests a tendency toward path movement signs in ASL. Wilbur and Schick (1987) found that signs without path movement typically gained path movement in stressed environments, and the presence or absence of path movement was the best predictor of the modifications signs would undergo when stressed. Several different sonority scales have been proposed for ASL (Blevins, 1993; Brentari, 1993; Corina, 1990; Sandler, 1993), but they generally agree that signs with path movement are more visually sonorous than signs without path movement.

Here, we compare signs of four phonological types, representing two gross places of articulation and two movement types. For place of articulation, we contrast signs on the *face* versus signs in *neutral space*. For movement type, we contrast *path movement* and *nonpath movement,* as these move-

TABLE 2 1
Participants and Sessions, With Children's Ages in Months and Weeks at Each Videotaped Session

Parent–Child Pair	Session 1	Session 2	Session 3	Session 4	Session 5
Mother–daughter	10;0	10;2	11;1	12;1	12;2
Mother–son	8;3	10;3	11;0	11;3	
Father-daughter	8;2	9;0	9;2	10;2	
Father–son	10;0	10;3	11;0	11;2	12;2

ment types are representative of two extremes: the largest and smallest possible movement types.

METHODS

Participants and Procedures

Each of four parent–child pairs was videotaped at least four times during a period of approximately 2 months. Children were between 8 and 12 months of age at the time of the tapings. All parents themselves had at least one deaf parent and thus all were native signers of ASL. Sessions typically lasted 30 to 45 minutes and were usually conducted in the families' homes. Parents were asked only to interact and play naturally with their children. Two researchers were also present at most videotaping sessions. Participant and session information is summarized in Table 2.1.

Sample Selected for Analysis

For our analysis, we chose the signs FOOD, MILK, MOMMY, DADDY, MORE, BALL, DOG, HORSE, CAT, DUCK, ORANGE, COLOR, and RED.[2] Each child-directed token of one of the selected signs in the videotaped samples was transcribed, yielding a total of 194 sign tokens. To examine how parents may differentially modify signs as a function of their phonological characteristics, signs were assigned to four categories or types based on the place of articulation (neutral space or face) and movement (path or nonpath movement) of the citation adult-directed form. Sign type and token information is summarized in Table 2.2.

---

[2]Because they differ from DUCK only in handshape, the signs BIRD and GOOSE were counted as instances of DUCK. Likewise, PINK was included in the analysis of RED. Both the noun FOOD and the verb EAT were included in the analysis of FOOD. For illustrations of these signs, see Humphries, Padden, and O'Rourke (1980).

TABLE 2.2
Sign Types and Tokens Analyzed

Type	Place of Articulation	Movement	Examples	Tokens
I	Face	Path	FOOD, MOMMY, DADDY	46
II	Face	No path	DUCK, HORSE, CAT, COLOR, ORANGE, RED	70
III	Neutral space	Path	BALL, MORE	23
IV	Neutral space	No path	MILK, DOG	55

We expected all of the selected signs to be fairly common in the parents' signing to their children. Most have been previously found in children's early vocabularies (e.g., Conlin, Mirus, Mauk, and Meier, chap. 4, this volume) or were common in the environment of the children who participated in this study.[3] All of the families, for instance, had books or toys with pictures of animals and colors that the parents frequently labeled for the children.

Coding

Following identification of all signs, we noted for each sign token whether there was parent–child eye contact throughout the production of the sign. Each sign was then classified according to its movement (path or nonpath movement) and place of articulation (face or neutral).[4] Path movement was defined as movement having articulation at the shoulder, elbow, or both. Thus, signs with only forearm rotation or wrist movement (e.g., CAT), open–close movement (e.g., MILK), or trilled movement (e.g., COLOR) were not considered to have path movement. For cyclicity, we counted the number of repetitions of the sign's movement.[5] Subjective evaluations of sign duration, location in space, and size were then made (by the first

---

[3]The child in our mother–daughter pair was also one of the children ("Noel") in the Conlin et al. study (see chap. 4, this volume).

[4]The precise place of articulation was also coded (e.g., chin, mouth, cheek, nondominant hand, neutral space, etc.). However, as noted earlier, we focus here only on the difference between signs articulated at the face and signs articulated in neutral space. We did not include in our analysis signs on the body (other than the face) because there were no such signs for which we had sufficient data for all parents. Interestingly, in a study of children's early sign production, Conlin et al. (chap. 4, this volume) found that children produced few signs on the body; signs on the face and in neutral space accounted for 86% of their data.

[5]Other articulatory parameters, including handshape, palm orientation, handedness (one- vs. two-handed signs), and contacting region of the hand were also coded but are not relevant to the current discussion.

author) by comparing child-directed signs to adult-directed citation versions elicited from one of the participating parents. For sign duration, signs were coded as normal, long, or short. For location in space, signs that were judged to be displaced (i.e., not produced in their citation-form location) were coded as either high, low, or on child's body. Signs that were judged to be in their usual location in space were coded as nondisplaced. For sign size, each sign was coded as either normal, large, or small.

Reliability Coding

To assess the reliability of our coding, approximately 20% of the identified sign tokens were independently coded by a second coder. Reliability for eye gaze was 74%. Reliability scores for cyclicity, duration, location in space, and size ranged from 74% to 85%.[6] In cases of disagreement, the original coder's judgments were used.

RESULTS

We first summarize overall findings regarding eye contact between the parent and child. Following that summary, results for cyclicity, duration, location in space, and size are presented, and the relation of these parameters to both eye gaze and the movement and place of articulation of the sign are discussed.

Eye Gaze

In approximately half (55%) of all tokens, there was eye contact between parent and child. In the remaining 45% of the tokens, either the parent or the child was looking somewhere other than at the interlocutor's face. However, it was unusual for the parents' signs not to be accessible to the child. In those 87 instances during which there was no eye contact, the parent typically either provided tactile input by signing on the child's body (24 of 87 or 28%) or made at least the hands visible by leaning or signing into the child's visual field (42 of 87 or 48%).

Cyclicity

In their citation forms, the signs analyzed here typically have two to three movement cycles. Consistent with previous studies of ASL motherese, we

---

[6]Coding for cyclicity was considered reliable if the two coders' judgments were within one cycle of each other.

found that parents sometimes increased the cyclicity, or repetitiousness, of their signs; 37% (64 of 173) of the signs coded for cyclicity had more than three repetitions.[7] We identified signs, for example MORE, with as many as 16 cycles. No differences in cyclicity were found between signs where there was parent–child eye contact (M = 3.8, SD = 3.0) and those where there was not (M = 3.5, SD = 2.3). However, we found a significant association between cyclicity and place of articulation. Signs articulated in neutral space had a higher average number of repetitions (M = 4.5, SD = 3.0) than signs articulated at the face (M = 3.2, SD = 2.3), $t(173)$ = 3.05, $p < .003$. We also found a trend in the direction of greater cyclicity for nonpath movement signs (M = 4.5, SD = 3.6) than for path movement signs (M = 3.6, SD = 2.8), $t(173)$ = 1.77, $p < .08$.

Duration

Increased duration was a common modification in our participants' signing. We coded as long all signs that appeared longer in overall duration than adult citation forms.[8] Overall, 104 (61%) of the signs were coded as having temporally lengthened movement. Of the remaining signs, 28% (48 of 170) were coded as normal, and 11% (18 of 170) were coded as short. Signs that were coded as short were roughly comparable to signs produced in conversational signing.

No perceived differences in duration were found between signs with path movement and those without. Approximately 60% (34 of 57) of path movement signs were coded as having increased duration, versus 63% (71 of 113) of nonpath movement signs. Likewise, place of articulation did not play a role in the perceived duration of signs: 63% (60 of 95) of signs on the face, and 60% (45 of 75) of signs in neutral space were judged to have longer or slower movement.

Interestingly, however, there was a significant association between eye gaze and the duration of parents' signs, $\chi^2(2)$ = 8.12, $p < .05$; see Table 2.3. Parents were more likely to increase the duration of a sign when they did not have eye contact with their child (75%) than when they did (54%). By contrast, parents produced normal or short signs more often when they had eye contact (46%) than when they did not (26%).

---

[7]Because its movement is not discrete enough to count cycles, the sign COLOR is excluded from this analysis. A few tokens of MILK are also excluded, because the father produced them with open–close movement cycles that were too small to accurately count.

[8]Signs produced on the child's body are excluded from consideration in the analyses of sign size and duration. Also, because we analyze cyclicity separately, it is not included in our analysis of sign duration. However, one possible effect of increased cyclicity is an increase in a sign's overall duration.

TABLE 2.3
Percentage (Frequency) of Signs With Normal, Long, and Short Duration, as a Function of Eye
Contact Between Parent and Child

Eye Contact	Normal	Long	Short
Yes	36% (38/107)	54% (58/107)	10% (11/107)
No	16% (10/63)	75% (47/63)	10% (6/63)

Location of Signs in Space

Parents often produced signs outside of the usual signing space, moving signs into their child's field of vision. Less than half (80 of 194 or 41%) of the tokens were judged to have been produced in their citation-form location.

However, as shown in Table 2.4, the most common value for signs on the face was nondisplaced (58%); only 26% were low. For signs in neutral space, on the other hand, the most common value was low (53%); only 17% were nondisplaced. Our finding that signs on the face were less often displaced than signs in neutral space is probably due to physical factors. To displace a sign on the face into a child's line of focus, the entire upper body must be moved; for a sign in neutral space, only the hands must be. Thus, for signs on the face, it is probably easier either to first gain the child's attention or to produce the sign on the child's body—a strategy that, like displacement of neutral space signs, involves displacement of only the arm(s) and hand(s). Still, on occasion parents did try to move signs articulated on the face into the child's visual field. In one example, a mother produced several tokens of the sign RED with her upper body positioned almost horizontal to the floor and her face at her daughter's eye level. However, the mother only resorted to this strategy after repeated attention-getting attempts failed to elicit any response from her child.

TABLE 2.4
Percentage (Frequency) of Signs Coded as Nondisplaced, High, Low, and on the Child, as a
Function of the Sign's Place of Articulation

Place of Articulation	Nondisplaced	High	Low	On Child
Face	58% (67/116)	3% (4/116)	26% (24/116)	18% (21/116)
Neutral space	17% (13/78)	27% (21/78)	53% (41/78)	4% (3/78)

The most common form of displacement was lowering. Overall, 34% (65 of 194) of the sign tokens coded (and 57% of the tokens coded as displaced) were judged to be lower in space than would be typical of their citation forms. The adult–child height difference resulted in parents often being situated somewhat above their children. This fact probably contributed to the large number of signs produced low in the parent's signing space. Perhaps more important, however, the child's focus of attention was often a book or object being manipulated at or near the floor. By lowering signs, parents moved them into the child's existing focus of attention.

Conversely, sometimes parents produced signs higher in space—typically by elevating neutral-space signs to a location near the shoulder or face. Signs produced higher in space constituted 13% (25 of 194) of the total signs and 22% (25 of 114) of the displaced signs. In general, displacement of signs was more typical of neutral space signs than of signs on the face. However, on occasion parents slightly elevated signs that are normally produced at the mouth (e.g., FOOD, DUCK) to a location just under (and sometimes on) the nose. Ten such examples of elevation of signs on the face were identified. Because parents only used this strategy during episodes of eye contact with the child, elevation of signs on the face does not seem to be an attention-getting device, although it might play a role in maintaining children's attention. For signs articulated on the face, parents occasionally used the strategy of producing these signs on their child's body instead of on their own. Of the 116 sign tokens articulated on the face, 21 (18%) were produced on the child (see Table 2.4). Overall, signs produced on the child accounted for 21% of the displaced signs.

Displacement of signs also seemed to vary as a function of the sign's movement type. Path movement signs were less frequently displaced than signs without path movement (see Table 2.5). Of the path movement signs coded, 59% were nondisplaced; only 12% were low. Conversely, almost half (46%) of the nonpath movement signs coded were produced low in the signing space, whereas only 31% were nondisplaced. The signs MILK and DOG (both signs articulated in neutral space) accounted for the preponderance (34 of 57 or 60%) of the nonpath movement signs coded as

TABLE 2.5
Percentage (Frequency) of Signs Coded as Nondisplaced, High, Low, and on the Child, as a Function of the Sign's Movement Type

Movement	Nondisplaced	High	Low	On Child
Path	59% (41/69)	12% (8/69)	12% (8/69)	17% (12/69)
Nonpath	31% (39/125)	14% (17/125)	46% (57/125)	10% (12/125)

TABLE 2.6
Percentage (Frequency) of Signs Coded as Nondisplaced, High, Low, and on the Child, as a
Function of Parent–Child Eye Contact

Eye Contact	Nondisplaced	High	Low	On Child
Yes	55% (59/107)	23% (25/107)	21% (23/107)	0% (0/107)
No	24% (21/87)	0% (0/87)	48% (42/87)	28% (24/87)

low. Only 40% (23 of 57) of the nonpath movement signs coded as low
were signs articulated at the face.

Not surprisingly perhaps, displacement of signs occurred more often
when the parent and child did not have eye contact (76%) (see Table
2.6). When there was eye contact, slightly more than half (55%) of the
parents' signs were produced in their usual location. Typically, when there
was not eye contact, parents moved signs lower and thus into their child's
field of vision (48%) or made the sign on the child's body (28%). Signing
on the child's body occurred only in interactions in which there was not
eye contact, usually when the child was seated on the parent's lap and
facing away from the parent. In contrast, signing higher in space occurred
only when there was eye contact between the parent and child.

Size

Most of the signs in our corpus were coded as normal size (119 of 170 or
70%). However, because all comparisons were made relative to citation
forms, not casual signing, many of the normal signs reported here would
be considered large for conversation. In this sense, parents' signs are comparable to especially clear signing.

A few sign tokens that appeared smaller than the citation forms were
coded as small (27 of 170 or 16%). For the most part, these tokens were
comparable to conversational signing, in which sign size, as well as repetitions and other parameters, may be reduced. In some instances, however,
parents produced signs with many repetitions but with small movement.
There were several examples of MILK for instance, for which we were unable
to count the number of open–close hand-internal movements. In these
examples, the father produced the sign with his hand almost touching his
face; reduced sign size in these cases seemed due not to phonological
reduction as in casual signing but rather to the father's expression of affect.[9]

---

[9]This use of small signs may be similar to a hearing parent's use of a high, "little" voice
with a hearing child.

TABLE 2.7
Percentage (Frequency) of Normal, Large, and Small Signs, as a Function of the Sign's Place of
Articulation and Movement Type

Articulatory Parameters	Normal	Large	Small
Place of articulation			
Neutral space	68% (51/75)	7% (5/75)	25% (19/75)
Face	72% (68/95)	20% (19/95)	8% (8/95)
Movement type			
Nonpath	66% (75/113)	19% (21/113)	15% (17/113)
Path	77% (44/57)	5% (3/57)	18% (10/57)

Some of the parents' signs were larger than citation forms (24 of 170 or 14%). In several cases, this increase in sign size involved the addition of path movement, and a resulting shift in the articulator(s) used to produce the sign. For instance, 8 of 17 tokens of RED were produced with elbow or shoulder movement away from the face, in addition to the hand-internal movement of the citation form. One father also produced two tokens of ORANGE with added path movement away from the face. Meier, Mauk, Mirus, and Conlin (1998) reported a similar tendency toward proximalization of movement in deaf children's early signing.[10] Interestingly, none of the parents in the current study added path movement to the sign MILK; however, we have observed two other deaf parents produce the noun MILK with downward path movement in addition to the typical hand-internal move-ment. This addition of path movement resulted in a form similar to the verb MILK. Significantly perhaps, both parents who produced the noun MILK with path movement were fluent but nonnative signers.

Results for sign size differ from those for cyclicity and location in space in that size appears to be increased more often for signs on the face than for signs in neutral space. Signs in neutral space were more likely than signs on the face to be small (25% and 8%, respectively) (see Table 2.7). Likewise, signs on the face were more likely than signs in neutral space to be large (20% vs. 7%, respectively). However, almost all of the signs at the face that were coded as large were signs without path movement. As shown in Table 2.7, more signs without path movement than signs with it were coded as large (19% and 5%, respectively).[11]

---

[10]By "proximalization," Meier et al. (1998) meant that their participants tended to use articulators closer to the torso than would be expected in adult citation-form signing.

[11]The seeming tendency for enlargement of nonpath movement signs on the face as opposed to those articulated in neutral space may be an artifact of our small sample size. As noted previously, the parents in this sample did not add path movement to the sign MILK; this sign contributed to the preponderance of our data on nonpath movement signs articulated in neutral space.

TABLE 2.8
Percentage (Frequency) of Normal, Small, and Large Signs, as a Function of Parent–Child
Eye Contact

Eye Contact	Normal	Small	Large
Yes	68% (73/107)	21% (22/107)	11% (12/107)
No	73% (46/63)	8% (5/63)	19% (12/63)

Eye gaze also may have affected the size of parents' signs (see Table 2.8). Parents increased the size of a sign when there was no eye contact slightly more often (19%) than when there was (11%). Parents used small signs more often when there was eye contact than when there was not. Of signs with eye contact, 21% were coded as small, versus 8% for signs without eye contact.

DISCUSSION

It has been suggested that child-directed language serves an attention-getting purpose (e.g., Fernald, 1984, 1992; Gottlieb, 1985; Newport et al., 1977). Consistent with this, the parents in this study were more likely to make adjustments to their signing when their children were not directly focused on them, with casual signing generally reserved for instances of clear eye contact. Displacement of signs into a child's field of vision or onto a child's body largely obviates the need for first attracting the child's attention. Other modifications parents made probably also increased the probability that signs would be perceived by the child. For instance, the greater the number of repetitions and the longer the duration of a sign, the more opportunity the child has to see the sign. Likewise, larger signs would seem more likely to be successfully perceived through a child's peripheral vision than would smaller signs. It is notable that virtually all the signs analyzed here were accessible to the children—either because there was direct eye contact, because parents moved signs into their children's line of vision, or because parents produced the signs on the child's body.

The fact that signs produced on the face are in a region of high visual acuity may explain our finding that signs on the face were less repetitious than signs in neutral space. In ASL, and presumably in other signed languages, a greater number of contrastive places of articulation are distinguishable on the face than in neutral space, perhaps because signs in neutral space are typically perceived through the less acute peripheral vision system (Siple, 1980). If motherese does serve an attention-getting role and if there is indeed an inherent perceptual advantage for signs on the face, there might be less reason to make these signs more repetitious. A related possibility is that because signs on the face are less easily moved into the child's field of vision, parents are more likely to require direct visual attention for these signs than for neutral space signs, which are easily displaced by moving the hands. Perhaps parents see less need to increase the cyclicity of their signs when the children's eye gaze makes it obvious that they are attending. This would be consistent with a view of child-directed signing as an attention-getting device.

It has also been suggested by several researchers that characteristics of child-directed language might help very young children segment the continuous stream of language into recognizable units (e.g., Garnica, 1977; Hirsh-Pasek et al., 1987; Kemler-Nelson et al., 1989). One way to facilitate segmentation might be to regularize the input. In English, words with a strong–weak (trochaic) stress pattern are very common. English-speaking parents, whether consciously or not, seem to enhance this strong–weak pattern. In adult-directed English, Cutler and Norris (1988) found that strong syllables coincided with word boundaries more than 70% of the time. However, in an analysis of mothers' speech, Kelly and Martin (1994) found that the correspondence between word boundaries and strong syllables was 95%. Kelly and Martin suggested that this effect is not due to conscious choices by the mothers, but rather to the fact that a greater proportion of the vocabulary used with young children is of Germanic origin and therefore naturally fits the strong–weak template. Regardless, however, of whether parents purposely regularize their child-directed speech, the result is language that may be more easily segmented into individual words.

By adding path movement to signs without path movement, parents in our study essentially made their signs look more like typical signs in ASL, as well as perhaps making them more salient. The lexical choices made by the parents in this study may also reveal a preference in ASL for signs with path movement. For instance, all of the tokens of MOMMY and DADDY reported here were produced with repeated movement to contact (i.e., one type of path movement). Parents never chose the lexical variants (which we call MOTHER and FATHER) that have only a hand-internal movement (finger wiggling). This is consistent with observations we have made of other deaf families. We have never seen parents use the variants MOTHER and FATHER when addressing young children. Erting et al. (1990) also found that the parents in their study always used the variant we call MOMMY. A similar lexical choice perhaps occurs with the sign DOG. Instead of the sign with only hand-internal movement that is common in adult-directed language, parents often use a version with a larger, "leg-slap" movement. Frequently, the segment with hand-internal movement is deleted entirely and only the downward slapping movement is used. Caregivers might exaggerate the predominant lexical shapes of their language (trochaic stress in English, path movement in ASL) through both their lexical and phonological choices.

In conclusion, child-directed signing in ASL has many similarities to child-directed speech. Whereas child-directed speech is characterized by its distinctive prosodic contours, simplicity, and redundancy, child-directed signing in ASL is characterized by slower sign speed, longer sign duration, and repetitiousness, as well as such modality-specific characteristics as signing on the child's body and moving signs into the child's visual field. Whether parents' child-directed signing facilitates children's language learning, we do not yet know. However, evidence suggests that deaf children of deaf parents fare better socially, academically, and linguistically (e.g., Allen, 1986; Moores, 1976; Vernon & Koh, 1970). What seems clear is that the deaf parents in this study, as well as those in other studies, are closely attuned to their child's focus of attention, and adjust their signing accordingly. Obviously, visual attention is crucial in signed communications. At least insofar as it increases the amount of input that children receive, child-directed signing may play an important role in deaf children's language acquisition.

ACKNOWLEDGMENTS

We thank Claude Mauk for his assistance with reliability coding and Ann Repp for the statistical analyses. We also thank Gene Mirus for sharing his native intuitions throughout the course of the project. We are especially grateful to the four families for their participation. Gene Mirus, Anne-Marie Guerra, and Raquel Willerman assisted with data collection. This work was supported by grants from the Texas Advanced Research Program and the National Institute on Deafness and Other Communication Disorders (RO1 DC01691-05) to RPM and by a Spencer Foundation Dissertation Fellowship to ASH.

REFERENCES

Allen, T. (1986). A study of the achievement patterns of hearing-impaired students: 1974–1983. In A. Schildroth & M. Karchmer (Eds.), *Deaf children in America* (pp. 161–206). San Diego, CA: College-Hill Press.

Baker, A. E., & Bogaerde, B. van den (1996). Language input and attentional behavior. In C. E. Johnson & J. H. V. Gilbert (Eds.), *Children's language* (Vol. 9, pp. 209–217). Mahwah, NJ: Lawrence Erlbaum Associates.

Blevins, J (1993). The nature of constraints on the non-dominant hand in ASL. In G. Coulter (Ed.), *Current issues in ASL phonology* (pp. 43–62). New York: Academic Press.

Brentari, D. (1993). Establishing a sonority hierarchy in American Sign Language: The use of simultaneous structure in phonology. *Phonology, 10,* 281–306.

Cooper, R., & Aslin, R. (1990). Preference for infant-directed speech in the first month after birth. *Child Development, 51,* 1584–1595

Corina, D (1990). Reassessing the role of sonority in syllable structure: Evidence from a visual-gestural language. *Chicago Linguistic Society, 26,* 33–44.

Cutler, A , & Norris, D. (1988). The role of strong syllables in segmentation for lexical access. *Journal of Experimental Psychology, 14,* 113–121.

Erting, C. J., Prezioso, C., & Hynes, M. (1990). The interactional context of deaf mother-infant communication. In V. Volterra & C. J. Erting (Eds.), *From gesture to language in hearing and deaf children* (pp. 97–106). Heidelberg, Germany: Springer-Verlag.

Fernald, A. (1984). The perceptual and affective salience of mothers' speech to infants. In L. Feagans, C. Garvey, & R. Golinkoff (Eds.), *The origins and growth of communication* (pp. 5–29). Norwood, NJ: Ablex.

Fernald, A. (1985). Four-month-old infants prefer to listen to motherese. *Infant Behavior and Development, 8,* 181–195.

Fernald, A. (1992). Human maternal vocalizations to infants as biologically relevant signals: An evolutionary perspective. In J. H. Barkow, L. Cosmides, & J. Tooby (Eds.), *The adapted mind. Evolutionary psychology and the generation of culture* (pp 391–428). Oxford, England: Oxford University Press

Gallaway, C., & Richards, B. (1994). *Input and interaction in language acquisition* Cambridge, England: Cambridge University Press.

Garnica, O. (1977). Some prosodic and paralinguistic features of speech to young children. In C. Snow & C. Ferguson (Eds.), *Talking to children Language input and acquisition* (pp. 63–88) Cambridge, England: Cambridge University Press.

Gottlieb, G. (1985). On discovering significant acoustic dimensions of auditory stimulation for infants. In G. Gottlieb & N A. Krasnegor (Eds.), *Measurement of vision and audition in the first year of life: A methodological overview* (pp 3–29). Norwood, NJ; Ablex.

Harris, M., Clibbens, J , Chasen, J., & Tibbitts, R. (1987). The social context of early sign language development. *First Language, 9,* 81–97

Heath, S B. (1983). *Ways with words· Language, life and work in communities and classrooms* Cambridge, England: Cambridge University Press.

Hirsh-Pasek, K., Kemler-Nelson, D., Jusczyk, P., Wright, K , & Druss, B. (1987). Clauses are perceptual units for young infants. *Cognition, 26,* 269–286

Holzrichter, A. (1995). *Motherese in American Sign Language* Unpublished master's thesis, University of Texas at Austin

Humphries, T., Padden, C., & O'Rourke, T. J. (1980). *A basic course in American Sign Language.* Silver Spring, MD: T. J. Publishers

Huttenlocher, J., Haight, W., Bryk, A., Seltzer, M , & Lyons, T. (1991). Early vocabulary growth: Relation to language input and gender. *Developmental Psychology, 17,* 236–248

Jamieson, J. R. (1994). Teaching as transaction: Vygotskian perspectives on deafness and mother-child interaction. *Exceptional Children, 60,* 434–449

Kantor, R. (1982) Communicative interaction: Mother modification and child acquisition of American Sign Language. *Sign Language Studies, 38,* 233–282.

Kelly, M., & Martin, S. (1994). Domain-general abilities applied to domain-specific tasks: Sensitivity to probabilistic information in perception, cognition, and language. *Lingua, 92,* 105–140.

Kemler-Nelson, D., Hirsh-Pasek, K., Jusczyk, P., & Wright-Cassidy, K (1989) How the prosodic cues in motherese might assist language learning. *Journal of Child Language, 16,* 55–68.

Klima, E., & Bellugi, U. (1979). *The signs of language.* Cambridge, MA: Harvard University Press.

Kyle, J., & Ackerman, J. (1987). Signing for infants: Deaf mothers using BSL in the early stages of development. In W. H. Edmondson & F. Karlsson (Eds.), *SLR'87. Papers from the Fourth International Symposium on Sign Language Research* (pp. 200–211). Clevedon, England: Multilingual Matters.

Launer, P. (1982). *'A plane' is not 'to fly': Acquiring the distinction between related nouns and verbs in ASL.* Unpublished doctoral dissertation, City University of New York.

Maestas y Moores, J. (1980). Early linguistic environment: Interactions of deaf parents with their infants. *Sign Language Studies, 26,* 1–13.

Masataka, N. (1992). Motherese in a signed language. *Infant Behavior and Development, 15,* 453–460.

Masataka, N. (1996). Perception of motherese in a signed language by 6-month-old deaf infants. *Developmental Psychology, 32,* 874–879

Meier, R. P., Mauk, C., Mirus, G. R., & Conlin, K. E. (1998). Motoric constraints on early sign acquisition. In E. Clark (Ed.), *Papers and reports on child language development* (Vol. 29, pp. 63–72). Stanford, CA: CSLI Press.

Moores, D. (1976). A review of education of the deaf. In L. Mann & D. Sabatino (Eds.), *Third review of special education* (pp. 19–52). New York: Grune & Stratton.

Newport, E., Gleitman, H., & Gleitman, L. R. (1977). Mother, I'd rather do it myself. Some effects and non-effects of maternal speech style. In C. E. Snow & C. A. Ferguson (Eds.), *Talking to children: Language input and acquisition* (pp. 109–149). Cambridge, England: Cambridge University Press.

Ratner, N. B., & Pye, C. (1984). Higher pitch in BT is not universal: Acoustic evidence from Quiche Mayan. *Journal of Child Language, 11,* 515–522.

Sandler, W. (1993). A sonority cycle in American Sign Language. *Phonology, 10,* 243–279.

Schieffelin, B. (1990). *The give and take of everyday life: Language socialization of Kaluli children.* Cambridge, England: Cambridge University Press.

Siple, P. (1980). Visual constraints for sign language communication. In W. C. Stokoe (Ed.), *Sign and culture: A reader for students of American Sign Language* (pp. 319–333). Silver Spring, MD: Linstok Press.

Snow, C. E. (1977). Mothers' speech research: From input to interaction. In C. E. Snow & C. A. Ferguson (Eds.), *Talking to children: Language input and acquisition* (pp. 31–49). Cambridge, England: Cambridge University Press.

Spencer, P. E., & Gutfreund, M. K. (1990). Directiveness in mother-infant interactions. In D. F. Moores & K. P. Meadow-Orlans (Eds.), *Educational and developmental aspects of deafness* (pp. 350–365). Washington, DC: Gallaudet University Press.

Swisher, M. V. (1992). The role of parents in developing visual turn-taking in their young deaf children. *American Annals of the Deaf, 137,* 92–100.

Vernon, M., & Koh, S. D. (1970). Early manual communication and deaf children's achievement. *American Annals of the Deaf, 115,* 527–536.

Wilbur, R., & Schick, B. (1987). The effects of linguistic stress on ASL signs. *Language and Speech, 30,* 301–323.

Chapter 3

The Acquisition of Natural Signed Languages: Lessons in the Nature of Human Language and Its Biological Foundations

Laura Ann Petitto
McGill University and
Montreal Neurological Institute

THE OSTENSIBLE BIOLOGICAL FOUNDATIONS OF LANGUAGE

Prevailing views about the biological foundations of language assume that very early language acquisition is tied to speech. Universal regularities in the *timing* and *structure* of infants' vocal babbling and first words have been taken as evidence that the brain must be attuned specifically to perceiving and producing spoken language in early life. To be sure, a frequent answer to the question "how does early human language acquisition begin?" is that it is the result of the development of the neuroanatomical and neuro-physiological mechanisms involved in the perception and the production of speech. An assumption that also underlies this view is that spoken languages are better suited to the brain's maturational needs in development. Put another way, the view of human biology at work here is that evolution has rendered the human brain neurologically "hardwired" for speech (Liberman & Mattingly, 1985, 1989; Liberman, 1984).

A Reasonable Doubt

As a young student and researcher, I had reason to doubt such views. While still a college undergraduate, I moved into a large mansion on the Hudson Palisades in New York City with an infant, West-African male chimpanzee, whom we named "Nim Chimpsky" (after, of course, Noam

41

Chomsky). This animal was part of a research project at Columbia University in which I attempted to raise the chimp like a child and to teach him signed language. Our research question concerned whether aspects of human language were species specific, or whether human language was entirely learnable (and teachable) from environmental input.

Although there is still much controversy surrounding the ape language research, what has remained surprisingly uncontroversial about all of the ape language studies to date is this: All chimpanzees fail to master key aspects of human language structure, even when you bypass their inability to produce speech by exposing them to other types of linguistic input, for example, natural signed languages. In other words, despite the chimpanzee's general communicative and cognitive abilities, their linguistic abilities do not equal what we humans do with language, be it signed or spoken. This fact raised the hypothesis to me that humans possessed *something* at birth *in addition to* the mechanisms for producing and perceiving speech sounds. Indeed, whatever this elusive "something" was, I knew that attempts to understand it would provide the key to what it was that distinguished human language from the communication of other animals.

CRITICAL EVIDENCE REGARDING THE BIOLOGICAL FOUNDATIONS OF HUMAN LANGUAGE

As noted previously, most all contemporary thought about the biological foundations of language is based on the core assumption that language and speech are neurologically privileged from birth. There is, however, a flaw with this assumption: Given that only languages utilizing the speech modality are studied, it is, *a priori*, impossible to find data that would do anything but support this hypothesis. Only when a modality other than speech is analyzed can any generalization about the brain's predisposition for speech be evaluated.

Over the past 15 years, my research program has been directed at understanding the biological foundations of human language by examining both spoken and signed languages. The goal has been to discover the specific biological and environmental factors that together permit early language acquisition to begin in our species.

Studies of very early signed language acquisition offer an especially clear window into the biological foundations of all of human language. Spoken and signed languages utilize different perceptual modalities (sound vs. sight), and the motor control of the tongue and hands are subserved by different neural substrates in the brain. Comparative analyses of these languages, then, provide key insights into the specific neural architecture that determines early human language acquisition in our species. If, as has been argued, very early human language acquisition is under the exclusive control of the maturation of the mechanisms for speech production and speech perception (Locke, 1983; Van der Stelt & Koopmans-van Bienum, 1986), then spoken and signed languages should be acquired in radically different ways. At the very least, fundamental differences in the *time course* and *structure* of spoken versus signed language acquisition would suggest that each may be processed and represented in different ways, presumably due to their use of different neural substrates in the human brain.

To investigate these issues, I conducted numerous comparative studies of children acquiring two spoken languages, English and French, and children acquiring two autonomous signed languages, American Sign Language (ASL) and Langue des Signes Québécoise (LSQ), from birth through the age of 48 months.

The empirical findings from these cross-linguistic and cross-modal studies are clear, involving surprising similarities in the overall time course and structure of early signed and spoken language acquisition.

Timing Milestones in Signing and Speaking Children

Deaf children exposed to signed languages from birth acquire these languages on an identical maturational time course as hearing children acquire spoken languages. Deaf children acquiring signed languages do so without any modification, loss, or delay to the timing, content, and maturational course associated with reaching all linguistic milestones observed in spoken language (e.g., Charron & Petitto, 1987, 1991; Petitto, 1984, 1985, 1987a, 1988; Petitto & Bellugi, 1988; Petitto & Charron, 1988; Petitto & Marentette, 1990, 1991)—a finding that is also corroborated in the important findings of other researchers (e.g., Bellugi & Klima, 1982; Meier, 1991; Newport & Meier, 1985). Beginning at birth, and continuing through age 3 and beyond, speaking and signing children exhibit the identical stages of language acquisition. These include the (a) *syllabic babbling stage* (7–10 months) as well as other developments in babbling, including "variegated babbling," ages 10 to 12 months, and "jargon babbling," ages 12 months and beyond; (b) *first word stage* (11–14 months); (c) *first two-word stage* (16–22 months), and the grammatical and semantic developments beyond.

Surprising similarities are also observed in deaf and hearing children's timing onset and use of gestures (Petitto, 1992). Signing and speaking children produce strikingly similar prelinguistic (9–12 months) and postlinguistic communicative gestures (12–48 months). They do not produce more gestures, even though linguistic "signs" (identical to the "word") and communicative gestures reside in the same modality, and even though some signs and gestures are formationally and referentially similar. Instead, deaf children consistently differentiate linguistic signs from communicative gestures throughout development, using each in the same ways observed in hearing children.

Throughout development, signing and speaking children also exhibit remarkably similar complexity in their utterances. For example, analyses of young ASL and LSQ children's social and conversational patterns of language use over time, as well as the types of things that they "talk" about over time (the semantic and conceptual content, categories, and referential scope), have demonstrated unequivocally that their language acquisition follows the identical path seen in age-matched hearing children acquiring spoken language (Charron & Petitto, 1987, 1991; Petitto, 1992; Petitto & Charron, 1988).

Recent work focuses on two very unusual populations, involving hearing children in bilingual, "bimodal" (signing–speaking) homes, as well as hearing children who are not being exposed to spoken language at all, only signed languages. The *hearing* children exposed to *both* signed and spoken languages from birth (e.g., one parent signs and the other parent speaks) demonstrate no preference for speech whatsoever, even though they can hear. Instead, they acquire both the signed and the spoken languages to which they are being exposed on an identical maturational timetable (Petitto, Costopoulos, & Stevens, in preparation). That is, the timing of the onset of all linguistic milestones occurs at the same time in both the signed and spoken modalities. For example, the bilingual, bimodal children acquiring French and LSQ produced their first word in French and their first sign in LSQ within hours of each other. Crucially, such children acquire the signed and spoken languages to which they are being exposed in the same manner that other children acquire two different spoken languages from birth in bilingual homes—for example, one with spoken Italian and French.

Most surprisingly, *hearing* children who are exposed *exclusively* to signed languages from birth through early childhood, with no spoken language input, achieve all milestones in signed language on the identical time course as seen in hearing children acquiring spoken language and deaf children acquiring signed languages (manual babbling, first signs, first two-signs, and beyond) (Petitto et al., in preparation). Thus, normal language acquisition occurred in these hearing children—albeit signed— *without* the use of auditory and speech perception mechanisms, and *without* the use of the motoric mechanisms for the production of speech.

Having established that the overall time courses of signed and spoken language acquisition are highly similar, questions remain about just how deep the similarities are in acquisition at the specific, structural level. I now review studies that address this issue in an attempt to shed new light on the mechanisms that underlie early language acquisition.

Structural Homologies in Signing and Speaking Children

In trying to understand the biological roots of human language, researchers have naturally tried to find its "beginning." The regular onset of vocal babbling—the "*bababa*" and other repetitive, syllabic sounds that infants produce—led researchers to conclude that babbling represents the beginning of human language acquisition, albeit language production. Babbling—and thus early language acquisition in our species—is said to be *determined* by the *development of the anatomy of the vocal tract and the neuroanatomical and neurophysiological mechanisms subserving the motor control of speech production* (Locke, 1983; Van der Stelt & Koopmans-van Bienum, 1986). The behavior has been further used to argue that the human language capacity must be uniquely linked to innate mechanisms for producing speech in ontogeny (Liberman & Mattingly, 1985, 1989). Crucially, it has also been used to argue that human language has been shaped by properties of speech in phylogeny (Lieberman, 1984).

In the course of conducting research on deaf infants' transition from prelinguistic gesturing to first signs, a class of hand activity containing linguistically relevant, "babbling-like" units that was different from all other hand activity during the "transition period" (9–12 months) became apparent (Petitto, 1984, 1987a, 1987b). These deaf infants appeared to be babbling with their hands. Additional studies were undertaken to understand the basis of this extraordinary behavior. The findings reported in Petitto & Marentette (1991) revealed unambiguously a discrete class of hand activity in deaf infants that was structurally identical to vocal babbling observed in hearing infants. Like vocal babbling, manual babbling was found to possess (i) a restricted set of phonetic units (unique to signed languages), (ii) syllabic organization, and it was (iii) used without meaning or reference. This hand activity was also wholly distinct from all infants' rhythmic hand activity, be they deaf or hearing. Even its structure was wholly distinct from all infants' communicative gestures.

The discovery of babbling in another modality confirmed the hypothesis that babbling represents a distinct and critical stage in the ontogeny of human language. However, it disconfirmed existing hypotheses about why babbling occurs: It disconfirmed the view that babbling is neurologically determined by the maturation of the speech-production mechanisms, per se. Specifically, it was thought that the *baba*, CV (consonant–vowel) alternation that infants produce is determined by the rhythmic opening and closing of the mandible (MacNeilage & Davis, 1990).

The Petittto and Marentette (1991) study also demonstrated the existence of "syllabic organization" in manual babbling. Like spoken language, the structural nucleus of the syllable in signed languages consists of the rhythmic opening and closing (or the rhythmic movement–hold) alternations of the hands/arms. Results indicated that the sign syllable alone possesses a special rhythmic (or temporal) organization that is unlike all other hand activity observed in all infants. The convergence of similar structures unique to babbling, be it on the hands or on the tongue, suggested that something else was contributing to the appearance of babbling in ontogeny; something other than the mandible, per se, was guiding this convergence of structure on two radically different modalities.

I hypothesized that this "something else" is the existence of *supra-modal constraints*, with the rhythmic oscillations of babbling being key (Petitto, 1997). Both manual and vocal babbling alone are produced in rhythmic, temporally oscillating bundles, which I hypothesized may, in turn, be yoked to constraints on the infant's perceptual systems. The next challenge then was to figure out how to study it.

A new study of manual babbling uses innovative technology, called the "OPTOTRAK Computer Visual-Graphic Analysis System," in an attempt to understand the rhythmic nature of babbling (Petitto, Ostry, Sergio, & Levy, in preparation). The precise physical properties of infants' manual activity were measured by placing tiny infrared emitting diodes (IREDs) on infants' hands and feet. The IREDs transmitted light impulses to cameras that, in turn, sent signals into the OPTOTRAK system. This information was then fed into computer software that provided us with information analogous to the *spectrographic representation of speech*, but involved the *spectrographic representation of sign*. Thus, for the first time, we were able to obtain recordings of the timing, rate, path movement, velocity, and "F_o"[1] for all infant hand activity, and to obtain sophisticated, 3-D graphic displays of each.

Preliminary results revealed the following: (a) Systematic *differences* exist between the rhythmic timing, velocity, and spectral frequencies of sign-exposed infants' manual babbling versus all infants' rhythmic hand activity (be they sign exposed or not); (b) Systematic *similarities* exist in the timing contours of infants' manual and vocal babbling; (c) Converging structures observed in infant *and* adult-to-infant signing–speaking productions suggest that all humans at birth may possess peak sensitivity to a rudimentary "timing envelope"—a rhythmic timing bundle in natural language prosody of about 1.2 seconds—as well as a sensitivity to any maximally contrastive units that fall within this temporal period (e.g., a unit the size of the syllable).

Thus, homologous structural organization was observed in manual and vocal babbling, even though the neural substrates for manual articulation differ from the neural substrates for the articulation of speech.

---

[1]The fundamental frequency (F_o) was calculated by decomposing the infants' 3-D movements into underlying spectral components (i.e., the different frequencies of movements that contributed to each hand, arm, and foot motion), and subsequently calculating these frequencies to their individual magnitude or power.

Significance of Studies of Early Signed and Spoken Language Acquisition

Despite the modality differences, signed and spoken languages are acquired in virtually identical ways. The differences that are observed between children acquiring a signed language versus children acquiring a spoken language are no greater than the differences observed between hearing children learning one spoken language, say, Italian, versus another, say, Finnish. Such findings cast serious doubt on the core hypothesis in very early spoken language acquisition: that the maturation of the mechanisms for the production and perception of speech exclusively determines the time course and structure of early human language acquisition. These findings further challenge the hypothesis that speech (and sound) is critical to normal language acquisition, and they challenge the related hypothesis that speech is uniquely suited to the brain's maturational needs in language ontogeny.

If speech alone were neurologically set or "privileged" in early brain development, then, for example, *hearing* infants exposed to both speech and sign from birth might be expected to attempt to glean every morsel of speech that they could get from their environment. Faced implicitly with a "choice" between speech and sign, the very young hearing infant in this context might be expected to turn away from the sign input, favoring instead the speech input, and thereby acquire signs differently (possibly later). Similarly, deaf *and* hearing infants exposed only to signed languages from birth should have demonstrated grossly abnormal patterns of language acquisition. None of this happened.

What is most remarkable about these findings is that the modality "switch" can be "thrown" *after* birth regarding whether a child acquires language on the hands or language on the tongue. We saw that children exposed to signed languages can acquire them just as easily as children exposed to spoken languages. Speech and sound are *not* critical to human language acquisition. Instead, there appears to be a stunning, biologically based *equipotentiality* of the modalities—be it spoken or signed—to receive and produce natural language in ontogeny. What, then, could this mean about the human brain at birth and how is language acquisition possible in our species?

THE BIOLOGICAL FOUNDATIONS OF LANGUAGE

The key issue for students of early brain development is not the fact *that* signed and spoken languages are acquired similarly, but to determine *why* this is so. Given the different neural substrates, where does the capacity to produce common linguistic structures come from? How is it possible that the modality of language transmission and reception can be changed at birth—from speech to sign, or vice versa—without any delay or alteration to the time course and nature of human language acquisition? How can the brain tolerate this radical change in the morphology of its expressive and receptive mechanisms for language, and what is the genetic basis for such stunning equipotentiality?

The present findings demonstrate that the brain at birth cannot be working under rigid genetic instruction to produce and receive language via the auditory–speech modality, per se. If this were the case, then both the maturational time course and the nature of signed and spoken language acquisition should be different. By contrast, using a wide variety of techniques and participant populations, I discovered that the acquisition of signed and spoken language is fundamentally similar.

What these findings do suggest is that the neural substrates that support the brain's capacity for language can be potentiated in multiple ways in the face of varying environmental pressures. The fact that the brain can tolerate variation in language transmission and reception, depending on different environmental inputs, and still achieve the target behavior provides support for there being a strong *amodal* genetic component underlying language acquisition, rather than the reverse. That is, the genetic foundations of language are not at the level of modality but at the level of abstract features of language structure such as its rhythmic and distributional patterning. Furthermore, there are multiple pathways by which language acquisition can occur. Thus, I suggest that a sensitivity to aspects of the specific distributional patterns found only in natural language is genetically determined and present at birth; this would constitute what is "rigid" or "fixed" about the brain in early language acquisition. At the same time, the language acquisition process is "flexible" in that language can be perceived and expressed via the hands or tongue.

In conclusion, the present findings led me to propose a new way to construe human language ontogeny. The only way that signed and spoken languages could be acquired with such startling similarity is if the brains of *all* newborns possess a mechanism that is sensitive to specific aspects of the distributional patterns and structural regularities of natural language, irrespective of the input modality. Rather than being exclusively hardwired for speech or sound, the young of our species are initially hardwired to detect aspects of the patterning of *language*—specifically, aspects of its rhythmic and distributional regularities—corresponding to the syllabic and prosodic levels of natural language organization. If the environmental input contains the requisite patterns unique to natural language, human infants will attempt to produce and acquire those patterns, irrespective of whether the input is on the hands or the tongue.

REFERENCES

Bellugi, U., & Klima, E. (1982). The acquisition of three morphological systems in American Sign Language. *Papers and Reports on Child Language Development, 21*, 1–35.

Charron, F., & Petitto, L. A. (1987). Semantic categories in the acquisition of Langue des Signes Québécoise (LSQ) and American Sign Language (ASL). *Abstracts of the Twelfth Annual Boston University Conference on Language Development*, 28.

Charron, F., & Petitto, L. A. (1991). Les premiers signes acquis par des enfants sourds en langue des signes québécoise (LSQ): Comparaison avec les premiers mots [The first signs acquired by deaf children in LSQ: A comparison with first words]. *Revue Québécoise de Linguistique Théorique et Appliquée, 10*(1), 71–122.

Liberman, A. M., & Mattingly, I. G. (1985). The motor theory of speech perception. *Cognition, 21*(1), 1–36.

Liberman, A. M., & Mattingly, I. G. (1989). A specialization for speech perception. *Science, 243*(4890), 489–494.

Lieberman, P. (1984). *The biology and evolution of language*. Cambridge, MA: Harvard University Press.

Locke, J. L. (1983). *Phonological acquisition and change*. New York: Academic Press.

MacNeilage, P. F., & Davis, B. (1990). Acquisition of speech production: Frames, then content. In M. Jeannerod (Ed.), *Attention & performance XII: Motor representation and control* (pp. 453–476). Hillsdale, NJ: Lawrence Erlbaum Associates.

Meier, R. (1991). Language acquisition by deaf children. *American Scientist, 79*, 60–70

Newport, E., & Meier, R. (1985). The acquisition of American Sign Language. In D. Slobin (Ed.), *The crosslinguistic study of language acquisition* (Vol. 1, pp. 881–938). Hillsdale, NJ: Lawrence Erlbaum Associates.

Petitto, L. A. (1984). *From gesture to symbol: The relationship between form and meaning in the acquisition of personal pronouns in American Sign Language*. Unpublished doctoral dissertation, Harvard University.

Petitto, L. A. (1985). Are signed languages acquired earlier than spoken languages? *Abstracts of The Society for Research in Child Development*, 269.

Petitto, L. A. (1987a). On the autonomy of language and gesture: Evidence from the acquisition of personal pronouns in American Sign language, *Cognition, 27*(1), 1–52.

Petitto, L. A. (1987b, July). *Theoretical and methodological issues in the study of sign language babbling Preliminary evidence from American Sign Language (ASL) and Langue des Signes Québécoise (LSQ)*. Paper presented at the Fourth International Symposium on Sign Language Research, Lappeenranta, Finland.

Petitto, L. A. (1988), "Language" in the pre-linguistic child. In F. Kessel (Ed.), *Development of language and language researchers· Essays in honor of Roger Brown* (pp. 187–221). Hillsdale, NJ: Lawrence Erlbaum Associates.

Petitto, L. A. (1992). Modularity and constraints in early lexical acquisition: Evidence from children's first words/signs and gestures. In M. Gunnar & M. Maratsos (Eds.), *Modularity and constraints in language and cognition The Minnesota Symposia on Child Psychology* (pp. 25–58). Hillsdale, NJ: Lawrence Erlbaum Associates.

Petitto, L. A. (1997). In the beginning: On the genetic and environmental factors that make early language acquisition possible. In M. Gopnik (Ed.), *The inheritance and innateness of grammars* (pp. 45–69). Oxford, England: Oxford University Press.

Petitto, L. A., & Bellugi, U. (1988). Spatial cognition and brain organization: Clues from the acquisition of a language in space. In J. Stiles-Davies, U. Bellugi, & M. Kritchevsky (Eds.), *Spatial cognition: Brain bases and development* (pp. 299–341). Hillsdale, NJ: Lawrence Erlbaum Associates.

Petitto, L. A., & Charron, F. (1988, May). *The acquisition of semantic categories in two sign languages* Paper presented at Theoretical Issues in Sign Language Research, Washington, DC.

Petitto, L. A., Costopoulos, N., & Stevens, L. (in preparation). The identity of linguistic milestones in signed and spoken languages: Evidence for a unitary timing mechanism in the ontogeny of language.

Petitto, L. A., & Marentette, P. (1990). The timing of linguistic milestones in sign language acquisition: Are first signs acquired earlier than first words? *Abstracts of the 15th Annual Boston University Conference on Language Development,* 34.

Petitto, L. A., & Marentette, P. (1991). Babbling in the manual mode: Evidence for the ontogeny of language. *Science, 251,* 1483–1496.

Petitto, L. A., Ostry, D., Sergio, L , & Levy, B. (in preparation) Linguistic versus non-linguistic manual activity in signing and non-signing infants under one year: The motoric underpinnings.

Van der Stelt, J. M., & Koopmans-van Bienum, F J. (1986). The onset of babbling related to gross motor development. In B. Lindblom & R. Zetterstrom (Eds.), *Precursors of early speech* (pp. 163–173). New York: Stockton.

Chapter 4

The Acquisition of First Signs:
Place, Handshape, and Movement

Kimberly E. Conlin
Texas School for the Blind

Gene R. Mirus
Claude Mauk
Richard P. Meier
University of Texas at Austin

Since Stokoe's pioneering work on the structure of American Sign Language (ASL), signs have generally been described in terms of three major parameters: hand configuration, place of articulation, and movement (Stokoe, Casterline, & Croneberg, 1965). The psycholinguistic literature on ASL has since uncovered effects that differ strikingly by phonological parameter; this is true both of short-term memory for signs and of slips of the hand (Klima & Bellugi, 1979). The general result that, under the stresses of human performance, signs sometimes cleave along the lines of one or the other of these formational parameters supports the psychological reality of sublexical structure in ASL (Klima & Bellugi, 1979). The specific result that handshape is particularly susceptible to being slipped can be used to support the claim that handshape has a unique status within the phonology of ASL (e.g., on a separate tier as in Sandler, 1989). In the acquisition literature, one diary study found that place of articulation is much more accurately produced in children's early signs than is handshape or movement (Siedlecki & Bonvillian, 1993). Here, we revisit early phonological development in children acquiring ASL as a first language; we use videotaped data of spontaneous conversations between deaf children and their deaf parents to probe the relative difficulty of the three major parameters of sign formation.

Although the acquisition literature on ASL is large (see Meier, 1991; Meier & Newport, 1990; and Newport & Meier, 1985, for reviews), the literature on the form of early signs is surprisingly scant. Research on early sign development has been largely driven by such issues as whether first signs appear earlier than first words and whether early signs are distinct from prelinguistic gestures (e.g., Meier & Newport, 1990; Orlansky & Bonvillian, 1985; Petitto, 1988; Volterra & Iverson, 1995). The articulatory properties of early signs have received occasional attention: McIntire (1977) and Boyes Braem (1990) examined the order by which ASL handshapes are acquired. Bonvillian and his colleagues have published a number of papers that report diary data on early vocabulary development in children of deaf, signing parents. On the basis of such data, Orlansky and Bonvillian (1984) argued, for example, that iconic signs are not overrepresented in the early vocabularies of signing children. Siedlecki and Bonvillian (1993) sought to probe early phonological development by recruiting parents to report how their children produce their first signs. Diary studies allow researchers to avoid well-known pitfalls of working with very young children: For example, when parents are collecting data, we worry less about the fact that children, during the earliest stages of language acquisition, may speak or sign only occasionally, and perhaps not at all in the presence of an observer.

Notwithstanding the advantages of diary studies, it is clear that a detailed understanding of early sign development demands access to videotaped data of children's sign productions. Only with careful transcription of videotaped data can we be confident that our description of trends in the phonological development of sign is not unduly affected by the biases of parental observers.

Studies of early sign development will prove important on several grounds. These studies may help us decide between competing models of the adult language: Like analyses of the slips of the hand produced by adults, analyses of children's errors may provide clues to how children represent the signs of their language. Models of the adult language will likely differ in how readily those insights are accommodated. More immediately, studies of early sign development may help us determine what constitutes a canonical sign (or perhaps, a canonical sign syllable), just as studies of early speech development have yielded evidence that, across children and across languages, the consonant–vowel syllable is the canonical, or "unmarked," syllable type of speech (cf. Oller & Lynch, 1992, for a review of early speech development).

Furthermore, studies of how children articulate their first signs may yield insights into motor development that will complement analyses of the development of reaching and manual dexterity in infants. Conveniently, in sign, unlike in speech, the articulators are readily visible. The large literature on the development of nonlinguistic manual behaviors may assist us in identifying constraints on early sign production that reflect general motoric development.[1] We hope to distinguish such constraints

---

[1] See Grove (1990) for a review of motoric factors that may affect the acquisition of "augmentative" sign systems in learning-disabled children.

from those deriving from the fact that sign production is a behavioral manifestation of the child's acquisition of a rule-governed linguistic system in which specific lexical items must be learned. In some instances, constraints on sign formation in adult sign languages may find their explanation in motor constraints that have minimal consequence for the adult, but that are quite limiting for the child. Inasmuch as languages must be learnable by the child and inasmuch as children may be peculiarly responsible for shaping sign languages (see, e.g., Kegl, Senghas, & Coppola, 1999; Meier 1984; Singleton, Morford, & Goldin-Meadow, 1993), such constraints may have enduring reflexes in adult grammar.

Last, a thorough understanding of how infants articulate their first signs is crucial to any account of the relation between so-called manual babbling and early sign development (cf. Meier & Willerman, 1995; Petitto & Marentette, 1991; and Velguth, 1995, for reports of manual babbling). In speech, there is no bright line between vocal babbling and early word production. Indeed, the articulatory propensities of babblers persist as they produce their first words and may even predict which words they choose to produce (Locke, 1983, 1985). Close attention to manual babbling must be matched by equally careful attention to how children articulate their first signs if we are to understand how manual babbling gives way to early sign production.

Here, we examine naturalistic data on the acquisition of first signs to compare children's performance with respect to the three major parameters by which ASL signs have traditionally been described: place of articulation, hand configuration, and movement.

METHODS

Participants

We followed 3 deaf children of deaf parents longitudinally from as early as 7 months of age to as late as 17 months; all 3 were girls. In all three families, ASL was the primary language of the home. Each child had at least one deaf grandparent and thus, each child received input from at least one native-signing parent. Because her family moved out of state, 1 child whom we refer to as Caitlin was followed only from 8 to 11 months of age. We followed Susie from 7 months, 3 weeks to 15 months and Noel from 9 months, 3 weeks through 17 months.[2]

Procedures

The children were videotaped biweekly while interacting at home with a parent, a native-signing experimenter, or both. We sought to identify all

---

[2]Subsequently, we report ages as follows: "7;3" is 7 months, 3 weeks.

ASL signs that the children produced on videotape. Among the three primary coders (KEC, GRM, & CM) was one native deaf signer of ASL (GRM). A gesture was considered a sign only if its form was recognizably related to an adult sign and if it was used in an appropriate context for that sign. For the purposes of this analysis, pointing signs other than the first-person pronoun ME were excluded. All candidate signs were coded according to their context of use and their articulatory shape. In essence, the coding of articulatory shape is a modified version of Stokoe's system for describing ASL signs (Stokoe et al., 1965). Thus, for current purposes, children's early signs are treated as a simultaneous bundle of phonological features and are not analyzed in terms of sequentially ordered segments. Videotapes were coded using a database program (Filemaker Pro) on a Macintosh computer.

The coded data were analyzed with respect to three major parameters of sign formation: place of articulation on the body, handshape, and movement. For place of articulation, the database provided the coder with a menu of 17 values, including seven regions on the face and head, the nondominant hand, the nondominant arm, three regions in the upper torso (ipsilateral side, middle, and contralateral side of the torso), the waist, and the leg.[3] We also coded whether or not a sign was articulated within neutral space, out of neutral space, or elevated beyond neutral space. Handshapes were coded using now-traditional labels drawn from the fingerspelling system of ASL, augmented by certain labels that are in effect featural (e.g., "bent" as in *bent-5*, a handshape with all fingers spread, extended from the first knuckle, but bent at the second, or "dot" as in *A-dot*, an A handshape with the thumb extended). Our coding system for handshape also included the handshape *lax*, which is a neutral handshape resembling a partially spread and extended 5-hand. In total, 25 handshape values were used in the coding of the dominant hand; the coding system allows additional values that were never needed in these data (e.g., the R-hand configuration did not appear in our data).

Within our movement parameter, we coded for the distinction between path movement signs and nonpath movement signs, as well as 11 types of path movements distinguished by direction of movement, shape of movement path, and uni- versus bidirectionality. This parameter in our coding system does not include hand-internal movements, wrist extension and flexion, or forearm rotation that results in pronation or supination of the hand.

---

[3]We could readily have added values for other places of articulation to our coding system (e.g., the neck as in the sign CURIOUS); however, the children produced no signs at these other places of articulation. By the terms *ipsilateral side* and *contralateral side* we refer to the sides of the torso that are, respectively, ipsilateral and contralateral to the signing hand.

We also coded each sign for an array of other articulatory dimensions that are not systematically discussed here; these include hand-internal movement, palm orientation, contacting region, hand arrangement (i.e., one- vs. two-handed), hand dominance, and number of movement cycles, among others. Last, we noted which joint(s) were involved in the execution of each sign (i.e., shoulder, elbow, the radioulnar joint of the forearm, the wrist, the first knuckles, and the second knuckles).[4]

Reliability

Approximately one third of the videotaped samples were coded by a second coder working independently. Agreement between the primary and secondary coders as to what gestural events constituted signs was 71%.[5] Agreement on place of articulation was 73%, but rose to 85% if we ignored discrepancies arising solely from the decision as to whether a sign was articulated in or out of the sign space. Agreement on the hand configuration of the dominant hand was 76%; this level of agreement was achieved by conflating certain handshapes that can be difficult to discriminate on videotape, specifically, handshapes with an extended index finger (the 1, G, D, and L-hands) and two handshapes with all fingers extended and spread (the 5-hand and its lax variant). Agreement on movement was 83%; this was achieved by conflating two movement categories (bidirectional up-and-down movement with repeated downward movement).

RESULTS

Overall Results

For the 3 participants in this study, 372 tokens of 79 different signs were coded; for a list of these signs by participant, see the Appendix. Because of the relatively small number of tokens, the data were pooled over age; consequently, we report no developmental analyses here. Figure 4.1 shows the frequency of errors by parameter, for each of the 3 participants. Summed across the children, this analysis revealed relatively few errors (18.6% of 372 tokens) on place of articulation. In contrast, handshape errors (75.0% of all tokens; dominant hand only) were much more frequent. Except in the data from Caitlin, movement was also less accurately

---

[4]An analysis of the cyclicity of our participants' sign productions and of the joints used in the execution of those signs is reported in Meier, Mauk, Mirus, and Conlin (1998).

[5]Subsequent analyses report data from the primary coders. Although we did not reconcile disagreements between the coders, we did compare our analysis of the full data set (reported in a later section) to an analysis of those signs that had been independently identified by two coders. With respect to the relative error rates for place of articulation, movement, and handshape, the two analyses revealed identical results.

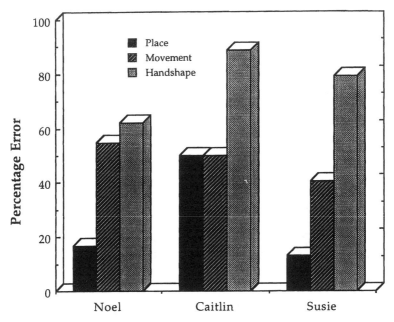

FIG. 4.1. Error rate on three parameters of sign formation in three deaf children of deaf parents: Noel (9;3–17;0), Caitlin (8;0–11;0), and Susie (7;3–15;0).

produced than place of articulation (46.0% of 372 tokens in error) but for all participants was more accurately produced than handshape.[6]

In the analysis just reported, a child's articulation of a sign outside the sign space was considered to be a place error. However, the articulatory distinction between inside and outside the sign space is not phonologically contrastive. In a follow-up analysis of the data on place of articulation, we restricted the class of place errors to exclude those tokens that were judged incorrect solely by virtue of their articulation outside the signing space. On this more conservative definition of a place error, there were 43 errors in 372 tokens (11.6%). Caitlin produced 8 such errors in 44 tokens (18.2%); Susie produced 22 errors in 215 tokens (10.2%); and Noel produced 13 errors in a set of 113 tokens (11.5%). Note also that on this new analysis, the place data from Caitlin are much more congruent with the data from the 2 other children (cf. Fig. 4.1).

We also compared the variability of each child's productions with respect to handshape, place of articulation, and movement. To be included in this

---

[6]As noted, our "movement" category does not include hand-internal movements. Were they to be included in the category, there would be no change on the relative error rates on place, movement, and handshape. Averaged over the 3 children, the error rate on hand-internal movement was 52%.

TABLE 4 1
Variability in Children's Sign Productions by Parameter

Child	Handshape	Place of Articulation	Movement
Caitlin	13/5 = 2.60	5/3 = 1.67	13/6 = 2.17
Susie	79/31 = 2.55	5/4 = 1.25	40/19 = 2 11
Noel	34/14 = 2 43	6/4 = 1.50	24/11 = 2.18
Mean	2.53	1.47	2.15

Note. Variability in children's productions is expressed as a ratio in which the denominator indicates the number of sign types on which the child produced at least one error for the parameter in question The numerator is the summation of the number of values (including the correct one, if produced) identified on that parameter for each of those sign types. A sign type was included here only if the child in question produced two or more tokens of it. The number of tokens of a given form is not considered here

analysis, a sign type must have been produced two or more times by the child. For a given parameter, we assessed variability only with respect to the set of signs on which the child erred in the production of that parameter. We then assumed that the expected number of values per sign type for handshape, for motion, and for place of articulation was in each case one.[7] The ratio of the actually encountered number of values to the predicted number of values gives an indication of the relative variability of handshape, place, and movement in each child's early sign production. The results appear in Table 4.1. In essence, the ratios reported here are type-to-type ratios: For example, Susie erred with respect to place on four signs. For three of those signs, she produced only one place value per sign. However, for one sign, she produced two different place values, making a total of five place values summed over these four sign types. These results on the variability of children's sign productions match those from the analysis of error frequency by parameter. Although the error data are sparse with respect to place, the current results suggest that, when children did err, their errors were relatively consistent across tokens. In contrast, children's productions were much more varied with respect to handshape.

Place of Articulation

A majority of the signs attempted by these three participants were produced either on the face and head (140 tokens or 37.6% of the corpus) or in

[7]Were we analyzing adult conversations, this assumption would be too strong because we would thereby be overlooking variation across registers. For example, the place of articulation of citation-form KNOW is the forehead. However, in colloquial conversation, that place may be "reduced" to the cheek.

neutral space (178 tokens or 47.8%); few signs had the nondominant hand (25 tokens or 6.7%) or some other region of the body such as the torso or nondominant arm (29 tokens or 7.8%) as their place of articulation.[8] Place errors that implicated signs articulated on the face included BED, FLOWER, DOLL, DADDY, CAT, COW, MOUSE, and TELEPHONE. For example, Noel at age 14;0 signed BED with palm contact on the ear instead of the cheek.

Phonologically contrastive errors with respect to neutral space signs were few. Not surprisingly perhaps, adult signs that are articulated in neutral space did not gain contact on the body in children's productions.[9] The errors that did occur in infant production of signs of this class arose from the child having articulated the sign outside the sign space (either too elevated in space or too far from the torso). The only exceptions were found in some of one child's tokens of a one-handed sign PET (Caitlin 10;2). In a subset of these tokens (4 of 24) in which she happened to be sitting on the floor, her hand contacted her upper leg.

The children produced a relatively small number of signs that in the adult language have the torso as the place of articulation (17 tokens or 4.6%), but such signs yielded a comparatively high error rate. They erred on 10 of these tokens. With two exceptions (two tokens of MONKEY in which the child substituted neutral space for ipsilateral torso), the errors substituted an ipsilateral location for an expected medial or contralateral location. For example, the one-handed sign BARNEY (i.e., the name of the purple dinosaur) contacted the ipsilateral side of the torso rather than the expected contralateral location (Noel: one token at 13;2 and two tokens at 16;1). Similarly, the place of articulation in one token of the sign BEAR—a two-handed sign in which each hand contacts the contralateral side of the chest—became ipsilateral; each hand contacted the ipsilateral side of the torso (Susie 14;2). Bonvillian and Seidlecki (1996) noticed a similar pattern in their parental report data; they attributed the phenomenon to difficulties that very young children have in reaching across the midline even in nonlinguistic manual activity.

As noted earlier, place of articulation errors tended to be consistent across tokens. For example, one child (Susie at ages 14;0 and 15;0) erred

---

[8]The frequency of signs made with the nondominant hand as the place of articulation seems strikingly low in our data. Klima and Bellugi (1979) reported that an analysis of the *Dictionary of American Sign Language* (Stokoe et al., 1965) revealed that such signs constitute 25% of the adult lexicon. Klima and Bellugi (1979) further reported that 37% of ASL signs are articulated in neutral space and 37% have some region of the body other than the nondominant hand as their place of articulation. Unfortunately, they did not break the data down further. We have no data on the frequency of different places of articulation in parental input to children.

[9]In four tokens, the opposite happened: Two tokens of MOUSE (Susie 11;0) and two tokens of MONKEY (Susie 14;2) were produced in neutral space. In the adult language, MOUSE has contact at the nose and MONKEY at the ipsilateral side of the torso.

consistently in her production of DOLL; in 7 tokens she produced DOLL at the lower lip, instead of at the nose. Another consistent place error, again from Susie (13;2), appeared in the production of the sign FLOWER: In 4 tokens the place of articulation was the ear, instead of the upper lip.[10]

However, we also encountered two instances of place of articulation errors in which the child erred in the production of signs that she typically produced correctly. For instance, Caitlin produced 5 tokens of the sign CAT in the videotaped samples from 10;2 and 11;1. The place of articulation was incorrect in just one instance. During this token, Caitlin's head was turned to search for her pet cat and she contacted her ear instead of her cheek. All other tokens of CAT produced by this child were correct in place of articulation. A similar—and more revealing—error occurred in a single token of the sign DADDY that Noel produced at 14 months. At the outset, this sign was correctly articulated at the center of the forehead. But during the production of the sign, Noel turned her head. Consequently, in the subsequent movement cycles of this sign, her hand contacted the side of her head, not her forehead. These two errors suggest that children may have some difficulty coordinating linguistic movements with nonlinguistic ones.

There were also more subtle differences in place of articulation between the participants' productions and the adult ASL models, most of which disappeared in subsequent taping sessions. These tokens did not constitute errors with respect to the contrastive values for place of articulation identified by Stokoe et al. (1965). For example, Susie produced many tokens of HAT using a 5-hand. In the tokens produced at 12;2, her palm contacted the side of her head, near the temple, while her fingers contacted the top of her head. By 14;0, Susie was consistently contacting the top of her head with her palm on every token of HAT.

Handshape

In contrast to place of articulation, handshape errors were found in 75% of 372 tokens. Unlike place of articulation errors, there was—sometimes even within a single taping session—considerable variability in what handshape a child produced for a given sign. For example, Caitlin produced five tokens of DADDY. Of these five tokens, two at 8;0 had the correct handshape. The remaining three tokens each had a different handshape (at 8;2, a loose O; and at 11;0, A and A with extended thumb). All were correctly placed on the forehead. In all, four different handshapes were used in the production of these five tokens of DADDY (see Fig. 4.2).

---

[10]Note that Susie's mother's production of FLOWER in child-directed signing may have promoted her daughter's error. The mother, who is a nonnative signer, produced an exaggerated form of FLOWER in which movement was from one cheek to the other, rather than from one side of the upper lip to the other.

FIG. 4.2.   Caitlin's productions of the sign DADDY. Panel (a) shows the correct
5-handshape. Panels (b) through (d) show three incorrect handshapes: a
loosely formed O-hand in (b), an A-hand in (c), and an A-dot handshape
in (d). The illustrations were drawn by Tony McGregor, copyright RPM.

We tallied the frequency of the various handshapes that appeared in
our data; in the analyses that follow, we consider only the initial handshape
of tokens that had handshape changes. In their production of ASL signs,
the children largely drew from a small subset of the possible ASL handshapes. Only eight handshapes appeared in more than 10 tokens in our
corpus; these eight handshapes are listed in Table 4.2. One handshape,
the 5-hand and its lax variant, was overwhelmingly more frequent than
any other.

These eight handshapes closely correspond to those that Boyes Braem
(1990) identified as the maximally unmarked handshapes in ASL. Using

TABLE 4.2
The Most Frequent Handshapes Identified in a Corpus of 372 Sign Tokens

Handshape	Frequency (% of Corpus)
5 (including lax)	186 (50.0)
G/Index/1	31 (8.3)
babyO	22 (5.9)
O	22 (5.9)
A	20 (5 4)
bent-5	18 (4.8)
C	15 (4 0)
S[a]	12 (3.2)
Total	326 (87.5)

Note. Only the initial handshape of tokens with handshapes change is included here.
[a]The S-hand category includes indeterminate fisted handshapes

physiological and cognitive factors to judge the relative complexity of hand-shapes, Boyes Braem assigned ASL handshapes to four groups. Those hand-shapes that fit her characterization of the maximally unmarked handshapes accounted for most of the signs that our participants produced. These handshapes are A, C, S, 5 (including lax), bent-5, L, baby O, and G (including the Index or 1-hands).[11] This set of eight hand configurations accounted for 83.6% of our data (311 of 372 tokens). Broken down by child, the results are as follows: For Susie, 169 out of 215 tokens (78.6%) drew on this set of eight hand configurations; for Caitlin, 38 of 44 tokens (86.4%) did so; and for Noel, 104 of 113 tokens (92.0%). The participants often substituted these handshapes for the more complicated models found in the adult versions of the signs they attempted. For example, one participant's productions of DOG (Susie from 10;3 to 14;2) usually involved open–close movement of an A, S or baby-O hand configuration instead of finger rubbing with the more complicated K handshape. Many signs with relatively complicated handshapes, such as COW and HORSE, were simplified to a 5-handshape. The handshapes in both COW and HORSE may be difficult because the anatomically favored grouping of little, ring, and middle finger is broken up (Ann, 1996).

We analyzed the children's handshape errors with respect to Boyes Braem's (1990) claims about the relative markedness of ASL handshapes. After excluding all signs in which the child's production or the adult target

[11]Boyes Braem (1990) did not mention bent-5, but it fits her criteria for the set of least-marked handshapes and thus we include it here. Note that this set of handshapes differs from that in Table 4.2 by its inclusion of L, which occurred in 7 of our 372 tokens, and its exclusion of O.

involved hand-internal movement, we had a set of 171 tokens in which the child substituted an incorrect handshape. In 100 tokens (58.5%), the child substituted a handshape that was less marked than the adult target; only in 14 tokens (8.2%) did the child substitute a more marked hand-shape. In all other instances, the target handshape and the child substitution were at the same markedness level.

Movement

Our analyses of movement remain preliminary. Interestingly, we have noted a tendency for children to proximalize movements in their early sign productions. By this we mean that children show generally better control of articulators that are close to the torso (i.e., the shoulder and elbow) than articulators that are distal from the torso (i.e., the forearm and wrist).[12] If an adult sign contains a proximal articulator, children are likely to retain it in their own productions; moreover, children show a tendency to substitute proximal articulators for distal ones (Meier et al., 1998). Below, we discuss a few examples of this tendency to proximalize movement.

In Noel's sign at 11;1, 12;1, and 13;2, we noticed 21 tokens (4 imitative, 16 elicited by her mother, and 1 spontaneous) of a nonce sign for "color." The recurring context was one in which Noel and her mother were flipping through a book in which each page displays a solid block of one of the colors.[13] Noel's form appears to have been based on the neutral-space color signs, for example, BLUE, GREEN, and YELLOW, that differ only in their handshape. These adult signs are executed with a repeated twisting movement of the forearm. However, along with this forearm rotation, Noel added a repeated up-and-down movement of the arm at the shoulder, thereby adding a proximal articulator to this sign; her handshape was a lax version of the 5-hand.

Two children, Noel at ages 12;2 and 14;0 and Susie at age 13;2, produced tokens of the signs MOMMY and DADDY in which the arm was raised from the shoulder to achieve contact at the chin or forehead as appropriate. The expected movement is a repeated extension and flexion of the elbow. We did not consider these productions to be errors with respect to the type of movement path. Nonetheless, the children's forms use an articulator that is more proximal than the expected articulator of the adult language.

---

[12]We do not consider hand-internal movements here.

[13]By *nonce sign* we mean that Noel's gesture may have been a sign of her own invention. The interpretation of this gesture as a nonce sign for "color" is buttressed by the fact that, in these same interactions, Noel also used the standard sign BLACK. The nonce sign was never used to refer to the black page in the book on which Noel and her mother were focused.

DISCUSSION

What's a Typical Early Sign?

On the basis of the data reported here, we can start to outline the form of a typical early sign. Further research, especially cross-linguistic research, may show whether the modal tendencies of these children correspond to some notion of what constitutes the canonical, or unmarked, sign type cross-linguistically. Our data suggest that an early sign will likely be articulated in neutral space or on the face. The handshape of an early sign will likely be a 5-hand (all fingers extended and spread) or its lax variant, although other handshapes will occur. Interestingly, the 5-hand, especially when lax, may approximate the neutral hand configuration. Although a plurality of early signs was articulated in neutral space, almost 38% were articulated on the face or head. Such signs were displaced far from the resting position of child's arms. Apparently, this displacement is not costly for the child.[14] It seems likely that the typical early sign may involve articulation at the relatively proximal articulators of the arm, elbow, and shoulder, although open–close movements of the hand may be frequent (Petitto, 1988). In another report (Meier et al., 1998) on the signing of the same children discussed here, these children showed reliable tendencies to proximalize sign movements, whether by omitting the action of a distal articulator or by introducing an unexpected proximal articulator. The typical early sign may also have repeated movement: Meier et al. (1998) reported a reliable tendency for children to produce a sign with repeated movement if the adult model was repeated; moreover, signs that have only a single movement cycle in the adult language tended to gain repetition in children's productions.

Explaining Early Sign Development

In studying slips of the hands, Klima and Bellugi (1979) found that the parameters of place of articulation and movement were more resistant to error than was hand configuration. Of 58 slips of the hand that involved only the value for one of the major parameters, 49 substituted an erroneous hand configuration into the target sign, whereas just 4 slips were restricted to place of articulation and 5 were restricted to the movement parameter.

---

[14]We would presume that children's early use of signs articulated on the face is promoted both by input factors (e.g., the large number of common ASL signs that have the face as their place of articulation) and by perceptual factors (e.g., signs articulated on the face are produced in a part of the addressee's visual field that is characterized by high acuity, as discussed by Siple, 1978).

In adult performance, handshape is more fragile than either place or movement.

Our study likewise showed substantial differences in performance as a function of parameter: Children's productions of the handshapes of ASL signs were typically incorrect, whereas their productions of the place values for those same signs were typically correct. Performance with respect to the movement parameter lay in between these two poles. Siedlecki and Bonvillian (1993) examined parental reports of the early signing of 9 children who were acquiring ASL as their first language. These children (1 deaf, 8 hearing) all had at least one deaf parent; their ages ranged from 6 to 18 months over the course of the study. Remarkably, their participants' error rate on place of articulation was approximately 16%; the figure that we report here is 18.6%. Error rates for movement and handshape were 38.5% and 50%, respectively; the figures we report are 46% and 75%. Thus, the analysis of our videotape data converges with the results from Siedlecki and Bonvillian's parental reports to indicate the same relative difficulty for the three parameters of place, movement, and handshape. In a case study of a hearing child of deaf parents whom she followed longitudinally from ages 12 to 25 months, Marentette (1995; Marentette & Mayberry, chap. 5, this volume) also found the same relative error rates for place, handshape, and movement that we observed.

There are several factors that may promote early—or at least seemingly early—correct use of place of articulation and later correct use of hand-shape. Infants may find the different places of articulation of ASL to be perceptually more distinctive than are the handshapes of the language. Another possibility is that adults, whether native signers or not, find place errors difficult to recognize. For example, on one occasion Noel produced a gesture articulated at her right hip that was otherwise identical to the sign DADDY. Her use of this gesture appeared highly communicative: that is, she was looking at her father and seemed to want something from him. But he showed no comprehension. At the current time, we cannot completely rule out the possibility that this gesture was, in fact, an erroneous form of DADDY and, more generally, that the absence of place errors in our data reflects our inability to identify them. Experimental approaches—for example, elicited production studies—would be informative, on the assumption that place errors persist past age 2, that is into the age range in which we could reasonably expect children to cooperate in an experimental setting.

However, the explanation that we favor for the absence of place errors from early signing is the following: Young children may lack the fine motor control to produce the array of distinct handshapes that occur in ASL, whereas the gross motor control required to reach a location, whether a toy or a location on the child's own body, appears firmly in place; Siedlecki and Bonvillian (1993) also made this proposal. Achieving a sign's correct place of articulation essentially requires reaching to a location on the child's own body. On the account developed by Marentette (1995), the child has a concept—a "body schema"—that tells him or her where significant body landmarks lie. The mistakes that we do find on place of articulation may be a product of erroneous mental representations of the pertinent signs, whereas hand configuration errors may be tied closely to developing motor control.

Another contributor to children's early success with place of articulation may be the general tendency in development for children to show better early motor skills with articulators, such as the shoulder or hip, that are proximal to the torso. With development, children gain better control over distal articulators, whether those articulators are segments of the arms or the legs (for an overview, see Payne & Issacs, 1995). Achieving a sign's correct place of articulation largely involves actions of the shoulder and elbow and therefore requires little coordination of distal articulators. In contrast, achieving correct handshapes is solely the province of distal articulators. We cited examples of children's production of sign movement that also reflect this early mastery of proximal articulators; our participants often substituted distal articulators with proximal ones. A more detailed discussion of the proximalization of sign movement is reported in Meier et al. (1998). This progressive mastery of proximal, then distal, articulators mirrors patterns seen in children's achievement of nonlinguistic motor milestones, such as kicking in infants and drawing in preschoolers (Jensen, Ulrich, Thelen, Schneider, & Zernicke, 1995; Saida & Miyashita, 1979).

The relative success with which children articulate the various handshapes of ASL may also have explanations that lie in the anatomy and physiology of the hand. Boyes Braem (1990) determined the markedness of handshapes based on the physiology of the tendons and muscles of the hand as well as on cognitive factors that may affect children's abilities to coordinate nonadjacent, but selected, fingers (as in the *horns* handshape in which the first finger and little finger are extended). On this basis, she proposed four stages of handshape acquisition. The hand configuration inventories of our participants in this early stage of language acquisition are very similar to the hand configurations composing her early stages (Stages I and II).

Our emphasis on motoric explanations for aspects of early sign development should not be interpreted to suggest that we would deny the significance either of perceptual effects in the acquisition of ASL or of input factors arising from the nature of child-directed signing. For instance, there are input factors that may promote the proximalization of sign movement. In child-directed signing, parents sometimes enlarge signs or assign a path movement to signs that have only hand-internal movements (e.g., RED). One consequence is that movement in child-directed signs is sometimes proximalized vis-à-vis what would be expected in adult-directed signing (Holzrichter & Meier, chap. 2, this volume). Further research may allow us to distinguish patterns of proximalization in children's signing from those in child-directed signing. Second, there may also be input factors that weight place of articulation over handshape. Holzrichter (1995) observed instances of what might be called handshape neutralization when parents sign on their children. For example, one of the parents whom she observed produced the sign DADDY in contact with her daughter's forehead. The place of articulation, albeit transferred to the child, was correct, but the handshape that the mother produced was an index-hand (index finger extended, all other fingers closed) rather than the expected 5-hand.

In conclusion, the emphasis we place on motoric constraints is similar to many current accounts of phonetic development in speech. Children may bring relatively rich perceptual abilities to the task of language acquisition (cf. Carroll & Gibson, 1986, on the perception of sign movement; Werker, 1989, on the perception of speech), but may also have distinctly limited motoric capacities. In this vein, MacNeilage and Davis (1993) argued that vocal babbling can be characterized as essentially an oscillation of the mandible; within a babbled syllable (i.e., within a mandibular oscillation), infants have, on their view, little independent control over the oral articulators. Is the signing infant also this constrained? We do not yet know. The answer may inform us about the extent to which infant motor constraints shape the forms of words versus signs, whether in child language or in the adult languages that children are acquiring.

ACKNOWLEDGMENTS

This chapter is an outgrowth of the first author's master's thesis that was presented to the Communication Sciences and Disorders program of The University of Texas at Austin. That thesis was codirected by Barbara J. Davis and Richard P. Meier. Raquel Willerman and Amanda Holzrichter assisted in data collection. Adrianne Cheek and Kearsy Cormier assisted in the analysis of the data reported here. This work was supported by a grant (RO1 DC01691-04) from the National Institute on Deafness and Other Communication Disorders to Richard P. Meier. Data collection was supported in part by a grant from the Texas Advanced Research Program, also to Richard P. Meier. We particularly thank the parents of Susie, Caitlin, and Noel for their cheerful participation in this study.

APPENDIX

Listed here are the sign types (number of tokens) identified in the signing of our participants. If no number is indicated, then only one token was produced by that child.

Caitlin	Noel	Susie
CAT (5)	BANANA (5)	ANIMAL
CROCODILE	BARNEY (3)	BABY
DADDY (5)	BED	BALL (7)
DIAPER	BIRD (4)	BEAR
DRINK	BLACK (11)	BIRD (4)
EAT (2)	CAR	BLACK
MORE (3)	CAT (2)	BOOK (4)
MOUSE (2)	CLOTHES (2)	CANDLE
PET (one-handed variant) (24)	COLD (temperature) (2)	CEILING-FAN (4)
	COLD (illness)	CHEESE (2)
	'color' (nonce sign) (21)	COOKIE (5)
	COW	COW (2)
	CRAB	CRAYON (3)
	CRACKERS	DADDY (14)
	DADDY (67)	DEER
	DIRTY	DIRTY
	DOG (on leg) (4)	DOG (19)
	DUCK	DOLL (7)
	EAT	DRINK (6)
	FALL (verb) (7)	EAT
	FINE	FARM (2)
	FINISH (4)	FINISH
	GRANDFATHER	FISH (4)
	GRAPE (3)	FLOWER (4)
	GREEN	HAMMER (7)
	HAIR	HAT (19)
	HAT	HORSE (2)
	HORSE	HURT
	HUG	LEAVE (as in 'leave it there') (10)
	KITE	LIGHT (noun) (19)
	LION	LION (4)
	LOLLIPOP	MILE (4)
	ME (2)	MINE (3)
	MICKY (3)	MONKEY (2)
	MILE (8)	MORE (2)
	MOMMY (4)	ORANGE (4)
	SLIDE (4)	OUT (4)
	SOCKS	PACIFIER (5)
		PICTURE
		PRAY (3)
		RED (2)
		TASTE
		TELEPHONE
		THANK-YOU (2)
		TOOTHBRUSH (2)
		TURTLE (10)
		WHAT (base-hand sign)
		WHAT (symmetrical 2-handed) (9)
		WHITE

REFERENCES

Ann, J. (1996). On the relation between ease of articulation and frequency of occurrence of handshapes in two sign languages. *Lingua, 98*, 19–41.

Bonvillian, J. D., & Siedlecki, T., Jr. (1996). Young children's acquisition of the location aspect of American Sign Language signs: Parental report findings. *Journal of Communication Disorders, 29*, 13–35.

Boyes Braem, P. (1990). Acquisition of the handshape in American Sign Language: A preliminary analysis. In V. Volterra & C. J. Erting (Eds.), *From gesture to language in hearing and deaf children* (pp. 107–127). Heidelberg, Germany: Springer-Verlag.

Carroll, J. J., & Gibson, E. J. (1986). Infant perception of gestural contrasts: Prerequisites for the acquisition of a visually specified language. *Journal of Child Language, 13*, 31–49.

Grove, N. (1990). Developing intelligible signs with learning-disabled students: A review of the literature and an assessment procedure. *British Journal of Disorders of Communications, 25*, 265–293.

Holzrichter, A. S. (1995). *Motherese in American Sign Language.* Unpublished master's thesis, University of Texas at Austin.

Jensen, J. L., Ulrich, B. D., Thelen, E., Schneider, K., & Zernicke, R. F. (1995). Adaptive dynamics in the leg movement pattern of human infants: III. Age-related differences in limb control. *Journal of Motor Behavior, 27*, 366–374.

Kegl, J., Senghas, A., & Coppola, M. (1999). Creation through contact: Sign language emergence and sign language change in Nicaragua. In M. DeGraff (Ed.), *Comparative grammatical change: The intersection of language acquisition, creole genesis, and diachronic syntax.* Cambridge, MA: MIT Press.

Klima, E. S., & Bellugi, U. (1979). *The signs of language.* Cambridge, MA: Harvard University Press.

Locke, J. L. (1983). *Phonological acquisition and change.* New York: Academic Press.

Locke, J. L. (1985). The role of phonetic factors in parent reference. *Journal of Child Language, 12*, 215–220.

MacNeilage, P. F., & Davis, B. L. (1993). Motor explanations of babbling and early speech patterns. In B. de Boysson-Bardies, S. de Schonen, P. Jusczyk, P. F. MacNeilage, & J. Morton (Eds.), *Developmental neurocognition Speech and face processing in the first year of life* (pp. 341–352). Dordrecht, Netherlands: Kluwer.

Marentette, P. F. (1995). *It's in her hand: A case study of the emergence of phonology in American Sign Language.* Unpublished doctoral dissertation, McGill University.

McIntire, M. L. (1977). The acquisition of American Sign Language hand configurations. *Sign Language Studies, 16*, 247–266.

Meier, R. P. (1984). Sign as creole. *Behavioral and Brain Sciences, 7*, 201–202.

Meier, R. P. (1991). Language acquisition by deaf children. *American Scientist, 79*, 60–70.

Meier, R. P., Mauk, C., Mirus, G. R., & Conlin, K. E. (1998). Motoric constraints on early sign acquisition. In E. Clark (Ed.), *Papers and Reports on Child Language Development* (Vol. 29, pp. 63–72). Stanford: CSLI Publications.

Meier, R. P., & Newport, E. L. (1990). Out of the hands of babes: On a possible sign advantage in language acquisition. *Language, 66*, 1–23.

Meier, R. P., & Willerman, R. (1995). Prelinguistic gesture in deaf and hearing infants. In K. Emmorey & J. Reilly (Eds.), *Language, gesture, and space* (pp. 391–409). Hillsdale, NJ: Lawrence Erlbaum Associates.

Newport, E. L., & Meier, R. P. (1985). The acquisition of American Sign Language. In D. I. Slobin (Ed.), *The crosslinguistic study of language acquisition Vol. 1: The data* (pp. 881–938). Hillsdale, NJ: Lawrence Erlbaum Associates.

Oller, D. K., & Lynch, M. P. (1992). Infant vocalizations and innovations in infraphonology. In C. A. Ferguson, L. Menn, & C. Stoel-Gammon (Eds.), *Phonological development. Models, research, implications* (pp. 509–536). Timonium, MD: York.

Orlansky, M. D., & Bonvillian, J. D. (1984). The role of iconicity in early sign language acquisition. *Journal of Speech and Hearing Disorders, 28,* 47–63.

Orlansky, M. D., & Bonvillian, J. D. (1985). Sign language acquisition: Language development in children of deaf parents and implications for other populations. *Merrill-Palmer Quarterly, 31,* 127–143.

Payne, V. G., & Issacs, L. D. (1995). *Human motor development: A lifespan approach.* Mountain View, CA: Mayfield.

Petitto, L. A. (1988). "Language" in the pre-linguistic child. In F. S. Kessel (Ed.), *The development of language and language researchers* (pp. 187–221). Hillsdale, NJ: Lawrence Erlbaum Associates.

Petitto, L. A., & Marentette, P. F. (1991). Babbling in the manual mode: Evidence from the ontogeny of language. *Science, 251,* 1493–1496.

Saida, Y., & Miyashita, M. (1979). Development of fine motor skill in children: Manipulation of a pencil in children aged 2 to 6 years old. *Journal of Human Movement Studies, 5,* 104–113.

Sandler, W. (1989). *Phonological representation of the sign: Linearity and nonlinearity in American Sign Language.* Dordrecht, Netherlands: Foris.

Siedlecki, T., Jr., & Bonvillian, J. D. (1993). Location, handshape, and movement: Young children's acquisition of the formational aspects of American Sign Language. *Sign Language Studies, 78,* 31–52.

Singleton, J. L., Morford, J. P., & Goldin-Meadow, S. (1993). Once is not enough: Standards of well-formedness in manual communication created over three different timespans. *Language, 69,* 683–715.

Siple, P. (1978). Visual constraints and the form of signs. *Sign Language Studies, 19,* 95–110.

Stokoe, W. C., Casterline, D. C., & Croneberg, C. G. (1965). *A dictionary of American Sign Language on linguistic principles.* Silver Spring, MD: Linstok.

Velguth, S. N. (1995). *Prelinguistic gestures in a deaf and a hearing infant.* Unpublished doctoral dissertation, University of Minnesota.

Volterra, V., & Iverson, J. M. (1995). When do modality factors affect the course of language acquisition? In K. Emmorey & J. Reilly (Eds.), *Language, gesture, and space* (pp. 371–390). Hillsdale, NJ: Lawrence Erlbaum Associates.

Werker, J. F. (1989). Becoming a native listener. *American Scientist, 77,* 54–59.

Chapter 5

Principles for an Emerging Phonological System: A Case Study of Early ASL Acquisition

Paula F. Marentette
Augustana University College

Rachel I. Mayberry
McGill University

Understanding how children acquire phonology is important to our attempt to explain language acquisition. Children who are acquiring a signed language as their first language provide researchers with a distinct observational advantage: We can see the articulators they use to produce words. However, they also provide us with a distinct challenge: discovering the nature and structure of phonological acquisition in languages where the articulators are the entire upper body and the perceptual sense is the eyes. In this chapter, we describe the emerging phonological system of a very young child acquiring American Sign Language (ASL) and propose the principles that guide this early phonological growth. Before we do so, however, we first describe the basic elements of signed language phonology and consider in detail the previous research that has investigated phonological acquisition in signed languages.

WHAT IS PHONOLOGY IN SIGNED LANGUAGE?

The study of phonology is concerned with the smallest parts of a language. These elements do not convey meaning on their own, however, particular combinations of these elements create signs that do convey meaning. The phonological structure of a sign consists of three major components: (a) where the hand is located relative to the body, called *location*—examples of location primes include [head, chin, nose, chest];[1] (b) how the hand moves in space, called *movement*—examples are [circle, arc, straight line, wiggle fingers]; and (c) the form of the hand itself, called *handshape*—examples are all fingers extended, written as [5], or all fingers closed with thumb to the side of the index finger, written as [A]. Other examples of ASL handshapes are shown in Fig. 5.1.

Of course, children have two hands and signs can be formed either with one or both hands. One-handed signs typically use the individual's dominant hand. The relation between the hands in two-handed signs is constrained by symmetry and dominance conditions (Battison, 1978). The symmetry condition states that if both hands move during the production of a sign, then (a) the handshapes must be the same, (b) the locations must be the same or symmetrical about the midline of the body, and (c) the movement must be the same and either simultaneous or alternating in phase (e.g., the hands can move up and down, together or in opposition). The dominance condition states that if both hands do not share the same handshape, then (a) only one hand produces the movement, and (b) the stationary hand is restricted to a small set of handshapes [A, S, 5, B, 1, C, O]. These conditions serve to limit the possible configurations of two-handed signs. Given that the phonological systems of signed languages are complex, but nevertheless rule bound, the question remains as to how very young children acquire these complex, but meaningless, phonological units and rules of signed languages.

PHONOLOGICAL ACQUISITION
IN SIGNED LANGUAGE

The signing child must master many different facets of the phonological structure of his or her language over the course of language acquisition. In order to understand phonological acquisition in signed languages, we must know a large number of details. These details include the handshapes, locations, and movements that are produced at the earliest stages of lexical development and the order in which these phonetic elements are acquired. However, knowledge of these details is insufficient. Complete understanding requires that two additional questions be asked. First, at what point in development does a child adhere to the formational constraints on signs, for example, the symmetry and dominance conditions? Second, when does the child show evidence of having a phonological system that guides the production of signs?

---

[1]Specific ASL primes are listed in square brackets to indicate that they are linguistic units.

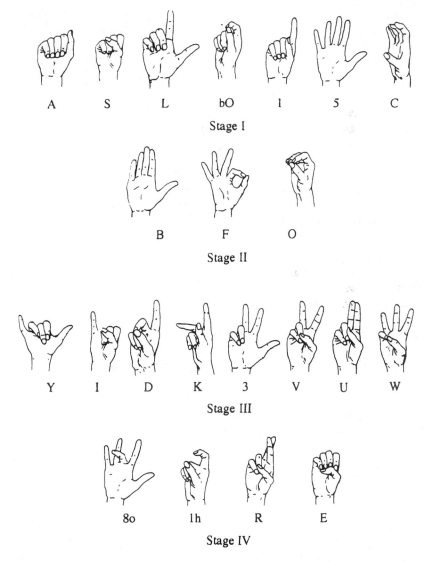

FIG. 5.1. The stages of acquisition for handshape primes according to Boyes Braem's (1990) theory. Handshapes © P. Marentette.

The few studies of ASL phonological acquisition have focused on the question of which primes are acquired and the order in which they appear. There has been relatively little explanation as to why children may be using these particular primes, and acquiring them in the order that they appear. This becomes apparent from a review of the studies of phonological acquisition in ASL. Of the small number of studies that have been conducted on phonological acquisition, the majority focused on handshape. In our present review, we focus on this aspect of ASL phonology in some detail before considering the limited information that is available about the acquisition of location and movement.

The Complex Process of Handshape Acquisition

Boyes Braem (1990) was the first investigator to study phonological acquisition in signing children. She developed a model of the order in which handshapes would be acquired. Using this stage model, Boyes Braem predicted the kinds of substitution errors that would be made by children. An evaluation of Boyes Braem's model must therefore consider both her predictions about the order of acquisition of handshapes and her predictions about the factors that affect handshape substitutions.

Order of Acquisition for Handshape. Boyes Braem hypothesized that the order in which a child learned to produce the handshapes of ASL would be influenced by two primary factors: the anatomical development of the hand and a factor she called *serial finger order.* Boyes Braem (1990) defined serial finger order as "whether the same features are applied to adjacent digits or to digits out of serial order" (p. 107). For example, the handshape [5], which requires all fingers to be extended and spread apart, should be acquired earlier than the handshape [V], which requires the index and middle fingers, but not the ring and pinkie fingers, to be extended and spread apart. Boyes Braem predicted that anatomical constraints on handshape formation would have the greatest influence in the early stages of acquisition, whereas serial finger order would affect the handshapes acquired later in phonological development.

The predicted order of handshape acquisition can be seen in Fig. 5.1. The handshapes of Stage I are those that the prelinguistic infant is capable of producing, for example, in reaching, grasping, and pointing (Fogel, 1981). Stage II handshapes are variants of those already mastered in Stage I. Stage III and IV handshapes are distinguished from those acquired earlier because they require inhibition and extension of the middle, ring, and pinkie fingers (e.g., [Y, K, 3, W]), as well as control of nonadjacent fingers (predicted to be difficult due to the serial finger order factor, e.g., [8o]).

The distinction between Stage I and II handshapes compared to those of Stage III and IV is supported by the work of Ann (1993). Ann examined the ease of production of handshapes in ASL and Taiwan Sign Language based on the anatomical structure of the hand and the physiological principles that guide its movement. According to Ann's (1993) classification, Stage I and II handshapes fall into the "easy" group, whereas Stage III and IV handshapes are classed as "difficult."

A number of studies investigated the order in which children begin to produce handshapes in the earliest stages of signing. Siedlecki and Bonvillian (1997; Siedlecki, 1991) provided data from a study of 9 children (8 hearing, 1 deaf) who were acquiring ASL as their primary language. The children's families were visited monthly between the ages of 0;6 and 1;6. Data analyses were based on the parents' reproduction of the children's sign types. That is, the data consisted of parental report of phonological form. Siedlecki and Bonvillian (1997) analyzed 448 sign types (range 16–139 per child). There is substantial overlap between the earliest handshapes acquired by Siedlecki and Bonvillian's participants and the first two stages of Boyes Braem's (1990) theory. Several handshapes (notably, [5, 1, B, A]) were produced early and frequently in these children's early signs. Earlier research using the same method of parental report with a different group of children also found that these same handshapes were produced with high frequency by young children (Bonvillian, Orlansky, Novack, Folven & Holley-Wilcox, 1985; Orlansky & Bonvillian, 1988).

Similar results were found in a case study of a deaf child of deaf parents (FF) between the ages of 1;1 and 1;9 (McIntire, 1977). Of the target signs that FF attempted to produce, the handshape required for the adult form was likely to be one of the Stage I handshapes (68%). When FF produced a sign, she depended almost exclusively on Stage I handshapes (98%). Of the Stage I handshapes, [5, 1, bO] were successfully produced for more than 80% of the signs in which they were required, and [S, A, C] were successfully produced for less than 50% of the signs in which they were required. Although FF attempted target signs that require Stage III and IV handshapes, she did not successfully produce any Stage III or IV handshapes during this time period.

Boyes Braem's (1990) own data provided further support of the primacy of Stage I handshapes. She studied an older child, Pola, age 2;7. Half of the target signs Pola produced required Stage I handshapes. With the exception of [S], the Stage I handshapes were correctly produced for 87% of the target signs in which they were required. Stage II handshapes were used with mixed success: [B] was produced correctly 95% of the time, but [O] was only correct 33% of the time. The handshape [F] was never required. Similarly mixed results occurred with Stage III handshapes. The handshapes [D, 3] were produced with complete accuracy, and handshapes [H, K] were used with moderate accuracy (66%, 50%), whereas handshapes [Y, V] were never accurately produced, and the others were not attempted. Boyes Braem concluded that Pola was at Stage III in her handshape development. Because these data were derived from a single session, however, it is impossible to assess the order in which Pola acquired these handshapes.

Finally, it is worth noting that Clibbens and Harris (1993) briefly reported on the acquisition of handshape between the ages of 1;2 and 2;4

in a deaf girl of deaf parents learning British Sign Language. The participant (Anne) depended heavily on the primes [5, A, 1] in her initial signs.

These studies provide supporting evidence for the primacy of a subset of Boyes Braem's (1990) Stage I handshapes (perhaps [5, A, 1, B, bO]). However, there is limited evidence to support the arrangement of handshapes among the other three proposed stages. None of the studies followed a child for a long enough period of time to observe the acquisition of handshapes from several different proposed stages. This makes it difficult to assess the stage aspect of the model.

Substitution Data. Boyes Braem (1990) also predicted the kinds of substitution errors that children would make. When a child produced the wrong handshape in a sign, Boyes Braem predicted that the handshape substituted for the target handshape would be one from the current stage or earlier stage of acquisition. That is, a child might substitute a [5] hand of Stage I for a [B] hand of Stage II, but she would not substitute a [U] hand of Stage III for a [B] hand. Boyes Braem identified six additional factors that she hypothesized to influence the particular handshape that replaced the target handshape. These were (a) a preference for fingertip contact, (b) the sympathetic extension of the thumb when the index finger is extended, (c) anticipation and retention of handshapes in other signs (or coarticulation), (d) the nature of the sensory feedback available to the child (i.e., can they see their own hands?), (e) the nature of the movement required by the sign (this suggests a limit to the level of linguistic complexity permitted in a sign, e.g., a more complex movement may be possible if the child simplifies a handshape), and (f) the use of handshapes as classifiers.

Bonvillian et al. (1985; Orlansky & Bonvillian, 1988) reported many handshape errors in their group of 13 children (12 hearing and 1 deaf) between 0;6 and 3;0. Five handshapes [B, 5, 1, A, C] accounted for 73% of the targets and 84% of the handshapes produced. These are all Stage I and II handshapes in Boyes Braem's model. Orlansky and Bonvillian (1988) reported three frequent errors: the primes [5] and [B] were frequently interchanged; the handshape [5] was often substituted for other Stage I handshapes such as [C, A, 1]; and the handshape [1] was often substituted for target primes from both Stages I and III [5, U, V, W, A]. However, these data were collapsed across all 13 children, making it impossible to know what an individual child's substitutions looked like. Nevertheless, these error data are largely consistent with the predictions made by Boyes Braem in that handshapes from earlier stages replace handshapes from later stages.[2]

---

[2]The prime [B] replacing [5] is not predicted from Boyes Braem's theory, as [B] is a Stage II handshape and [5] is a Stage I handshape.

Siedlecki (1991) reported a number of handshape substitutions for target signs in his group of children. The frequently produced handshapes [5, 1, A, B, bO] were also the most frequent substitutes in these children's signs. The handshape [5] was used to replace target handshapes [A, B, C, O] and the handshape [1] replaced [5, B, C, O]. One pattern of substitution that Siedlecki and Bonvillian (1997) noticed was that a [5] handshape was chosen if the target sign required contact between the heel of the hand and a location, and a [1] handshape was chosen if the target sign required contact between the fingertips and a location. Because these substitutions were collapsed across children, it is impossible to know if individual children showed distinct patterns of substitution.

Siedlecki and Bonvillian (1997) acknowledged the contribution of "ease of fine motor control" to handshape acquisition but found this factor to be inadequate to fully explain the children's handshape use. They found that several of Boyes Braem's (1990) secondary factors were influential. For example, they found that handshape production was influenced by the type of contact required with a location. In addition, having to produce a handshape in the context of a sign (i.e., simultaneously with a location and movement) reduced the accuracy of handshape production, as did the presence of differing handshapes in preceding and following signs.

In McIntire's (1977) case study of FF, she found that of the 186 substitutions made by FF, 182 (98%) were handshapes from Stage I. The prime [5] accounted for 54% of all substitutions. These data also support the primacy of Stage I handshapes in Boyes Braem's (1990) model. McIntire (1977) posited phonological rules to explain several of FF's substitutions. However, she further hypothesized that many of the secondary factors suggested by Boyes Braem would override these phonological rules. For example, there was a clear preference for fingertip contact in some signs that do not require that type of contact (i.e., SHOE, BIRD, GOAT, and WATERMELON). McIntire agreed with Boyes Braem's speculation that other secondary factors would also have a strong influence on the accuracy of handshape production. Due to the difficulty of assessing these factors, however, she did not provide data to evaluate this claim.

A study of the bilingual acquisition of ASL and English in a hearing child (Anya) with a deaf mother and a hearing father provides a few additional observations about phonological acquisition. Prinz and Prinz (1979) reported that phonological errors between the ages of 0;7 and 1;7 included handshape substitutions of [A] for the target [1h] in APPLE and [A] for the target [Y] in TELEPHONE. The prime [A] is a Stage I handshape, so its substitution for the later primes [Y, 1h] conforms to Boyes Braem's model.

Collectively, these studies provide supporting evidence for the early acquisition of Stage I handshapes. Boyes Braem hypothesized that these early handshapes are anatomically easy configurations for very young children to produce. In addition to frequent production, these same handshapes are often used as substitutions, in place of the target handshape. Although both Boyes Braem (1990) and McIntire (1977) posited phonological rules to govern these substitutions, they were working during a time when our theoretical understanding of ASL phonology was quite limited. The linguistic theories they used are no longer held. Current phonological theories may provide better explanations of some handshape substitutions. In addition, Boyes Braem proposed a number of other factors that may guide a child's substitutions. These include a mix of anatomical (sympathetic thumb extension), perceptual (fingertip contact, sensory feedback), phonetic (coarticulation, complexity of other parameters), and linguistic (classifier use) influences. These are all reasonable avenues of exploration. Few other attempts have been made to explain the particular handshape substitutions that children make in their early signs.

Location, Location, Location

In contrast with the study of handshape, there are few studies of the acquisition of location by signing children. Perhaps location has been the subject of less work because researchers have informally observed that children do not show much problem with its acquisition. Of the three major sign parameters, Siedlecki and Bonvillian (1993) found that location was the most accurately produced (overall accuracy calculated across children and ages was 83% compared to 50% for handshape and 61% for movement). Meier, Mauk, Mirus, and Conlin (1998) also found high accuracy for the production of location relative to the other parameters of a sign.

Bonvillian and Siedlecki (1996) proposed a model for the order of acquisition of location primes. The proposal is based on several characteristics of their data: accuracy of production of location primes, order of acquisition of primes across children, and frequency of appearance of primes in the children's lexicons. The earliest acquired primes in their study were [neutral space, trunk, chin, forehead]. Bonvillian and Siedlecki noted that these early primes are frequently used in the adult lexicon and suggested that they are easy to produce (although there is no explanation of how ease is measured). In addition, these primes were maximally contrastive, requiring much broader distinctions compared to those required among the location primes of later levels. Finally, Bonvillian and Siedlecki (1996) noted that many of the children's signs involved locations that contacted the body.

The accuracy difference between location and the other parameters, was explained by both Meier et al. (1998) and Bonvillian and Siedlecki (1996) as resulting from the level of motor control required. The production of a location prime requires a relatively gross level of control compared to the finer manipulations of the fingers needed to produce particular handshapes.

The Movement Puzzle

As with location, few studies have investigated the acquisition of movement primes. Bonvillian et al. (1985) reported the coding of movement primes to be particularly difficult. This is because children sometimes produced different movements with each hand, thus violating the symmetry and dominance conditions of ASL. The most frequently produced movement primes were [contact, in, pronate, out, down, and supinate].[3] Participants made frequent errors for movement primes.

The principal observation made by Siedlecki (1991; Siedlecki & Bonvillian, 1993) about the acquisition of movement primes was the children's reliance on the prime [contact]. Aside from the frequent and accurate production of this prime, and its dominant use as a substitute, few other patterns were noteworthy. The prime [contact] was the only movement prime produced by all of the children in the study. As a result, in his model of the order of acquisition of movement primes, Siedlecki (1991) placed [contact] alone in the first level. He hypothesized that this prime is mastered by the children, in part, because its production highlights location, a sign parameter that the children produced with greater accuracy.

Meier et al. (1998; see also Conlin, Mirus, Mauk & Meier, chap. 4, this volume) analyzed ASL acquisition in 3 deaf girls ranging in age from 0;7 to 1;5. They investigated the effect that the development of motor control may have on the production of early signs. Their results suggest that children may alter the movement of a sign by replacing a more distal articulator with a more proximal articulator (e.g., the elbow rather than the wrist), by deleting the movements made by more distal articulators, or both. The reduction of many of the movement primes to a movement of the shoulder or elbow often resulted in a simple contact to the target location. This fits well with Siedlecki and Bonvillian's (1993) finding of children's early reliance on the prime [contact].

The Early Phonological Repertoire in ASL

We can draw several generalizations about the early phonological repertoire of children acquiring ASL from our analysis of the available studies. First,

---

[3]The movement prime [pronate] refers to twisting the lower arm so that the palm of the hand faces down; the prime [supinate] refers to twisting the lower arm so that the palm faces up.

children produce a variety of location primes and do so with high levels of accuracy. Second, children tend to make heavy use of the movement prime [contact] but despite this, they manage to achieve a fair degree of accuracy in the production of movement. Third, most children produce a small set of common handshapes (i.e., [5, 1, A, B]) and achieve relatively low overall accuracy in handshape production. These observations describe aspects of the phonological repertoire of young signing children, including the phonetic elements they produce in the earliest signs as well as the order in which they produce various handshapes, locations, and movements.

Despite the accumulation of details regarding children's early ASL phonological acquisition, there has been little theoretical development in this field. Just as the phonological errors made by adults reveal something of their phonological system (Mayberry, 1995), phonological errors produced by children can reveal something about the child's emerging phonological system. In the following section, we investigate the phonological acquisition of a single child in the earliest stages of phonological acquisition. We then analyze her phonological errors and propose of a set of principles to account for her errors.

THE EMERGENT PHONOLOGICAL SYSTEM

The present study describes the emerging phonological system of 1 child through the identification of the principles that structure the form of her signs. A longitudinal case study was chosen to determine if principled relations existed between target signs and actual sign productions. This type of analysis can only be conducted within a single child's data because of the degree of individual variation in children's phonological repertoires and in the strategies used to reduce a target sign to a sign that the child can produce (Ferguson & Farwell, 1975; Vihman, 1993). Our analyses focus on the patterns that were evident during the first year of signing and we describe the principles that may underlie this child's developing phonological system.

The Child

The participant, SJ, was a female hearing child of deaf parents. ASL was the exclusive language used in her home and was SJ's primary language for the duration of the study. SJ was videotaped in her home, for about 1 hour, once every 2 months. The observations included in the present analysis begin with her first signs on tape at 1;0 and continue until 2;1. Table 5.1 shows SJ's age at each session included in the study. During the

TABLE 5.1
Sign Types and Sign Tokens by Age

Age (year, Month, Day)	Sign Types	Sign Tokens
1;00.07	5	10
1;02.24	11	32
1;04.26	18	50
1;06 13	42	136
1;08.18	63	162
1;10.27	49	154
2;00.26	70	145

taping sessions SJ, her mother, and occasionally her father played with various toys, books, and household items.

Coding and Analysis

Each session was coded twice: first to isolate the signs produced on each tape, then to determine the phonetic form of each of the signs. An important part of the first coding involved the assessment of whether a given manual action was a sign or not. This meant that nonlinguistic actions such as pointing and communicative gestures, and prelinguistic actions such as manual babbling, were excluded from the phonetic analysis.

A sign was defined as a manual action with an interpretable meaning and a phonetic form based on an adult sign. A form observed more than once had to have a consistent referent for it to be considered a sign. The majority of signs produced by SJ were easily recognized as an attempt at the form of an adult sign. The requirement that the form of the child's signs be based on the form of the adult sign was helpful in separating gestures from signs (Meier & Willerman, 1995). The requirement that the child's signs have a consistent meaning was helpful in separating manual babbling from signs. In this way, the definition of sign used in this study permitted the isolation of signs from the variety of manual actions that SJ produced. Reliability of sign identification was checked by a deaf research assistant for portions of the videotapes and found to be 86% (275 signs agreed on/321 signs observed by either coder).

The second coding involved recording the phonetic form of each sign. The following phonetic aspects of each sign were coded: handshape (right and left hand), palm orientation (right and left hand), location (vertical place of articulation and horizontal place of articulation, following Brentari, 1990), movement (path, hand internal), and contact (contact of hand to body, contact within hand). This yielded 10 bits of information for each sign. Handshapes that differed only by thumb location were not reliably distinguished in this study. A list of 105 randomly selected signs was coded to check for reliability. Reliability was calculated as the number of bits of phonetic information agreed on divided by the total number of bits of phonetic information: Intercoder reliability was 86% for phonetic form.

The data analysis was designed to discover any patterns in the form of SJ's early sign production. An important element of this analysis was to determine which primes SJ substituted for the target prime when she produced an error. To this end, two types of frequency data were collected: target frequency (how often she attempted signs that required a prime) and production frequency (how often she produced a prime). These counts provided information about the frequency of various substitutions (e.g., SJ substituted a handshape prime [5] when she was attempting to produce [B] on 16 occasions at the 1;11 session).

The Acquisition of Sign Parameters

A total of 1,699 data points were coded from the seven videotaped sessions. Signs represent 48% of these data points (689 spontaneous signs, 115 imitated signs). The distribution of sign types and spontaneous sign tokens across sessions is shown in Table 5.1. SJ produced a range of other empty-handed manual activities including points, empty-handed gestures, manual babbling, attention-seeking actions, and a few uninterpretable actions.

The results of this study show that development was not uniform across all aspects of ASL phonology. Instead, this child demonstrated a distinct acquisition process for each aspect of ASL phonology. The systematicity of SJ's phonological acquisition is most clearly demonstrated by an analysis of the location and handshape parameters. Movement is mentioned only briefly as it provides an excellent contrast to the patterns observed in the acquisition of location and handshape. The full analyses can be found in Marentette (1995).

Location. SJ produced location primes with a high degree of accuracy throughout the study. Horizontal place of articulation, which encodes how far away from the body a sign is produced (either in contact, slightly away from the body, or with extended arms), was produced with an overall accuracy of 89%. The few errors that she did produce primarily involved substituting a fully extended arm for one that should have been positioned close to but not touching the body.

Vertical place of articulation (VPOA) was encoded with respect to the body part near which a sign is produced. The overall accuracy of locations SJ produced in the vertical plane was also quite high at 74%. SJ produced the primes [trunk, cheek, hand, chin, head] most frequently. These five primes accounted for 75% of VPOA primes produced.

The three primes that SJ used as substitutes most often were [trunk, head, mouth]. She did not make substitutions randomly. SJ used anatomy as an organizing principle for VPOA production. Of the errors produced, 91% involved anatomical neighbors. Consider the most frequent substitutions made by SJ:

[temple] replaced by [head]
[chin] replaced by [mouth]
[shoulder] replaced by [trunk]
[cheek] replaced by [ear]
[trunk][4] replaced by [hand]
[hand] replaced by [trunk]

The first four substitutions show a less salient anatomical part being replaced with a more salient location. These errors may have occurred because the target body parts (e.g., temple, chin, shoulder, cheek) were not as well represented in her body schema as other body parts such as mouth and head and chest. Examples of these errors include COW (produced at [head] not [temple]) as shown in Fig. 5.2, DUCK (produced at [mouth], not [chin]), COP (produced at [trunk] not [shoulder]), and TELEPHONE produced at [ear] not [cheek].

These last two types of substitution do not seem to fit with an explanation based on anatomical representation. Instead, they involve errors in the dominance and symmetry conditions that apply to two-handed sign production (Battison, 1978). Examples include SHOE and BOOK, two-handed signs that require both hands to move. SJ occasionally produced these with one stationary hand, while the other moved to contact it (replacing [trunk] with [hand]). The opposite error also happened, in which SJ would replace a [hand] location with [trunk], that is, when one hand should have been stationary, but both hands produced the movement. Examples of this type of error are the signs COOKIE, and SCHOOL. These violations of dominance and symmetry are distributed throughout the data with a peak occurring at the 1;11 session.

Handshape. In contrast to location primes, handshape primes were the least accurately produced by SJ. Accuracy did not improve over the course

---

[4]Note that [trunk] does not mean the sign was made in contact with the body as it could be produced at differing horizontal places of articulation. All of the signs involved in this error type were produced in neutral space.

FIG. 5.2. The child's sign COW (in comparison with the mother's target sign) shows several noteworthy errors; she replaced the handshape [Y] with [1] and added a second hand (a tendency for signs made outside SJ's visual field); she also replaced the location [temple] with [head]. Illustration by Michel Shang, © R. Mayberry & P. Marentette.

of the year of observation. The overall accuracy of handshape production with the dominant hand was 27%. Even though SJ used a restricted range of handshapes on the nondominant hand, these were no more accurate, showing an overall accuracy of 26%.

SJ produced a wide variety of handshapes, but the central trio were [5, 1, A]. These primary handshapes represent a particular set of relations: (a) they are a subset of easy to produce handshapes (Ann, 1993); (b) they are produced with high frequency in the adult language (Klima & Bellugi, 1979); and (c) they are perceptually distinctive (i.e., fully open fingers, fully closed fingers, extended single digit). These handshapes were also the earliest to appear, with [5] appearing first, followed by [1], and then [A].

SJ's handshape substitutions provide clear evidence of a phonological system influenced by anatomical, linguistic, and possibly perceptual factors. The most frequent substitutions are listed below:

[B 5h C Bb][5] replaced by [5]
[1b 1h Y] replaced by [1]
[S bO] replaced by [A]
[F] replaced by [bO]

---

[5]The handshape [5h] is produced by bending the fingers of the [5] hand at the distal joints, or by spreading the [C] hand. The handshape [Bb] is produced by bending the fingers of the [B] hand at the proximal knuckle, so that all fingers are straight but perpendicular to the palm of the hand.

FIG. 5.3. The child's sign APPLE replaced the handshape [1] for [1h] and the movement [twist] with [contact] in comparison to the mother's target sign. Illustration by Michel Shang, © R. Mayberry & P. Marentette.

These substitutions are patterned and do not represent the random use of any prime for any other prime. This pattern is demonstrated in part by their independence. First, SJ rarely substituted frequent handshapes for each other. This pattern is true for the three frequent substitutes [5, 1, A]. For example, consider the handshape pair [5] and [A]. The prime [5] was never produced in place of [A] and [A] never produced in place of [5]. Second, there was a unidirectional relation between the substitute and the intended target. For example, the prime [5] replaced [C], but [C] did not replace [5]. Third, each handshape was used as a substitute for a different set of handshapes: [A] substituted for [bO] but [5] did not substitute for [bO]. Because SJ's error patterns demonstrate an internal structure, this provides strong evidence of a phonological system at work.

Examples of signs involving these errors include DRINK (with [C] replaced by [5]), SHOE (with [S] replaced by [A]), and APPLE (with [1h] replaced by [1]), as seen in Fig. 5.3. The sign COW, depicted in Fig. 5.2 shows two noteworthy errors. First, the handshape error, where SJ replaced a [Y] with a [1], and second, the addition of the second hand. Unlike Siedlecki and Bonvillian (1993), who reported that their participants often deleted a required second hand, SJ was more likely to add a second hand, particularly to signs produced out of her field of vision.

Movement. Movement primes were produced with moderate accuracy across all sessions. For path primes (involving the movement of the arm through space), accuracy was 57%. The most frequently produced path primes were [contact] (e.g., MOMMY) and a brushing movement (e.g., HAPPY). These two primes accounted for 59% of path primes in the database. Hand-internal primes (movements within the hand and fingers) were produced with an overall accuracy of 48%. The most frequent hand-internal movement primes were bending the proximal finger joints (e.g., DUCK) and rotation of the lower arm (e.g., BOOK), accounting for 58% of hand-internal primes produced. SJ often replaced a target hand-internal prime with a path prime (44 of 329 required primes, 13%), suggesting that she did not distinguish the two types of movement. SJ produced those primes that were most frequently required in the target signs she attempted. No pattern accurately describes her substitutions.

There are (at least) two possible explanations for the rudimentary nature of the system observed in SJ's production of movement. First, movement is complex and it may develop later in the child's acquisition process. During the early period covered in this study, it may be that SJ relied on frequency, producing movement primes with the same frequency that she observed them. Perhaps later in her development SJ began to make substitutions for movement primes based on some other principle, as she did with handshape and location. A second possibility is that the coding scheme used in this analysis does not capture the important factors relevant to the acquisition of movement. Unlike handshape primes, movement primes are not all articulator based and this fact may obscure any systematicity that exists in SJ's data. However, the hand-internal movement primes are primarily articulator based and they do not exhibit any systematicity in SJ's data. The absence of systematicity of hand-internal movements may be accounted for by the Meier et al. (1998) hypothesis that hand-internal movements are distal and therefore less likely to be used by the child.

In summary, SJ showed different levels of accuracy in the production of location, handshape, and movement. Her production of location was most accurate, followed by movement, and then handshape, just as has been observed in other children. SJ also relied on many of the same primes that have been observed in other children's early signs. What is particularly revealing about SJ's early signs, however, is the distinct nature of the paths that she followed in acquiring each of the parameters of ASL over her first year of signing. We next propose the principles that guided this child's emerging phonological system.

Principles Guiding Phonological Acquisition

Location was produced with high accuracy from the very earliest of SJ's signs. This finding replicates that of Bonvillian and Siedlecki (1996) and Meier et al. (1998). Although the earlier mastery of gross motor control is undoubtedly a significant factor in the acquisition of location, this does not provide an explanation for the errors that children make. SJ's accuracy in producing location primes, along with the anatomical organization of her errors, suggests that she used a body schema as an initial representation of this parameter.

Throughout the first year of life, children develop a sense of how their body is organized and how it functions in the world (Butterworth, 1992; Neisser, 1991). Using a body schema would permit SJ to connect locations that are visually identified on another person's body with locations on her own body that she must identify through tactile and kinesthetic feedback. The capacity to link information that is received by visual and tactile means is crucial to the infant's capacity to imitate facial expressions (Meltzoff & Moore, 1993). This cross-modal link, connected to a well-developed body schema, may also subserve the child's capacity to acquire the location aspect of sign phonology.

With respect to handshape, the first primes to be acquired are those that are (a) easy to produce, (b) perceptually salient, and (c) frequent in the target language. For SJ (and many other children reported in the literature), these first handshapes include [5, 1, A, B]. Once SJ mastered these handshapes, she systematically substituted them for other handshapes. Three principles explain her handshape substitutions. First, SJ showed a preference for spread handshapes. Boyes Braem (1990) argued that it is more natural for fingers to spread than for fingers to be held tightly together and predicted that children would prefer [5] over [B] as a result. This is clearly true for SJ, as the substitution of [5] for [B] is her most frequent error.

The second principle is a preference is for unmarked primes. It is not surprising that unmarked primes appear early in a child's phonological repertoire. What is noteworthy, however, is the relation between the target primes that SJ attempted and the unmarked primes with which she replaced them. For example, SJ never produced the prime [Y] correctly. Instead, she frequently replaced it with [1]. Although this is certainly an example of anatomic ease, ([1] is easier than [Y] for the young child), the use of [1] as opposed to [5] or [A] as a substitute appears to be motivated by the phonological structure of ASL. In several current theories of ASL phonology, the prime [Y] is most closely related to [1] in structure (Brentari, 1990; Brentari, van der Hulst, van der Kooij, & Sandler, 1996; Sandler, 1995). The substitution of [bO] for [F] is also explained by this phonological principle.

The third principle underlying the substitution of handshape primes is a preference for open finger position. For example, SJ substituted [5h, C, Bb], all handshapes in which either the proximal or distal knuckle is bent, with the handshape [5]. This could be an anatomical preference for fully extended fingers, although Ann (1993) argued against this. It could also be a perceptual preference for fully open handshapes. In Brentari's (1990) phonological analysis of ASL, fully open or fully closed handshapes are more perceptually salient and therefore are preferred over handshapes with partially extended fingers.

To summarize, the structure of SJ's emerging phonological system is complex and varied. She relies on a body schema for location and a set of anatomically and linguistically influenced principles for handshape. It appears that she has not developed beyond a rudimentary system for movement within the time frame studied, although it may also be that better explanation of movement primes in ASL is required to explain the aspect of phonological acquisition in very young children.

One generalization describes all of the children studied to date. Location and handshape are acquired differently by children. Previous studies have established that location is easier for children; young children produce location primes with a greater degree of accuracy relative to other sign parameters. This study provides one possible explanation for this result. We propose that location is easier because children can rely on an emerging cognitive representation of their body to anchor their acquisition of the location primes of signs. For handshape acquisition, by contrast, the child has no preexisting mental representation or schema to provide an easy entry into the phonological system. Instead, factors such as ease of production, frequency in the input, and perceptual salience highlight a small set of primes for the child. The young child's substitutions of handshape primes reveal structured relations rather than random replacements.

ACKNOWLEDGMENTS

We thank SJ and her family for their willingness to be in the spotlight and Jill Morford and Lori Steckle for comments on earlier versions of this chapter. We also thank Michel Shang for drawing the sign illustrations and Patrick Boudreault for converting the illustrations to computer files. The research reported here was supported by postgraduate fellowships from the National Sciences and Engineering Research Council (NSERC); a J. W. McConnell Fellowship from McGill University; a research grant from the Faculty of Graduate Studies, McGill University to P. Marentette; a NSERC grant to L. A. Petitto; and NSERC research grant 171239 to R. Mayberry.

REFERENCES

Ann, J. (1993). *A linguistic investigation of the relationship between physiology and handshape.* Unpublished doctoral dissertation, University of Arizona, Tucson.

Battison, R. (1978). *Lexical borrowing in American Sign Language.* Silver Spring, MD: Linstok.

Bonvillian, J. D., Orlansky, M. D., Novack, L. L., Folven, R. J., & Holley-Wilcox, P. (1985). Language, cognitive, and cherological development: The first steps in sign language acquisition. In W. Stokoe & V. Volterra (Eds.), *SLR '83: Proceedings of the third international symposium on sign language research* (pp. 10–22) Silver Spring, MD: Linstok.

Bonvillian, J. D., & Siedlecki, T., Jr. (1996). Young children's acquisition of the location aspect of American Sign Language signs: Parental report findings. *Journal of Communicative Disorders, 29,* 13–35.

Boyes Braem, P. (1990). Acquisition of the handshape in American Sign Language: A preliminary analysis. In V. Volterra, & C. J. Erting (Eds.), *From gesture to language in hearing and deaf children* (pp. 107–127). New York: Springer-Verlag.

Brentari, D. (1990). *Theoretical foundations of American Sign Language phonology, Volume One* Unpublished doctoral dissertation, University of Chicago.

Brentari, D., van der Hulst, H., van der Kooij, E., & Sandler, W. (1996, September). *One over all and all over one: A dependency-based decomposition of selected fingers* Poster presented at Theoretical Issues in Sign Language Research, Montreal, Quebec.

Butterworth, G. (1992). Origins of self-perception in infancy. *Psychological Inquiry, 3,* 103–111.

Clibbens, J., & Harris, M. (1993). Phonological processes and sign language development. In D. J. Messer & G. J. Turner (Eds.), *Critical influences on child language acquisition and development* (pp. 197–208). New York: St. Martin's Press.

Ferguson, C. A., & Farwell, C. (1975). Words and sounds in early language acquisition. *Language, 51,* 419–439.

Fogel, A. (1981). The ontogeny of gestural communication: The first six months. In R. E. Stark (Ed.), *Language behavior in infancy and early childhood* (pp. 17–44). New York: Elsevier North Holland.

Klima, E., & Bellugi, U. (1979). *The signs of language.* Cambridge, MA: Harvard University Press.

Marentette, P. F. (1995). *It's in her hands A case study of the emergence of phonology in American Sign Language* Unpublished doctoral dissertation, McGill University, Montreal.

Mayberry, R. I. (1995). Mental phonology and language comprehension, or What does that sign mistake mean? In K. Emmory, & J. S. Reilly (Eds.), *Language, gesture, and space* (pp. 355–370). Hillsdale, NJ: Lawrence Erlbaum Associates.

McIntire, M. L. (1977). The acquisition of American Sign Language hand configurations. *Sign Language Studies, 16,* 247–266.

Meier, R. P., Mauk, C., Mirus, G. R., & Conlin, K. E. (1998). Motoric constraints on early sign acquisition. In E. Clark (Ed.), *Proceedings of the Child Language Research Forum* (Vol. 29, pp. 63–72). Stanford: Center for the Study of Language and Information Press.

Meier, R. P., & Willerman, R. (1995). Prelinguistic gesture in deaf and hearing infants. In K. Emmorey, & J. S. Reilly (Eds.), *Language, gesture, and space* (pp. 391–409). Hillsdale, NJ: Lawrence Erlbaum Associates.

Meltzoff, A. N., & Moore, M. K. (1993). Why faces are special to infants—On connecting the attraction of faces and infants' ability for imitation and cross-modal processing. In B. de Boysson-Bardies, S. de Schonen, P. Jusczyk, P. MacNeilage, & J. Morton (Eds.), *Developmental neurocognition: Speech and face processing in the first year of life* (pp. 211–225). Dordrecht, Netherlands: Kluwer.

Neisser, U. (1991). Two perceptually given aspects of the self and their development. *Developmental Review, 11,* 197–209.

Orlansky, M. D., & Bonvillian, J. D. (1988). Early sign acquisition. In M. D. Smith & J. L. Locke (Eds.), *The emergent lexicon. The child's development of a linguistic vocabulary* (pp. 263–292). New York: Academic Press.

Prinz, P. M., & Prinz, E. A. (1979). Simultaneous acquisition of ASL and spoken English. *Sign Language Studies, 25,* 283–296.

Sandler, W. (1995). Markedness in the handshapes of sign language: A componential analysis. In H. van der Hulst & J. van der Weijer (Eds.), *Leiden in Last HIL phonology papers I* (pp. 369–399). The Hague, Netherlands: Holland Academic Graphics.

Siedlecki, T., Jr. (1991). *The acquisition of American Sign Language phonology by young children of deaf parents.* Unpublished doctoral dissertation, University of Virginia.

Siedlecki, T., Jr., & Bonvillian, J. D. (1993). Location, handshape, and movement: Young children's acquisition of the formational aspects of American Sign Language. *Sign Language Studies, 78*, 31–52.

Siedlecki, T., Jr., & Bonvillian, J. D. (1997). Young children's acquisition of the handshape aspect of American Sign Language signs. Parental report findings. *Applied Psycholinguistics, 18*, 17–39.

Vihman, M. M. (1993). Variable paths to early word production. *Journal of Phonetics, 21*, 61–82.

Chapter 6

Early Sign Combinations in the Acquisition of Sign Language of the Netherlands: Evidence for Language-Specific Features

Jane A. Coerts
University of Amsterdam

In this chapter, I demonstrate that children can acquire language-specific features at an early age. This will become clear from research on the acquisition of basic order in Sign Language of the Netherlands (SLN) in relation to the acquisition of another language-specific feature, namely, subject pronoun copy.

To explain the acquisition of language-specific features, the theory of parameter setting was proposed within a generative syntactic framework (Chomsky, 1981). Within this theory, children find out how the values of a restricted set of parameters are set in the language they are acquiring. The choice for a particular parameter value is made on the basis of information available in the input.

The description of the possible set of parameters is far from complete, but it is generally assumed by researchers working within a parametric framework that there is a parameter for basic order and a so-called pro-drop parameter. The description of the initial states of parameters is another area that needs more attention. Is there an initial default value (as suggested by Hyams, 1986, for the pro-drop parameter)? Or are the parameters initially not set, that is, are the various options, for a limited time, simultaneously present in the developing grammar (cf. Meisel, 1995)? The third area that needs further investigation relates to the moment at which children are able to definitely link the correct value to a specific parameter. The parameter for basic order is assumed to be acquired early (Clahsen & Muysken, 1986; Weissenborn, 1990).

Within the acquisition context, pro-drop and basic order have been investigated most extensively from a parametric point of view. The acqui-

91

sition of null arguments and basic order also formed the focus of a study on early combinations in SLN carried out by Coerts and Mills (now Baker) in 1994. Coerts and Mills found a considerable amount of variation with respect to order, which made it difficult to determine whether the children had set the parameter for basic order. In this chapter I show that part of this variability can be explained by the children's mastery of another language-specific feature, namely, subject pronoun copy (Bos, 1995). This feature had not been identified for SLN at the time of the Coerts and Mills study and was therefore not integrated in their analysis procedure. Bos, however, convincingly argued that subject pronoun copy, in combination with subject-drop, results in a superficially different order than basic order. Consequently, a study of the acquisition of basic order in SLN must incorporate this feature. An analysis procedure that takes subject pronoun copy into account can shed new light on the question of when children acquiring SLN master the language-specific feature of basic order. For this purpose, the Coerts and Mills data are reanalyzed.

Before presenting this reanalysis, a brief sketch of the syntactic rules of adult SLN is given insofar as they are relevant to this study. The rules cover constituent order and null arguments. Current views on the acquisition of these language-specific aspects provide the theoretical context for the studies in this chapter. Subsequently, a summary of an earlier study on the acquisition of basic order and null arguments in SLN (Coerts & Mills, 1994) is given so that it can be compared with Study II (discussed later). The next step is to describe the language-specific feature of subject pronoun copy (Bos, 1995); the early occurrence of this feature in our children's data might be responsible for the high degree of variability with respect to order reported by Coerts and Mills. In the central part of this chapter, I show first that subject pronoun copy is indeed acquired early in SLN (Study I) and second, that the presence of this language-specific feature explains to a great extent the variation that Coerts and Mills (1994) found earlier (Study II).

BASIC ORDER AND NULL ARGUMENTS IN ADULT SLN

SLN appears to be a language with SOV or verb-final order (Bos, 1995; Coerts, 1994). Different orders are possible, but these seem to be the result of a movement rule. For example, SOV can change into O,SV via topicalization of the object. Therefore, both (1) and (2) are possible in SLN:[1]

---

[1]Signs are represented in capitalized glosses. The subscripts, 1, 2, and 3 refer to the locations of the signer, the addressee, and created locations for nonpresent referents, respectively. 3a is a location on the signer's right, 3b on his left. Nonmanual markings of sentence types are indicated with a line above the glosses; the length of the line corresponds to its duration. Commas represent pauses; "t" stands for the nonmanual grammatical marker for topicalization. The source of the examples is given in quotes on the right-hand side.

(1) WOMAN THREAD$_{3b}$ CUT$_{3b}$
   "The woman cuts the thread"   (Coerts, 1994, p. 78)

$$\overline{\hspace{3cm}}^{\,t}$$

(2) TELEVISION, GIRL WATCH
   "As for the television, the girl is watching it" (Coerts, 1994, p. 76)

Locative phrases can also appear in first position as the result of a movement rule, as is shown in (3):

(3) CHAIR CAT SIT-ON
   "The cat is sitting on the chair"   (Coerts, 1994, p. 79)

Another feature of adult SLN is the licensing of null arguments. Subjects as well as objects do not necessarily have to be expressed overtly by a pronominal or nominal sign (Bos, 1993). Several researchers found evidence for a relation between the possibility of null arguments and the "richness" of an agreement system (cf. Jaeggli & Safir, 1989). Rich agreement systems show an elaborate verbal paradigm with fixed positions within the verb for the elements that cross-reference the subject and object. These cross-referential elements can be unambiguously associated with nominal constituents in the clause and are therefore viewed as pronominal themselves. Null arguments are often allowed in languages with a rich agreement system, because these arguments can be identified on the basis of these cross-referential elements. Bos (1993, 1994) argued that this is also true for SLN. According to her, the paradigm of multiple agreement verbs exhibits different forms for every combination of person category of subject and object. For example, in its citation form, the verb sign GIVE moves from the signer toward a place directly in front of the signer, meaning "to give." If the beginning and end points of the same movement are stressed, it means "I give to you." By changing the direction of the movement, for example, a movement from location 3a (the signer's right; associated with third-person singular) toward location 2 (the location in front of the signer; associated with second person), the meaning of the sign changes into "She/he gives to you." All possible singular agreement forms of GIVE are presented in (4):

(4) $_1$GIVE$_2$ "I give to you"
    $_1$GIVE$_{3a/3b}$ "I give to her/him"
    $_2$GIVE$_1$ "You give to me"
    $_2$GIVE$_{3a/3b}$ "You give to her/him"
    $_{3a/3b}$GIVE$_1$ "She/he gives to me"
    $_{3a/3b}$GIVE$_2$ "She/he gives to you"
    $_{3a/3b}$GIVE$_{3b/3a}$ "She/he$_i$ gives to her/him$_j$"

Despite this extensive possibility to mark verbs for agreement, agreement in SLN and other sign languages is not always realized. That is, it is not unusual for a multiple agreement verb to agree with only one argument instead of two or even with no argument at all. If there is agreement with only one argument, this argument is generally the object. This asymmetry between subjects and objects was also found with regard to null arguments, in the sense that object-drop occurs approximately twice as often as subject-drop (Bos, 1993, 1994). There is, however, no one-to-one correspondence between the presence of agreement and the absence of independent expression of the subject and object. That is, subjects and objects can be expressed independently by a lexical or pronominal sign and also be signaled by agreement, or they can be null in the absence of agreement. How null arguments in SLN are identified in the absence of agreement marking is currently the object of research (Bos, in prep). It is possible that, like ASL, these types of null arguments are null variable arguments (*var*), as in Chinese, and that identification takes place on the basis of topic chaining (see Lillo-Martin, 1986, 1990, for further details on the existence of two types of null arguments, i.e., null pronominal arguments [*pro*] and null variable arguments [*var*] in one language).

ACQUISITION OF BASIC ORDER
AND NULL ARGUMENTS

To explain the acquisition of language-specific features within a generative framework, Chomsky (1981) proposed the theory of *parameter setting*, as described earlier. According to this model, children's basic task in language learning is to set values on each parameter according to the requirements of their native language. The choice for a particular setting is made on the basis of positive evidence in their input language. Hyams (1986) developed this idea further. For the pro-drop parameter, she suggested that children have an unmarked form or default setting of the parameter, before they make a choice on the basis of the evidence in their language. This proposal, however, is not undisputed (Clahsen, 1991; Lebeaux, 1987).

Within a parametric framework, it is assumed that children quickly set the parameter for basic order and later learn the movement rules for the other possible orders (Clahsen & Muysken, 1986; Weissenborn, 1990). As shown earlier, SLN appears to be a language with SOV order. Children acquiring this language as a first language would therefore be expected to rapidly produce subjects in initial position and verbs in final position.

For all the languages that were investigated from a parameter perspective, it was reported that subjects are dropped in early child utterances (e.g., Italian, English: Hyams, 1986; Japanese: Mazuka, Lust, Wakayama,

& Snyder, 1986; Hebrew: Berman, 1990; French, German: Weissenborn, 1992; ASL: Lillo-Martin, 1992). There is, however, much variation in the proportion of null subjects between children and across languages. This raises the general question of how large the rate of missing subjects must be for there to be plausible interpretation that the omission of subjects is syntactic (cf. Coerts & Mills, 1994; Krämer, 1995). Hyams (1992) argued that frequency is not important but that the two significant aspects for interpretation are the change over time (for children acquiring a non-pro-drop language) and an asymmetry of missing subjects compared to missing objects. Because adult SLN allows missing subjects, change over time is not relevant. The subject–object asymmetry is relevant for SLN because, as I described previously, this language allows both types of null arguments. Hyams's (1992) prediction that there will always be a subject–object asymmetry in the child's use of null arguments is based on the assumption that null subjects are acquired as *pro*, whereas null objects are dependent on *var*. According to Hyams (1992), *pro* is present from the beginning, whereas *var* will appear on the basis of maturation. Lillo-Martin (1991), among others, rejected this claim; she believes that children do have variables at a very early age. The study of the acquisition of SLN can contribute to our knowledge with respect to the acquisition of null arguments. Are null subjects more frequently used in early combinations than null objects, as Hyams would predict, or is there in fact no asymmetry or even an asymmetry in the opposite direction, reflecting the adult SLN pattern?

PREVIOUS WORK ON SYNTACTIC ACQUISITION OF SLN

Coerts and Mills (1994) examined the early sign combinations of deaf twins, Laura and Mark, with respect to null arguments and basic order. The mother of the twins is deaf and their father is a hearing child of deaf parents; both parents are native signers of SLN. The children and their mother were filmed at home in a freeplay situation. The data of the children were taken from monthly recordings between the ages of the first occurrence of a signed combination and 2;6 (years; months).[2]

Coerts and Mills found that the children dropped subjects and objects frequently up to age 2;6. A comparison of the mean percentages of null subjects (35%) and null objects (31%) does not reveal a clear asymmetry between subject- and object-drop. This quantitative result challenges Hyams's (1992) prediction that all early grammars will show a subject–object asymmetry. Coerts and Mills suggested that the relatively high fre-

---

[2]No recording was made at the age of 2;3.

quency of object-drop is a reflection of the children's early mastery of this language-specific feature.

The results of Coerts and Mills with respect to the acquisition of basic order show a preference for subjects in initial position and a tendency to produce verbs in final position. However, they found a considerable degree of individual variation and no clear development over time. It is therefore difficult to conclude that the children have acquired this language-specific feature early, as Clahsen and Muysken (1986) and Weissenborn (1990) predicted. Coerts and Mills suggested that the variability that they found might have been caused by a blurred picture of the regularities with respect to order in the input. For example, an analysis of verb position in the input at age 1;11 showed that the verb was in final position in approximately 50% of the mother's utterances (van den Bogaerde & Baker, 1996), as opposed to 90% in adult–adult sign (Coerts, 1994).

An alternative explanation, however, might be that the children have already mastered the position of the subject and also another language-specific feature, namely, subject pronoun copy. This feature of SLN was not known at the time of the Coerts and Mills study. In combination with subject-drop, subject pronoun copy leads to a superficially different order from SOV. It is possible that Mark and Laura acquired this language-specific feature at an early stage and that the mastery of this feature is responsible for the variability found in our acquisition data.

In the next section, I first give the characteristics of this feature. Next, I demonstrate how subject pronoun copy can lead to a superficially different order, followed by a description of the linguistic context in which subject pronoun copy frequently occurs.

SUBJECT PRONOUN COPY

Bos (1995) found that in adult SLN, subject pronoun copy is a regular phenomenon. She defined subject pronoun copy as "the incidence of a subject pronoun in final position, or at least in a position after the main verb, which is a copy of the features of the subject argument, which may either be overt, in that case itself most likely also being pronominal, or non overt" (p. 133). In her data, pronoun copy occurred in about 20% of the main clauses. In about half of all instances of pronoun copy, there was no preceding independent lexical expression of the subject, which led to a superficially different order from the basic order. Bos argued that this OVS order is in fact not different but related to the basic SOV order: SOV + subject pronoun copy becomes SOVS; SOVS + subject-drop becomes OVS.

Bos (1995) argued that the use of subject pronoun copies, whether preceded or not by the overt expression of a subject in its initial position, is a strategy to identify the subject of the clause. This strategy is in keeping with the overall tendency in SLN to express the subject lexically. Evidence for her claim comes from the fact that subject pronoun copy occurs approximately twice as often in main clauses without subject agreement than in clauses with subject agreement. She also found that when there is a double lexical expression of the subject, the antecedent of the final subject pronoun is predominantly an INDEX and rarely an NP. The double presence of subject pronouns, Bos suggested, creates some necessary redundancy considering the low perceptual saliency of INDEXes.

The presence of subject pronoun copies may explain the variability with respect to order found in the Coerts and Mills data. I therefore decided to reexamine their data with respect to subject and verb position. To do so, I first needed to investigate if the children used subject pronoun copies and, if so, when they acquired this language-specific feature; this was done in Study I. Then, I reanalyzed the data of Coerts and Mills with respect to constituent order in relation to subject pronoun copy (Study II). The results of Study II show that a great deal of the variation in order that was found earlier can in fact be attributed to the children's use of subject pronoun copy in combination with subject-drop.

STUDY I: THE ACQUISITION OF SUBJECT PRONOUN COPY

The first question I asked was the following: Are there instances of subject pronoun copy present in the input data? It is assumed, based on positive evidence from the input data, that children acquire this language-specific feature. The mother is expected to use this feature while communicating with her children. Because the children should learn that final INDEXes are copies of previously expressed subjects, I expected the input data to include utterances in which the subject was expressed twice: once in its initial position and once postverbally or sentence finally (in utterances that lack a verb).

The second question is this: When do children acquiring SLN produce utterances with subject pronoun copy? If the acquisition of subject pronoun copy is responsible for the variation with respect to basic order found in the Coerts and Mills study, then this feature should be acquired early in the development.

Data and Analysis

For this study, I made use of the videorecordings of the Coerts and Mills study. On a monthly basis, Mark and Laura were each filmed individually with their mother in a free-play situation for at least 20 minutes, as part of a longitudinal study. Both children were born with severe hearing loss. Mark has a loss of more than 90dB in his best ear; Laura has a loss of 70dB. Laura had a hearing aid, but she did not wear it in recording sessions and wore it infrequently in general (see van den Bogaerde, 1994, and Coerts & Mills, 1994, for further details).

To answer the first research question, I transcribed 10 minutes of the input data of the mother to both Mark and Laura at the ages of 1;6, 2;0, and 2;6. For the analysis, I selected all declarative clauses that consisted of at least two constituents. Utterances with a labeling function and ambiguous utterances were excluded from the analysis. Utterances with a labeling function were excluded because in these utterances, it is impossible to distinguish between the use of an INDEX as a referring pronoun and the use of an INDEX to indicate location (see Coerts & Mills, 1994). Ambiguous utterances were excluded from the analysis because different interpretations can lead to different syntactic categories for one and the same constituent.

To answer the second research question, I reanalyzed all declarative combinations produced by the children in 20 minutes of the monthly recordings between the ages of the first occurrence of a signed combination and 2;6. Mark produced his first combination at 1;4 and Laura at 1;10. Utterances with a labeling function and ambiguous utterances were excluded from analysis, as were direct imitations of the mother, because they are not considered spontaneous productions.

The following criteria were used to determine whether a sign was a subject pronoun copy. The sign must

- occur postverbally (in utterances containing a verb) or sentence finally (in utterances that lack a verb)
- have the form of a pronoun (i.e., an INDEX)
- be a copy of the features of the subject argument
- (for the children): occur after the children had produced one utterance where the subject was expressed twice: once in sentence-initial position and again in either postverbal or sentence-final position

The last criterion was added to ensure that a sign referring to the subject and occurring postverbally or sentence finally could plausibly be interpreted as subject pronoun copy even in the absence of a realization of subject in initial position. A child's utterance in which a double lexical expression of a subject had occurred was taken as evidence that the child had analyzed a final subject INDEX as a subject pronoun copy.

The majority of subjects in sentence-final or postverbal position met the second criterion; that is, they were predominantly pronouns (only those utterances of the children that were produced after the fourth criterion had been met are considered): 79% for Mark (27 from 34), 93% for Laura

(13 from 14), and 100% (30 from 30) for their mother. Subjects realized in initial position, on the other hand, were both independently expressed INDEXes and full NPs, with the exception of the recordings up to 2;0, during which both the mother and the children almost exclusively produced lexical pronouns.

Results

First, there are clearly instances of subject pronoun copy present in the input data. The twins' mother produced utterances containing subject pronoun copies in every recording analyzed here. The results of this analysis are presented in Table 6.1. The table shows that where subject pronoun copy occurs, it also coincides with subject-drop in approximately 50% of all cases. Although the numbers are small, there seems to be a tendency to drop subjects more often as the children grow older. Initially, subject pronoun copy occurs in the context of double expression of the subject: once in initial position and once in postverbal or sentence-final position. This kind of utterance may help the children find out that final INDEXes are copies of an earlier expressed subject. Examples of double expressed subjects are presented in (4) and (5):

(4) INDEX$_{beppie}$ FILM INDEX$_{beppie}$
    "Beppie is filming"   Mother–Laura: 1;6

(5) INDEX$_{building-block}$ BLUE INDEX$_{building-block}$
    "The building block is blue"   Mother–Mark: 2;0

In examples (4) and (5), not only the subject pronoun copy but also the first expression of the subject have the form of a pronoun. This seems to

TABLE 6.1
Total Number of Mother's Utterances That Contain Subject Pronoun Copy and Number of Subject Pronoun Copy in Combination With Subject-Drop

Age	Mother–Mark		Mother–Laura	
	No. SPC[1]	No. SPC + SD[2]	No. SPC	No. SPC + SD
1;6	4	0	7	3
2;0	5	3	4	2
2;6	2	2	8	5

[1] = total number of utterances containing subject pronoun copy (SPC)
[2] = number of utterances containing subject pronoun copy in combination with subject-drop (SD).

be the regular pattern up to age 3;0. In sentences that do not contain a subject pronoun copy, but only a sentence-initial subject, however, the mother produces both subject pronouns and lexical subject NPs from age 2;0. It is possible that the use of the same form for the initial subject as well as for the postverbal or sentence-final subject also facilitates the interpretation of the latter subject pronoun as a copy of the initial subject.

With the increasing age of the children, subject pronoun copy seems more often to coincide with subject-drop. This results in utterances with one overtly expressed subject pronoun in postverbal or sentence-final position. This is shown in examples (6) and (7). In (6), the subject pronoun copy follows the main verb; in (7) it follows the complement. Complement structures do not contain a verb in SLN:

(6) CRY INDEX$_{dolls}$
"The dolls are crying"   Mother–Laura 2;6

(7) YELLOW INDEX$_{building-block}$
"The building block is yellow"   Mother–Mark: 2;0

The results of the analysis of the mother's utterances indicate that the children do receive the structure of postverbal or sentence-final INDEXes being subject pronoun copies in their input. This may trigger their own use of this feature.

To determine the onset of subject pronoun copy in the language production of the children, I looked for the first combination with a double expression of the subject, once in sentence-initial position and once postverbally or sentence finally. As stated earlier, I considered double expression of the subject as evidence that the children had analyzed a final subject pronoun as a subject pronoun copy. Laura produced such an utterance at 1;10 and Mark at 2;0. The utterances are presented in (8) and (9) respectively:

(8) INDEX$_{sonja}$ FILM INDEX$_{sonja}$
"Sonja is filming"   Laura: 1;10

(9) INDEX$_{building-block}$ YELLOW INDEX$_{building-block}$
"The building block is yellow"   Mark: 2;0

The next occurrence of an INDEX that met the first three criteria for the identification of subject pronoun copy was taken as the onset of the mastery of this language-specific feature. Mark met these criteria at 2;1 and Laura at 2;2. Although both children showed an increase in their use of subject pronoun copy over the period under study, this is much clearer for Mark than for Laura. This is demonstrated in Table 6.2.

TABLE 6 2
Total Number of Children's Utterances That Contain Subject Pronoun Copy and Number of
Subject Pronoun Copy in Combination With Subject-Drop

Age	Mark		Laura	
	No SPC[1]	No SPC + SD[2]	No. SPC	No. SPC + SD
2;0	0	0	0	0
2,1	1	0	0	0
2;2	4	4	2	2
2;4	0	0	3	3
2;5	5	5	3	2
2;6	17	12	5	5

[1] = total number of utterances containing subject pronoun copy (SPC).
[2] = number of utterances containing subject pronoun copy in combination with subject-drop (SD).

As can be deduced from Table 6.2, most instances of subject pronoun copy coincide with subject-drop (21 out of 27 for Mark, and 12 out of 13 for Laura). Coerts and Mills (1994) did not interpret postverbal or sentence-final subjects as subject pronoun copies, but as normal expressions of the subject. This might have led to the reported variability in the relative order of the subject and verb.

In conclusion, we can say that the results of Study I show that the children get positive evidence for the language-specific feature of subject pronoun copy and that they acquire this feature reasonably early in their syntactic development. The co-occurrence of subject pronoun copy and subject-drop from age 2;1 (Mark) and 2;2 (Laura) may have caused the variability with respect to order in our earlier study. A reanalysis of the Coerts and Mills data that takes into account the feature of subject pronoun copy forms the basis for the second part of my research.

STUDY II: A REANALYSIS OF THE ACQUISITION OF BASIC ORDER

Data and Analysis

For this study, I reanalyzed the spontaneous language of the children taken from the monthly recordings of Coerts and Mills (1994) from 2;1 (first occurrence of subject pronoun copy) up to and including 2;6, and also the recordings at 3;0. An analysis of this latter recording was added to get a clearer picture of the developmental path of basic order. The recordings at 3;0 lasted only 6 minutes for Mark and 10 minutes for Laura. This is short compared to the other recordings, which lasted at least 20 minutes. Because I also wanted to know to what extent the input data was consistent with respect to basic order, I analyzed 10 minutes of the input to the children at ages 2;0, 2;6, and 3;0 with regard to the position of subjects and verbs and subject pronoun copy.

For the analysis, I selected all declarative clauses that consisted of at least two constituents, except utterances with a labeling function, ambiguous utterances, and (for the children) direct imitations of the mother (see Study 1 for a motivation of this decision).

The position of the subject was noted for each declarative clause that contained a subject, except for those utterances in which the only expression of the subject was a subject pronoun copy. In clauses with a double lexical expression of a subject, the first occurrence of the subject was taken as the subject position. For declarative clauses in which the subject was not in first position, it was noted whether this subject was a pronoun or a full noun phrase and, if it was a pronoun, whether it occurred after the verb (when present) or sentence finally (in combinations without a verb). Only postverbal or sentence-final subject pronouns were interpreted as subject pronoun copies. Utterances in which the subject was expressed only once and in which the subject met all the criteria for subject pronoun copy, namely, utterances in which subject-drop co-occurred with subject pronoun copy, were excluded from the analysis of subject position because the position of the dropped subject could not be determined objectively.

The position of the verb was noted for all combinations that included a verb. In clauses where the main verb was expressed twice, the first occurrence of the verb was taken as the verb position. In utterances where the subject was expressed twice, the position of the verb was evaluated as final if the verb was followed only by the second lexical expression of the subject. In clauses where the verb was in nonfinal position and where there was only one lexical expression of the subject, I examined whether pronoun copy had taken place. If this was the case, the verb position was considered sentence final. So for the analysis of verb position, I did not exclude utterances with OVS order where the subject was a subject pronoun copy.

The results of the children are grouped in two periods: from 2;1 up to 2;6, and at 3;0. For reasons of completeness, I added the results of the period from 1;4 for Mark and from 1;10 for Laura up to and including 2;0 in Tables 6.3 and 6.4. This division of age groups is slightly different from that of Coerts and Mills (1994), who included the data of 2;0 in the period from 2;0 up to 2;6. The decision for this altered division is based on the moment of first occurrence of subject pronoun copy in the children's data. To be able to compare the new results with respect to order with those of the Coerts and Mills study, I summarized their 1994 results according to this altered division in age groups in Tables 6.5 and 6.6. In addition, I calculated the proportion of subjects in initial position and verbs in final position of the mother at 2;0 and 2;6, using the criteria of Coerts and Mills (1994). In this way, the effect of our new analysis procedure for regularities in the input also becomes clear.

Results

The percentage of subjects in initial position for the total number of combinations that included a subject are presented in Table 6.3. Contrary to Coerts and Mills (1994), I excluded all utterances with a subject pronoun

TABLE 6 3
Percentages of Subjects in Initial Position in Utterances With and Without a Verb
(Utterances in Which Subject-Drop Co-occurred With a Subject Pronoun Excluded)

	Declarative Clauses With Subjects in Initial Position							
	Mark		Mother–Mark		Laura		Mother–Laura	
Age	%	No[1]	%	No.	%	No.	%	No.
(→) 2;0	67	21	93	28	86	7	100	19
(→) 2,6	70	110	79	24	83	70	83	23
3,0	93	15	100	8	82	11	100	13

[1] = total number of combinations including a subject minus utterances in which subject-drop co-occurred with subject pronoun drop.

TABLE 6 4
Percentages of Verbs in Final Position (Ignoring Subject Pronoun Copy)

	Declarative Clauses With Verbs in Final Position							
	Mark		Mother–Mark		Laura		Mother–Laura	
Age	%	No[1]	%	No	%	No	%	No.
(→) 2,0	42	12	75	12	40	5	79	14
(→) 2;6	76	78	63	19	76	34	44	9
3,0	56	9	78	9	91	11	47	34

[1] = total number of combinations including a verb

TABLE 6 5

Percentages of Subjects in Initial Position in Utterances With and Without a Verb According to the Analysis Procedure Used by Coerts and Mills (1994)

	Declarative Clauses With Subjects in Initial Position							
	Mark		Mother–Mark		Laura		Mother–Laura	
Age	%	No [1]	%	No.	%	No.	%	No
(→) 2,0	67	21	84	31	86	7	90	21
(→) 2;6	58	131	73	26	71	82	68	28

[1] = total number of combinations including a subject

TABLE 6.6

Percentages of Verbs in Final Position According to the Analysis Procedure Used by Coerts and Mills (1994)

	Declarative Clauses With Verbs in Final Position							
	Mark		Mother–Mark		Laura		Mother–Laura	
Age	%	No [1]	%	No	%	No.	%	No.
(→) 2;0	42	12	41	12	40	5	71	14
(→) 2;6	51	78	58	19	65	34	33	9

[1] = total number of combinations including a verb.

copy being the only expression of the subject from age 2;1 for Mark and age 2;2 for Laura. As was shown in Study I, there was no evidence that children considered a sentence-final subject pronoun as a subject pronoun copy prior to that time. As described earlier, the number and proportion of subjects in initial position is reported for three age groups. I also added the proportion of initial subjects for the mother. In Table 6.3, no distinction is made between utterances containing a verb and utterances that do not contain a verb, because in the data I describe here, the presence or absence of a verb does not influence the proportion of subjects in first position.

Compared with the original analysis (see Table 6.5), the percentages are clearly higher as an effect of excluding utterances in which the only overt expression of the subject is a subject pronoun copy. Now, development also becomes clearer for Mark; at age 3;0, his percentage of subjects in initial position increases to 93%. Laura does not show development, but her percentage was already above 80% in the period from 2;1 to 2;6.

The proportions of the mother's subjects in initial position show a high degree of consistency with respect to the placement of the subject. Her mean percentage of subjects in initial position, when we take subject pronoun copy into account, is 93%, as opposed to 79% when subject pronoun copy is not taken into account. Table 6.3 also shows that the mother's productions increase to 100% of subjects in initial position in three recording sessions (one with Mark and two with Laura). This implies that the input to the children is much more homogeneous with respect to subject position than we thought during the Coerts and Mills study.

Of the remaining subjects in noninitial position, approximately one third occur in second position after a locative phrase. This is true for both the mother and her children. As stated previously, locative phrases can occur in sentence-initial position as the result of a movement rule. Although both Laura and Mark produce locative phrases in first position, the numbers for Mark are more convincing. He places the locative phrase in first position in 14 of a total of 42 utterances containing both a subject and a locative phrase; Laura does this 4 times out of 14. Almost all of Mark's utterances with a locative phrase in first position were produced in the period from 2;1 to 2;6 (13 of 14). If we exclude these utterances from the analysis, assuming that they indicate Mark's mastery of the movement rule for locative phrases, his proportion of subjects in initial position for this period increases to 80%.

On the basis of these results, it can be concluded that the children have acquired subject position by age 2;6. An analysis procedure for subject position that takes subject pronoun copy into account gives a much clearer picture of both the children's production and that of their mother. The variability reported by Coerts and Mills (1994) can to a great extent be attributed to the researchers' lack of knowledge of adult SLN at the time of their first analysis. Another interesting result is that the input of the mother is highly consistent with respect to the position of the subject. Earlier suggestions that the input does not reveal clear information with respect to subject position must therefore be revised.

To examine the effect of subject pronoun copy on the position of the verb, I reanalyzed all combinations containing a verb from age 2;1 for Mark and 2;2 for Laura. According to the new analysis procedure, a verb was counted as final when no constituent followed it or when it was followed only by a subject pronoun copy, that being the only lexical expression of the subject in the utterance. (In our earlier analysis, we scored this verb position as medial.) The results of this analysis are presented in Table 6.4.

Again, the reanalysis leads to higher percentages of verbs in final position for the most relevant ages (compare Table 6.4 with Table 6.6). The children show a strong preference for verbs in final position in the period from 2;1 up to and including 2;6. For Mark, this preference is less clear at 3;0. The proportion at age 3;0 is, however, not very reliable because of the small number of combinations including a verb produced in that short recording. Laura does show a continuing increase in the verb-final placement at age 3;0.

If we look at the input figures, we see a less consistent pattern with respect to verb position compared to subject position. The mean percentage of subjects in initial position for the mother is 93%; the mean percentage of verbs in final position is 64%. This difference can be explained by the fact that adverbial phrases can easily follow the verb in SLN. Constituents that follow the verb in the input data are primarily adverbial phrases for direction or manner. Occasionally, the verb is followed by an object. By contrast, lexical subject NPs never follow the verb.

The children show the same pattern as their mother with respect to constituents that follow the verb, with the exception of lexical subject NPs, which they do sometimes place after the verb. These utterances are ungrammatical in adult SLN.

Although the position of adverbial phrases for direction and manner has not yet been investigated for SLN, it seems that their preferred position is at the end of the sentence. If this is true, an analysis procedure that defines a verb as final if it follows the subject and (in)direct object would be more accurate.

Summarizing, it can be said that an analysis of verb position that deals with the phenomenon of subject pronoun copy results in a more convincing picture of the children having acquired the basic position of the verb. The lower percentages of final position of the verbs compared to initial position of the subjects may be the result of a too strict definition of verb finality. More knowledge of the ordering principles in SLN will help us to further develop our analysis procedures, especially with respect to verb position.

CONCLUSION AND DISCUSSION

The aim of the studies reported in this chapter was to investigate at what age children acquiring SLN master language-specific features of SLN. I concentrated on two features: subject pronoun copy and basic order. I investigated whether an early mastery of subject pronoun copy by children acquiring SLN as a native language might have affected the results of an earlier study carried out by Coerts and Mills in 1994 on the acquisition of basic order. Bos (1995) found that subject pronoun copy occurs very regularly in adult SLN. This language-specific feature of SLN was not known at the time of the Coerts and Mills study on the acquisition of basic order.

One important outcome of these studies is that they show that knowledge of the adult language steers the choice of analysis procedures used for acquisition data. The variation with respect to order phenomena reported in Coerts and Mills (1994) can to a large extent be attributed to our lack of knowledge of adult SLN at that time. Coerts and Mills suggested that the variability they found could partly be explained by irregularities in the input data. This suggestion, however, should be rejected. The mother of the twins gives them a very stable picture with regard to subject position; 93% of her subjects occur in first position. The position of the verb is less clear (64%), but this percentage on reanalysis exceeds the percentage reported in the Coerts and Mills study by 15%. A possible explanation for the fact that the percentage for verbs in final position is much lower than that for subjects in initial position is that adverbial phrases in SLN, especially those for manner and direction, tend to occur postverbally. If this is true, our definition of verb-final position in this chapter still has been too broad. This is an extra motivation to go back to data of adult SLN users and look for regularities with respect to the order of arguments other than subjects, objects, and verbs.

A second important outcome of the studies is that they demonstrate that subject pronoun copy is acquired at an early stage of syntactic development. Mark acquired this feature at age 2;1, and Laura at age 2;2. Further, in Study II, I reanalyzed the Coerts and Mills data and also the data of the children at age 3;0. It turned out that an analysis procedure that takes subject pronoun copy into account results in a much clearer picture with respect to the acquisition of subject and verb position. The results show that children have acquired basic order by age 2;6.

The results of both Study I and II suggest that children can acquire language-specific features at a very early stage in their language development. The assumption of Clahsen and Muysken (1986) and Weissenborn (1990) that children set the parameter for basic order early can thus be confirmed.

ACKNOWLEDGMENTS

I am very grateful to Anne Baker, Heleen Bos, Beppie van den Bogaerde, and the editors of this book for their valuable comments on earlier versions of this chapter.

REFERENCES

Berman, R. (1990). On acquiring an (S)VO language: Subjectless sentences in children's Hebrew. *Linguistics 28*, 1135–1166.

Bos, H. F. (1993). Agreement and pro-drop in Sign Language of the Netherlands. In F. Drijkoningen & K. Hengeveld (Eds.), *Linguistics in the Netherlands 1993: AVT Publications 10* (pp. 37–47). Amsterdam: Benjamins.

Bos, H. F. (1994). An auxiliary verb in Sign Language of the Netherlands. In I. Ahlgren, B. Bergman, & M. Brennan (Eds.), *Perspectives on sign language structure. Papers from the Fifth International Symposium on Sign Language Research* (Vol. 1, pp. 37–53). Durham, NC: The International Sign Linguistics Association/The Deaf Studies Research Unit, University of Durham.

Bos, H. F. (1995). Pronoun copy in Sign Language of the Netherlands. In H. F. Bos & T. Schermer (Eds.), *Sign language research 1994. Proceedings of the 4th European Congress on Sign Language Research* (pp. 121–148). Hamburg, Germany: Signum Press.

Bos, H. F. (in prep.). *Person and location marking in Sign Language of the Netherlands.*

Chomsky, N. (1981). *Lectures on government and binding.* Dordrecht, Netherlands: Foris.

Clahsen, H. (1991). *Child language and developmental dysphasia: Linguistic studies of the acquisition of German.* Amsterdam: Benjamins.

Clahsen, H., & Muysken, P. (1986). The availability of universal grammar to adult and child learners: A study of the acquisition of German word order. *Second Language Research, 2,* 93–119.

Coerts, J. A. (1994). Constituent order in Sign Language of the Netherlands and the functions of orientations. In I. Ahlgren, B. Bergman, & M. Brennan (Eds.), *Perspectives on sign language structure. Papers from the Fifth International Symposium on Sign Language Research* (Vol. 1, pp. 69–88). Durham, NC: The International Sign Linguistics Association/The Deaf Studies Research Unit, University of Durham.

Coerts, J. A., & Mills, A. E. (1994). Early sign combinations of deaf children in Sign Language of the Netherlands. In I. Ahlgren, B. Bergman, & M. Brennan (Eds.), *Perspectives on sign language usage. Papers from the Fifth International Symposium on Sign Language Research* (Vol. 2, pp. 319–331). Durham, NC: The International Sign Linguistics Association/The Deaf Studies Research Unit, University of Durham.

Hyams, N. M. (1986). *Language acquisition and the theory of parameters.* Dordrecht, Netherlands: Reidel.

Hyams, N. M. (1992). A reanalysis of null-subjects in child language. In J. Weissenborn, H. Goodluck, & T. Roeper (Eds.), *Theoretical issues in language acquisition: Continuity and change in development* (pp. 249–268). Hillsdale, NJ: Lawrence Erlbaum Associates.

Jaeggli, O., & Safir, K. J. (Eds.). (1989). *The null subject parameter. Studies in natural language and linguistic theory, Vol 15* Dordrecht, Netherlands: Kluwer.

Krämer, I. (1995). *The occurrence of subjects and objects in child Dutch. A longitudinal study of the spontaneous speech of seven children aged 1;8 to 3;1.* Unpublished master's thesis, Department of General Linguistics, University of Amsterdam.

Lebeaux, D. S. (1987). Comments on Hyams. In T. Roeper & E. Williams (Eds.), *Parameter setting* (pp. 23–39). Dordrecht, Netherlands: Reidel.

Lillo-Martin, D. C. (1986). Two kinds of null arguments in American Sign Language. *Natural Language and Linguistic Theory, 4,* 415–444.

Lillo-Martin, D. C. (1990). Studies of American Sign Language syntax and the principles and parameters of universal grammar. In W. Edmondson & F. Karlsson (Eds.), *SLR '87. Papers from the Fourth International Symposium on Sign Language Research* (pp. 86–93). Hamburg: Signum Press.

Lillo-Martin, D. C. (1991). *Universal grammar and American Sign Language. Setting the null argument parameters.* Dordrecht, Netherlands: Kluwer.

Lillo-Martin, D. C. (1992). Comments on Hyams and Weissenborn: On licensing and identification. In J. Weissenborn, H. Goodluck, & T. Roeper (Eds.), *Theoretical issues in language acquisition Continuity and change in development* (pp. 301–308). Hillsdale, NJ: Lawrence Erlbaum Associates.

Mazuka, R., Lust, B., Wakayama, T., & Snyder, W. (1986). Distinguishing effects of parameters in early syntax acquisition: A cross-linguistic study of Japanese and English. *Papers and Reports on Child Language Development, 25,* 73–82.

Meisel, J. M. (1995). Parameters in acquisition. In P. Fletcher & B. MacWhinney (Eds.), *The handbook of child language* (pp. 10–35). Cambridge, MA: Blackwell.

van den Bogaerde, B. (1994). Attentional strategies used by deaf mothers. In I. Ahlgren, B. Bergman, & M. Brennan (Eds.), *Perspectives on sign language structure Papers from the Fifth International Symposium on Sign Language Research* (Vol. 2, pp. 305–318). Durham, NC: The International Sign Linguistics Association/The Deaf Studies Research Unit, University of Durham.

van den Bogaerde, B., & Baker, A. E. (1996, April). *Verbs in the input of a deaf mother to one deaf and one hearing child.* Paper presented at the Child Language Seminar, Reading, United Kingdom.

Weissenborn, J. (1990). Functional categories and verb movement: The acquisition of German syntax reconsidered. In M. Rothweiler (Ed.), *Spracherwerb und Pragmatik. Linguistische Untersuchungen zum Erwerb von Syntax und Morphologie. Linguistische Berichte* (Special Issue 3, pp. 190–224).

Weissenborn, J. (1992). Null subjects in early grammars: Implications for parameter-setting theories. In J. Weissenborn, H. Goodluck, & T. Roeper (Eds.), *Theoretical issues in language acquisition· Continuity and change in development* (pp. 269–300). Hillsdale, NJ: Lawrence Erlbaum Associates.

Chapter 7

A Reexamination of "Early Exposure" and Its Implications for Language Acquisition by Eye

Jill P. Morford
University of New Mexico

Rachel I. Mayberry
McGill University

The importance of early exposure to language is gaining widespread recognition as a result of accumulating data from studies that investigate language development in deaf individuals who are first exposed to language at different ages. What precisely, however, does the term *early exposure* mean within the context of recent research and theory on language acquisition? Two bodies of research are relevant to the concept of early exposure, and bridging these research areas gives us a fuller understanding of the critical importance of early exposure to language acquisition.

The first research area compares early as opposed to later exposure to language. These studies demonstrate that individuals who are exposed to language at earlier ages consistently outperform individuals exposed to language at later ages for first and second language acquisition of both signed and spoken languages. The second research area identifies the aspects of language that are developing during the first year of life. These studies focus on the phonological development of infants exposed to spoken and signed languages and underscore the parallels in the development of the perceptual and productive systems of signed and spoken languages, as well as the similarities in the language environments to which infants are exposed in sign and speech. Together, these bodies of research illuminate the ways in which language exposure shapes the acquisition process. Consideration of these research findings allows us to reexamine the term *early exposure* to specify more precisely how the development of the phonological system during the first months of life affects ultimate outcomes of language acquisition by eye.

THE "EARLY" OF EARLY EXPOSURE:
TIMING AND LANGUAGE ACQUISITION

Early and Later Learners Compared

Exposure to language from birth is not the norm for deaf children. Thus, a number of researchers have investigated the effects of delayed language acquisition in this population. There are now three independent sets of research that converge on a single conclusion: Deaf individuals who are exposed to language at earlier ages consistently outperform deaf individuals exposed to language at later ages on tests of signed language knowledge and processing.

Mayberry and her colleagues (Mayberry, 1993; Mayberry & Eichen, 1991; Mayberry & Fischer, 1989) investigated the effects of delayed language acquisition on sentence shadowing and recall in American Sign Language (ASL). Shadowing (repeating a sentence while watching it) and recall (repeating a sentence after its completion) both require several processes: perception, recognition, comprehension, and memory of signs. Participants can enhance their performance on shadowing and recall if they are able to predict upcoming signs in a sentence based on grammatical and contextual knowledge. Thus, these tasks closely parallel day-to-day interaction in ASL. By comparing the performance of individuals first exposed to ASL at different ages, Mayberry was able to demonstrate that participants who were exposed to ASL earlier produced fewer omissions and substitutions in their shadowing and recall of sentences, and comprehended shadowed material better than participants who were exposed to ASL later in life. Her studies compared adults who were exposed to ASL at three different ages: 0 to 3 years, 5 to 8 years, and 9 to 13 years. Substitutions produced by the adults in the oldest age of exposure group indicated that their processing of the linguistic form of ASL was very superficial. These participants replaced target signs with phonologically similar but semantically inappropriate signs, suggesting that they did not immediately access the meaning of signs and thus retained only features of the surface form. Although earlier learners also modified recalled sentences, their modifications resulted in sentences that maintained the semantic relations of the target sentence and that were more grammatically acceptable when compared with the recalled sentences of later learners.

Newport (1990) reported research that she and colleagues conducted comparing the performance of adult signers exposed to ASL at different ages on the production and comprehension of ASL morphology and syntax. Three groups of participants participated in this research: native signers, individuals first exposed to ASL between the ages of 4 and 6, and individuals first exposed to ASL after age 12. Regardless of their initial exposure to ASL, all of the participants had at least 30 years experience using ASL on a daily basis. The results show that age of exposure to language did not affect participants' use of basic word order in ASL. However, there was a gradual decline in participants' ability to produce and comprehend a variety of ASL morphological structures, depending on the age of initial exposure to ASL. Individuals who were exposed to ASL earlier consistently outperformed individuals who were exposed to ASL later on these tasks.

A series of studies carried out by Emmorey and her colleagues (Emmorey, Bellugi, Frederici, & Horn, 1995; Emmorey & Corina, 1990, 1992) provided strong evidence that early exposure to language is important for efficient language processing. Native signers of ASL recognize isolated signs approximately 20 msec earlier than individuals who learned ASL between the ages of 4 and 16. Thus, early exposure to language allows the language user to depend more on linguistic knowledge and less on the actual signal to identify signs during perception. These investigators also found that native signers are more sensitive to errors in verb agreement and classifier usage during online processing than later learners of ASL. Even though all of the participants were able to detect errors in verb agreement, only native signers identified them rapidly enough for them to interfere with an online measure of sensitivity. Thus, it is not only at the level of phonological processing of individual signs, but also at the level of grammatical processing that we have evidence of much more rapid and efficient processing of language by individuals who are exposed to language earlier in life.

The related findings reported by these independent investigators demonstrate that early exposure to language is essential for rapid, efficient, and correct language usage in both production and comprehension. When language exposure is delayed, even by as little as a few years, language processing deficits become apparent. These deficits do not prevent late learners from using ASL as their primary language, but they provide a clear illustration of why early exposure to a first language is preferable for positive long-term outcomes.

Advantages Extend Beyond First Language Acquisition: Second Language Learners Compared

Second language acquisition does not parallel first language acquisition in every respect, but there do appear to be advantages to early exposure to a second language just as there are for the acquisition of a first language. Although older learners may outperform younger learners over a short period of time (e.g., up to a year), younger learners eventually gain a higher level of mastery in a second language than older learners (Krashen,

Long, & Scarcella, 1979). For example, in a study of Italian immigrants to the United States, Oyama (1976) found that the age of first exposure to English (between 6 and 20 years of age) predicted mastery of English phonology, whereas the length of time the immigrants had resided in the United States (between 5 and 18 years) did not. In a more recent study, Munro, Flege, and Mackay (1996) studied English vowel production in 240 native Italian speakers who arrived in Canada at ages ranging from 2 to 23 years. Age of arrival was a strong predictor of perceived "accentedness," with increases in perceived accent corresponding to older ages of arrival. Thus, early exposure to the second language ensures acquisition of the phonology, whereas later exposure, even if longer, does not.

Similar findings have been reported for second language learners' acquisition of morphology and syntax. For example, Patkowski (1980) analyzed transcripts of the spontaneous speech of a group of immigrants who arrived in the United States at different ages, and thus, were first exposed to English as a second language at different ages. Because written transcripts were used, the morphology and syntax could be evaluated without being influenced by accent. Individuals who had been exposed to English prior to puberty were judged to be more "native-like" than individuals who were first exposed to English after puberty. Because all participants had resided in the United States at least 5 years, the length of exposure to English did not predict native-like mastery of English. In a related study, Johnson and Newport (1989) found that age of first exposure to English predicted the ability of immigrants to the United States to identify errors in an auditory grammaticality judgment task. They studied immigrants who had arrived in the United States between the ages of 3 and 39 years, and had lived in the United States between 3 and 26 years. Like the previous study, these investigators found no effect of length of exposure to the second language, but they did find that the age when immigrants arrived in the United States was related to task performance. Thus, age of exposure predicts performance on both production and comprehension of the morphology and syntax of a second language.

These studies of second language learners demonstrate that early exposure can influence not only first language acquisition but second language acquisition as well. However, Johnson and Newport (1989) reported one finding that has yet to be replicated among first language learners. They found that earlier exposure is beneficial to second language mastery only up to a certain point. In their study, the performance of individuals who began learning English before age 15 could be predicted by age. But age of first exposure to English did not predict variability within the poorer performance of the participants who arrived between the ages of 17 and 39. This suggests there may be a threshold age, after which variation in language acquisition is better accounted for by other factors than age of exposure.

First and Second Language Learners Compared

In the only research to date that directly compared age of acquisition effects in first and second language learners, Mayberry (1993) found that *late-deafened adults* outperformed typical late learners of ASL on a sentence recall task even though both groups of signers were first exposed to ASL between the ages of 9 and 13. Late-deafened adults are individuals who were born hearing and acquired a spoken language from birth, but became deaf during adolescence and subsequently learned ASL. All of the participants in this study had used ASL for an average of 50 years. Hence, the only distinction between the participant groups was their linguistic experience prior to their acquisition of ASL: One group had no prior conventional language (first language learners), and the other group used a conventional spoken language, namely English (second language learners). The latter group produced as many lexical substitutions as the first language learners on Mayberry's processing task, but their errors were primarily semantically appropriate, unlike the errors of the first language learners.

A second study replicated and extended this finding (Mayberry & Lock, 1998). Late first-language learners (i.e., deaf individuals who acquired scant language, signed or spoken, in early childhood) who were first exposed to ASL and written English between the ages of 5 and 9 performed much worse than hearing second language learners of English on a grammatical processing task. The same was not true for native ASL learners. Native ASL signers, who acquired ASL from birth and English as a second language between the ages of 5 and 9, performed just like hearing participants, who had learned English as a second language at the same ages, on the grammatical processing task. These findings demonstrate that early exposure to a first language facilitates, and perhaps is necessary for, later language learning at older ages, as in second language learning.

In sum, the benefits of early as opposed to late exposure to language have been demonstrated across a wide variety of language tasks, across individuals of different ages, for both spoken and signed languages, and for both first and second language acquisition. These results come from several independent laboratories. The convergence of results from several different studies provides very strong evidence for the importance of early exposure to language acquisition and processing. This raises the following question: What characteristics of language exposure are influencing acquisition at its earliest stages? We address this question by examining studies of spoken and signed language acquisition during the first year of life.

THE "EXPOSURE" OF EARLY EXPOSURE: LANGUAGE ACQUISITION IN THE FIRST YEAR OF LIFE

The most obvious effect of language exposure on language acquisition is the fact that a child exposed to Portuguese learns Portuguese and not Bantu, and a child exposed to Langue des Signes Québécoise (LSQ) learns LSQ and not ASL. This influence is most apparent when children begin speaking their first words or signing their first signs, around their first birthday. Prior to this point, infants communicate primarily through nonlinguistic means. Nevertheless, they are learning a great deal about language, but only if they are exposed to it. We, in turn, can learn a great deal about what aspects of language exposure infants are sensitive to by observing the aspects of language that develop at this very early time in life. In this section, we describe aspects of language acquisition in the first year that illustrate how very early development is shaped by exposure to language.

Spoken Language Acquisition in the First Year

The earliest developments in language concern receptive rather than pro-ductive skills. So without ever making a sound or lifting a hand, the infant begins to acquire language simply by listening and watching. Research on the early perceptual development of children exposed to spoken languages is extensive. Infants exposed to spoken languages spend their first year learning about the sound system of the language, including identifying the phonemes and allophones (the distinctive sounds and how much those sounds can vary acoustically), the phonotactics (what sounds can occur together and what sounds cannot), and the prosody (the intonation).

   The view that language is a blur of sounds to infants was completely overturned by a landmark study in 1971 by Eimas and colleagues (Eimas, Siqueland, Jusczyk, & Vigorito, 1971). These investigators gave infants a pacifier connected to a tape recorder in such a manner that when the infants sucked on the pacifier, the tape recorder played synthetic speech sounds, specifically the syllables /ba/ and /pa/, which differ by a single phoneme. Although some of the infants were as young as 1 month old, the pattern of their sucking demonstrated that they noticed a difference between these phonemes. After listening to one sound repeatedly, the infants' sucking slowed, but if the sound changed, they began to suck more rapidly. Eimas et al. ruled out the possibility that the infants were respond-ing to a simple acoustic difference by repeating the experiment with two syllables that were as acoustically distinct as /ba/ and /pa/ but that are both categorized by adults as /ba/. In this condition, the infants did not display any response to the change in sound. Thus, tiny infants are already processing speech sounds in much the same way as adults.

In subsequent research, several investigators showed that infants are even sensitive to phoneme differences that do not occur in the language they are exposed to (Streeter, 1976; Trehub, 1973, 1976). These results lead many to conclude that at birth, hearing infants are able to distinguish between all of the phonemes used in the world's spoken languages. In other words, a child born in Argentina is prepared to learn Hungarian, Tagalog, or Spanish, in the sense that this child will be able to discern the phonemic contrasts that distinguish two words with different meanings in any of these languages. The same is not true for adults. An adult living in Argentina can distinguish all the phonemic contrasts of Spanish and some contrasts from Hungarian and Tagalog but not all.

This surprising difference in infant and adult speech perception abilities raised an important question for language researchers: If infants are born with the ability to process many different languages, when does exposure to the native language influence an individual's speech processing abilities? The answer is astonishing. Right from birth, infants are already sensitive to some characteristics of their native language, and over the course of the first year, there is more and more evidence of differentiated responses to the phonological structure of the native language.

To explain this research, it is helpful to make a distinction between two types of phonological structure in language. Segmental structure refers to the individual sounds such as vowels and consonants that are combined to create spoken words. Suprasegmental structure refers to sound characteristics that affect several segments, such as stress and intonation, also referred to as prosody. It is possible to take a recording of speech and remove most of the segmental information through a process called *low-pass filtering*. The resulting speech sounds muffled—you cannot identify specific words, but you still hear the pitch rising and falling and the voice becoming louder or softer. In order to investigate an infant's sensitivity to segmental structure, investigators often use the type of approach described in the Eimas et al. (1971) experiment—using two syllables or words that differ in a single segment or phoneme. By contrast, experiments designed to look at an infant's sensitivity to suprasegmental structure will often use long stretches of connected speech but with the segmental information removed through low-pass filtering.

Studies of infant speech perception suggest that infants are first sensitive to the suprasegmental structure of their native language. For example, one study demonstrated that newborns just 4 days out of the womb have the ability to distinguish their own language from a foreign language (Mehler et al., 1988). Mehler and colleagues recorded passages of speech produced by a French-Russian bilingual and played them to newborns in a hospital in France. The infants heard either French only, Russian only, French followed by Russian, or Russian followed by French. While the infants listened to the speech, the investigators measured the rate of sucking on a pacifier. They found that infants whose parents spoke French responded differently than infants whose parents spoke a variety of other languages. Infants who had been exposed to French in the womb produced a higher sucking rate when listening to French than to Russian. Further, for the group of infants who heard Russian followed by French, there was a sudden increase in sucking rate. By contrast, the group that heard French followed by Russian did not differ from the group that heard only French, suggesting that the novelty of hearing something different was equivalent to the general preference the infants showed for hearing their native language. This difference in the infants' responses to the French-Russian versus the Russian-French conditions was replicated with speech passages that had been low-pass filtered, suggesting that the infants were discriminating their native language from another language on the basis of prosodic cues. The infants who were not exposed to French (or Russian) in the womb exhibited sucking rates for both French and Russian similar to the French infants' response to Russian, that is, they did not appear to discriminate the two languages. Further, there was not a significant increase in sucking rate when the language changed from French to Russian or vice versa. The investigators concluded that infants become sensitive to prosodic characteristics of their native language by hearing the speech of their mothers that is naturally "filtered" as it passes through the wall of the uterus.

Sensitivity and attention to the prosodic characteristics of speech allows infants to begin detecting important boundaries in the speech stream. We might expect that infants start by identifying single words, and combine them into larger units, but instead they do the reverse. They begin by identifying large units, such as the clause, and gradually learn to identify smaller units of language, such as phrases and words. Jusczyk (1989) found that infants as young as 4 and a half months preferred to listen to speech with pauses inserted at clause boundaries rather than to speech with pauses inserted within clauses. He further demonstrated that it was the prosodic cues that influenced infants' listening preferences by replicating the effect with speech that was low-pass filtered. Infants still preferred the speech with pauses inserted at clause boundaries. Using the same technique, Jusczyk et al. (1992) found that 9-month-olds are sensitive to the location of sub-clausal phrase boundaries.

Myers et al. (1996) found that infants are sensitive to word boundaries by 11 months. Thus, even before infants know the words or the grammatical structure of their native language, they know how to break up the stream of speech into parts to which they will later learn to attach meaning. They depend primarily on prosodic cues to achieve this segmentation process. However, Myers et al. found that 11-month-olds no longer preferred listening to speech with pauses inserted at word boundaries instead of syllable boundaries after the stimuli had been low-pass filtered. These investigators suggested that identifying word boundaries may be a later development than clause or phrase boundaries because prosodic cues alone are not always sufficient to identify a word boundary. Infants must coordinate prosodic cues with their knowledge of phonotactic and allophonic constraints, a topic to which we turn now.

Because the segmental structure of speech cannot be perceived in the womb like the suprasegmental structure of speech, it is perhaps not surprising that infants do not show a particular sensitivity to the consonants and vowels of their native language right from birth. Nevertheless, research by Werker and colleagues (Polka & Werker, 1994; Werker, Gilbert, Humphrey, & Tees, 1981; Werker & Tees, 1983, 1984) showed how exposure to language gradually shapes the way that infants perceive phoneme contrasts within the first year. In their experiments, infants from 5 months of age and older were trained to turn their head to the side when they heard a novel sound. If they did, they saw a panel light up on the wall, revealing an engaging toy. With younger infants, they used a habituation technique. Comparing infants, children, and adults who were native speakers of English, German, or Hindi, Werker and her colleagues found that the transition from language-general to language-specific phoneme perception skills occurs between 8 and 10 months for consonant contrasts and at around 6 months for vowel contrasts. In other words, prior to 6 months, English-exposed infants are just as responsive to a vowel contrast from German as they are to a vowel contrast from English, but by 6 months, this pattern changes. Likewise, 6-month-olds exposed to English will turn their heads when they hear a consonant contrast from Hindi or English, but 10-month-olds turn only when they hear the English contrast.

Werker and her colleagues (1994; Werker, Lloyd, Pegg, & Polka, 1997) did not think that these results could be simply explained as a loss of the ability to distinguish phoneme contrasts that are not reinforced in the environment. They believed that there is a more constructive process taking place in the first year, during which infants reorganize their perceptual categories in response to language exposure. One implication of this reorganization is that infants are displaying an awareness of variation in sound that signals meaning in their language. Thus, these early developments, although related to the sound structure of the language, have implications for the acquisition and processing of language structure at other levels as well.

Simultaneous with these perceptual developments, infants are also learning to produce the sounds of their language in the first year of life. There are interesting parallels in perception and production. Although infants are not born with the ability to produce all sounds, once they begin producing speech-like sounds, they do not produce only sounds that they hear. They begin by producing anatomically and physiologically possible sounds as they explore the motor capacity of the tongue, throat, and mouth. Some generalizations have been observed across the early babbling of infants exposed to very different languages suggesting that babbling at the earliest stages is not a response to language exposure (Locke, 1983). Another indication that early vocal babbling is exploratory rather than responsive to language exposure is the fact that deaf infants participate in the earliest stages of babbling (Oller & Eilers, 1988). But hearing infants gradually shift to producing babbling that exhibits phonological characteristics of their native language. Interestingly, production parallels perception in the order of the influence of suprasegmental and segmental structure on babbling.

The effects of exposure to language can be observed in infants' babbling beginning at around 8 months. At this age, babbling begins to exhibit the suprasegmental characteristics of the native language (Whalen, Levitt, & Wang, 1991). Subsequently, at around 9 to 11 months, phonemes and syllable types that are most frequent in the native language become more common in babbling and first words (de Boysson-Bardies & Vihman, 1991). For example, Levitt and Aydelott Utman (1992) recorded the babbling of an American and a French infant longitudinally and analyzed the babbling acoustically. Between 5 and 11 months, the investigators found a good deal of overlap in the babbling of both infants, including the inventory of consonants and vowels produced and their success in producing specific features of phonemes. Between 11 and 14 months, however, the babbling of the two infants showed more and more indication of diverging along language-specific characteristics, such as syllable structure and timing.

To summarize, in production as in perception, language exposure gradually shapes the path of language acquisition beginning at a very early age, influencing first the suprasegmental structure and then the segmental structure of speech.

Signed Language Acquisition in the First Year of Life

In stark contrast to the progress that has been made in understanding perceptual development in children acquiring spoken languages, this area is mostly unexplored for children acquiring signed languages. Most of the methods used for investigating speech perception could be easily modified for sign perception by replacing audio recordings of speech with video recordings of sign. Based on the findings for speech perception, we could predict that infants should develop a sensitivity to the suprasegmental and segmental characteristics of signed languages in the first year.

Because very little visual stimulation can be perceived in utero, we would not expect infants to show any language-specific responses right from birth. However, Masataka (chap. 1, this volume) showed how exquisitely sensitive the language environment is to the perceptual capabilities of infants, in this case, the infant's eyes. All infants are visually captivated by signed motherese. Masataka has described how motherese in Japanese Sign Language emphasizes the suprasegmental patterns of language, not the segmental ones, with wider angles of arm articulation and slowed, repetitive cycles of movement uncharacteristic of adult-directed signed language. The emphasis in signed motherese on suprasegmental patterning has immediate effects on infants, even those who have never seen signs before. They attend longer to signed motherese and display a more pleasant affect when doing so in comparison to adult-directed sign. Here, we observe a critical parallel between the nature of language that infants are exposed to in signed and spoken languages in the first year of life: Signed and spoken motherese are tailored to fit the infants' attentional capacities, by eye or by ear, and direct and hold the infants' attention to the suprasegmental patterning of language.

The goodness of fit between infants' eyes and the signed language to which they are exposed in a naturalistic setting in the first year was shown by Holzrichter and Meier (chap. 2, this volume). They found that parents carefully monitor the infant's visual gaze so that nearly every sign they make to the infant falls within the infant's visual field. Signs made to the periphery of the infant's visual field are articulated with wide, cyclic, and repetitive motions, thereby attracting the infant's central visual focus. Infant-directed sign may differ from infant-directed speech in an important way. Hearing infants are able to receive and perceive the language spoken around them without their caretakers having to monitor their attentional state. By contrast, deaf infants are unable to receive and perceive the language signed around them unless adults take care to sign within or at the periphery of the infant's visual field. For these reasons, infant-directed sign may play a greater role in early signed language development than infant-directed speech plays in early spoken language development. This is an important question for which we have little data at present.

Infants' first attempts to produce language are very similar for signers and speakers. The earliest manual production of all infants, like the early vocal production of both deaf and hearing infants, is probably influenced primarily by anatomical and physiological constraints. Meier and Willerman (1995) suggested that early manual exploratory babbling can be explained in terms of motor stereotypies, that is, repetitive movements that infants engage in while gaining voluntary motor control over various parts of the body. Masataka (chap. 1, this volume; Ejiri & Masataka, 1999) found that early, precanonical (or marginal) vocal babble was accompanied by rhythmic hand movements in hearing infants exposed to speech and a deaf infant who was not. After continued exposure to language, hearing infants exposed to speech produce canonical vocal babble. Infants exposed to a signed language from birth begin producing manual babbles that exhibit characteristics of the signed language phonology. These babbled productions, like the earlier exploratory babbling and perhaps like signed motherese, are highly repetitive in structure. For example, a signed babble might consist of repeatedly contacting the open palm of one hand with the index finger of the other (Meier & Willerman, 1995). Petitto and Marentette (1991) argued that manual babbles resemble vocal babbles because they make use of only a subset of the possible target language phonemes and because they exhibit syllabic organization. Further, by distinguishing manual babbling from other motor behaviors, these investigators found that manual babbling constituted a much larger proportion of all motor behavior in infants ages 10 to 14 months who were exposed to a signed language than in infants in this age range who were not exposed to a signed language. This suggests that the articulatory characteristics of these early manual babbles are influenced by the child's exposure to language. One question that remains open is whether or not the suprasegmental characteristics of the native signed language are exhibited in the infant's manual babbling prior to the segmental characteristics.

There is emerging evidence that children's first signed productions are derived from the segmental structure of the language to which they are exposed. As with manual babble, the child's initial attempts at sign production are influenced by anatomical maturity and motor control. The child tends to proximalize arm and hand movements but nonetheless captures the "place" parameter of sign structure as Conlin, Mirus, Mauk, and Meier (chap. 4, this volume) and Siedlecki and Bonvillian (1993) found. Like the early word attempts of young hearing infants exposed to spoken language, the early word attempts of young infants exposed to signed language are segmentally structured with a limited repertoire of organized phonemes and syllables that the child has extracted from the signed language to which he or she has been exposed to from birth (Marentette & Mayberry, chap. 5, this volume). Not surprisingly, then, the early sentence attempts of children exposed from birth to the Sign Language of the Netherlands show clear word order patterns and movement rules that reflect the sentence patterning of their Sign Language of the Netherlands input (Coerts, chap. 6, this volume).

THE ADVANTAGES OF EARLY EXPOSURE: IMPLICATIONS FOR LANGUAGE ACQUISITION BY EYE

The research summarized thus far allows us to conclude without a doubt that early exposure to language is critical to language acquisition. We can argue this on two counts. First, there is ample evidence that the long-term outcomes for individuals exposed to language early are better than the long-term outcomes for individuals who are not. Second, there is a great deal of accumulated evidence that language exposure influences how humans acquire language from the first days of life. In the final section of this chapter, we now bridge these two bodies of literature by proposing a possible explanation of how early phonological development is related to the types of long-term advantages observed in deaf individuals who learn language at an early age.

Recall that deaf adults who acquired ASL as their native language exhibit advantages on a number of language production and processing tasks when compared to nonnative ASL signers. These advantages were primarily related to the ability to manipulate the morphological and syntactic structure of the language without producing phonological errors. For example, in Mayberry's (1993) shadowing task, native signers were able to break down the meaning of complex sentences without suffering from intrusion errors from phonologically similar signs to the target signs. Likewise, Newport (1990) found that early learners were able to comprehend and produce structures that required multiple morphemes to be produced simultaneously, as in classifier and spatial verb agreement constructions. Emmorey's studies (Emmorey, Bellugi, Frederici & Horn, 1995; Emmorey & Corina, 1990, 1992) all indicated that native signers are much faster in accessing lexical information, which is only possible after phonological processing is complete. Thus, although these tasks are very different in nature, and use language stimuli that differ in complexity and content, the native signers' performance in comparison to nonnative signers' performance on all of the tasks indicates that individuals exposed to a signed language from birth are more efficient in their processing of phonological information than those whose exposure first occurred later.

Given these results, it is telling that it is precisely the suprasegmental and segmental features of language that caretakers emphasize in their exchanges with infants, be it in sign or speech. This type of modification appears to be highly tuned to the infant's perceptual and attentional capabilities. Moreover, it is precisely the phonological system that develops during the first year of life in terms of perception and segmentation of the suprasegmental and segmental elements of the language signal. Further, it is during this earliest developmental stage that many deaf individuals are not exposed to language. Why doesn't the phonological system develop appropriately later, when deaf individuals are finally exposed to language? We believe that there are multiple factors, such as a difference in the attention patterns of the older learner, a difference in the type of language to which later learners are exposed, and a difference in the neural structure of the learner's brain.

Consider a hypothetical deaf child who is not exposed to language until the age of 5 or 10 or 15. During the first day of preschool, middle school, or high school, this child will need to negotiate personal relationships and interact with academic materials. There will be an immediate focus on learning signs and their mapping to meaning. This child will not simply watch the signing all day long for interesting patterns in the phonological structure! To the contrary, this individual's attention will be focused on the task of immediately trying to derive meaning from all communicative signals. Similarly, the teachers and fellow students of this child will sign about things that are cognitively appropriate to the level of his or her chronological development. They will not use the slow, exaggerated, and repetitive signing that deaf parents use with their infants, which is tailored to capture and transfix visual attention (Holzrichter & Meier, chap. 2, this volume; Masataka, chap. 1, this volume). Finally, it may well be the case that individuals introduced to language this late in life are no longer able to reorganize their perceptual categories to subserve phonetic ones, as Werker (1994) described in the case of the 10-month-old infant becoming highly sensitive to native language phoneme contrasts. It may be that the neural consequences of delaying exposure to language until these older ages prevents the individual from developing language-specific, neural processing patterns.

In more general terms, what we are proposing is that the true advantage of early exposure to language is the development of the phonological system prior to the development of the lexical-semantic and morpho-syntactic systems. During the first year of life, the language infants are exposed to tunes their perceptual systems and shapes their production systems. Early language exposure is implicated in this process in at least three ways. First, there are neural consequences of early exposure. The language infants are exposed to shapes the neural connections being made in their brains, neural connections that underlie processes of perceptual reorganization. Language exposure at a later time in life may not affect the individual's neural connections and perceptual organization in precisely the same way. Second, there are attentional consequences of early exposure. The infant is attracted to prosodic characteristics of language, particularly when they are exaggerated in infant-directed speech or sign (Fernald, 1985; Masataka, chap. 1, this volume). In the first year of life, infants learn what to watch for in signed languages and what to listen to in spoken languages. Finally, there are advantages in terms of the type of language that infants are exposed to. Adults interact with infants, toddlers, and school-aged children in very different ways. Not surprisingly, the language they use with children of different ages also differs. As several of the chapters in this volume document and describe, deaf parents who sign with their infants exaggerate phonological characteristics of their signs and take care to sign in the infants' line of vision (Conlin et al., chap. 4, this volume; Holzrichter & Meier, chap. 2, this volume; Masataka, chap. 1, this volume).

How can a difference in phonological development and subsequent adult phonological perceptual skills account for the wide range of long-term effects associated with delayed language acquisition? Mayberry (1994) proposed that problems in phonological processing will have cascading effects on all other levels of language processing. Lexical access will be inefficient if the phonological structure of the sign is not identified rapidly. Subsequent morphological and syntactic processing will be slowed because short-term memory is not freed from holding phonological parameters as lexical access is delayed. Incomplete or fragmented processing of the morphology and syntax on top of laborious lexical access are all barriers to identifying the semantic content.

If our proposal is correct, one of the greatest barriers to early language exposure is the fact that many deaf infants are not identified until after the first year. Thus, one concern for future research involves improving the early identification of deafness and the early provision of services to families with deaf children. A second challenge for the field is to map out the perceptual development of the deaf child exposed to a signed language in the first year of life. Without knowing more about typical development, we cannot hope to address the problems that arise from delayed exposure. Although there has been considerably more attention to babbling than to perceptual development in infants exposed to a signed language, cross-linguistic research on signed language production in the first year is necessary to identify language-specific effects of early exposure on phonological production.

In sum, although the importance of early exposure to language is widely accepted among researchers and practitioners involved in the area of deafness and language, development of these areas of research is necessary to lead us to a more adequate understanding of why early exposure is particularly critical to language acquisition by eye.

ACKNOWLEDGMENT

Preparation of this chapter was supported by a grant from the National Sciences and Engineering Research Council of Canada (NSERC 171239) to R. Mayberry.

REFERENCES

de Boysson-Bardies, B., & Vihman, M. (1991). Adaptation to language: Evidence from babbling and first words. *Language, 67*, 297–319.
Eimas, P. D., Siqueland, E. R., Jusczyk, P., & Vigorito, J. (1971). Speech perception in infants. *Science, 171*, 303–306.

Ejiri, K., & Masataka, N. (1999). Synchronization between preverbal vocal behavior and motor action in early infancy. II. An acoustic examination of the functional significance of the synchronization. *Japanese Journal of Psychology, 69*, 433–440.

Emmorey, K., Bellugi, U., Frederici, A., & Horn, P. (1995). Effects of age of acquisition on grammatical sensitivity: Evidence from on-line and off-line tasks. *Applied Psycholinguistics, 16*, 1–23.

Emmorey, K., & Corina, D. (1990). Lexical recognition in sign language: Effects of phonetic structure and morphology. *Perceptual and Motor Skills, 71*, 1227–1252.

Emmorey, K., & Corina, D. (1992, January). *Differential sensitivity to classifier morphology in ASL signers.* Paper presented at the Linguistic Society of America, Chicago, IL.

Fernald, A. (1985). Four-month-olds prefer to listen to motherese. *Infant Behaviour and Development, 8*, 181–195.

Johnson, J. S., & Newport, E. L. (1989). Critical period effects in second-language learning: The influence of maturational state on the acquisition of English as a second-language. *Cognitive Psychology, 21*, 60–99.

Jusczyk, P. W. (1989, April). *Perception of cues to clausal units in native and non-native languages.* Paper presented at the Society for Research in Child Development, Kansas City, MO.

Jusczyk, P. W., Hirsh-Pasek, K., Kemler Nelson, D. G., Kennedy, L., Woodward, A., & Piwoz, J. (1992). Perception of acoustic correlates of major phrasal units by young infants. *Cognitive Psychology, 24*, 252–293.

Krashen, S. D., Long, M. H., & Scarcella, R. C. (1979). Age, rate, and eventual attainment in second language acquisition. *TESOL Quarterly, 13*, 573–582.

Levitt, A. G., & Aydelott Utman, J. G. (1992). From babbling towards the sound systems of English and French: A longitudinal two-case study. *Journal of Child Language, 19*, 19–49.

Locke, J. (1983). *Phonological acquisition and change.* New York: Academic Press.

Mayberry, R. I. (1993). First-language acquisition after childhood differs from second-language acquisition: The case of American Sign Language. *Journal of Speech and Hearing Research, 36*, 1258–1270.

Mayberry, R. I. (1994). The importance of childhood to language acquisition: Evidence from American Sign Language. In J. C. Goodman & H. C. Nusbaum (Eds.), *The development of speech perception The transition from speech sounds to spoken words* (pp. 57–90). Cambridge, MA: MIT Press.

Mayberry, R. I., & Eichen, E. B. (1991). The long-lasting advantage of learning sign language in childhood: Another look at the critical period for language acquisition. *Journal of Memory & Language, 30*, 486–512.

Mayberry, R. I., & Fischer, S. D. (1989). Looking through phonological shape to sentence meaning: The bottleneck of non-native sign language processing. *Memory and Cognition, 17*, 740–754.

Mayberry, R. I., & Lock, E. (1998, May). *Critical period effects on grammatical processing Privileged status of the first language.* Paper presented at the American Psychological Society Convention, Washington, DC.

Mehler, J., Jusczyk, P., Lambertz, G., Halsted, N., Bertoncini, J., & Amiel-Tison, C. (1988). A precursor of language acquisition in young infants. *Cognition, 29*, 143–178.

Meier, R. P., & Willerman, R. (1995). Prelinguistic gesture in deaf and hearing infants. In K. Emmorey & J. Reilly (Eds.), *Language, Gesture and Space* (pp. 391–409). Hillsdale, NJ: Lawrence Erlbaum Associates.

Munro, M. J., Flege, J. E., & Mackay, I. A. (1996). The effects of age of second language learning on the production of English vowels. *Applied Psycholinguistics, 17*, 313–334.

Myers, J., Jusczyk, P. W., Kemler Nelson, D. G., Charles-Luce, J., Woodward, A. L., & Hirsh-Pasek, K. (1996). Infants' sensitivity to word boundaries in fluent speech. *Journal of Child Language, 23*, 1–30.

Newport, E. L. (1990). Maturational constraints on language learning, *Cognitive Science, 14*, 11–28.

Oller, K., & Eilers, R. (1988). The role of audition in infant babbling. *Child Development, 59*, 441–449.

Oyama, S. C. (1976). A sensitive period for the acquisition of a phonological system. *Journal of Psycholinguistic Research, 5*, 261–283.

Patkowski, M. (1980). The sensitive period for the acquisition of syntax in a second language. *Language Learning, 30*, 449–472.

Petitto, L. A., & Marentette, P. F. (1991). Babbling in the manual mode: Evidence for the ontogeny of language. *Science, 251*, 1493–1496.

Polka, L., & Werker, J. F. (1994). Developmental changes in perception of non-native vowel contrasts. *Journal of Experimental Psychology: Human Perception and Performance, 20*, 421–435.

Siedlecki, R., Jr., & Bonvillian, J. D. (1993). Location, handshape, and movement: Young children's acquisition of the formational aspects of American Sign Language. *Sign Language Studies, 78*, 31–52.

Streeter, L. A. (1976). Language perception of 2-month-old infants shows effects of both innate mechanisms and experience. *Nature, 259*, 39–41.

Trehub, S. E. (1973). Infants' sensitivity to vowel and tonal contrasts. *Developmental Psychology, 9*, 91–96.

Trehub, S. E. (1976). The discrimination of foreign speech contrasts by infants and adults. *Child Development, 47*, 466–472.

Werker, J. F. (1994). Cross-language speech perception: Development change does not involve loss. In J. C. Goodman & H. C. Nusbaum (Eds.), *The development of speech perception: The transition from speech sounds to spoken words* (pp. 93–120). Cambridge, MA: MIT Press.

Werker, J. F., Gilbert, J. H. V., Humphrey, K., & Tees, R. C. (1981). Developmental aspects of cross-language speech perception. *Child Development, 52*, 349–353.

Werker, J. F., Lloyd, V. L., Pegg, J. E., & Polka, L. B. (1997). Putting the baby in the bootstraps: Toward a more complete understanding of the role of the input in infant speech processing. In J. Morgan & K. Demuth (Eds.), *Signal to syntax. The role of bootstrapping in language acquisition* (pp. 427–447). Mahwah, NJ: Lawrence Erlbaum Associates.

Werker, J. F., & Tees, R. C. (1983). Developmental change across childhood in the perception of non-native speech sounds. *Canadian Journal of Psychology, 37*, 278–286.

Werker, J. F., & Tees, R. C. (1984). Cross-language speech perception: Evidence for perceptual reorganization during the first year of life. *Infant Behavior and Development, 7*, 49–63.

Whalen, D. H., Levitt, A. G., & Wang, Q. (1991). Intonational differences between the reduplicative babbling of French- and English-learning infants. *Journal of Child Language, 18*, 501–516.

Part II

READING DEVELOPMENT

Chapter 8

Is American Sign Language Skill Related to English Literacy?

Michael Strong
University of California, Santa Cruz

Philip Prinz
San Francisco State University

The topic of bilingual education for deaf students is receiving increased attention among educators in North America (e.g., Mashie, 1995). As American Sign Language (ASL) is incorporated more and more into the instructional process, questions are being raised regarding the appropriateness of bilingual approaches for deaf learners. Of particular interest is the issue of whether the relation between ASL proficiency and English literacy can be considered analogous to the proposed underlying relation between first and second spoken language skills, a concept that serves as one of the theoretical justifications for bilingual programs in hearing populations.

One of the anachronisms in education is that new instructional approaches are usually adopted before their effectiveness is researched, but in order to assess the effectiveness of a new program it must first be used for a substantial period of time. Furthermore, the relative effectiveness of educational programs for deaf children is especially difficult to assess because of the numerous intervening variables such as degree and etiology of deafness, parental hearing status, and language exposure. Thus, educators and parents of deaf children are often faced with having to make instructional choices without the benefit of scientific research to inform their decisions.

The notion of using ASL and English in bilingual instruction for deaf children has been discussed, advocated, and (following similar projects in other countries such as Denmark and Sweden) even incorporated into some programs over the past 10 years (Mashie, 1995; Strong, 1995). Although no evaluations have been published on these so-called bilingual-bicultural or *Bi-Bi* programs, several groups of researchers have conducted studies that focus in one way or another on the relation between ASL and English literacy acquisition, an essential factor in determining the potential efficacy of bilingual educational approaches for deaf children (Hoffmeister, de Villiers, Engen, & Topol, 1997; Padden & Ramsey, 1996; J. Singleton & S. Supalla, personal communication; Strong & Prinz, 1997).

In this chapter, we report on one such study, attempting to relate it to other work. In addition, we also address the issue of Cummins's (1981, 1989) linguistic interdependence theory. This theory states that all languages share a common underlying proficiency and that cognitive and academic skills acquired in a first language will transfer to related skills in a second language. Thus, learning to read and write in Spanish will facilitate the same activities in English. Cummins's theory is frequently brought to bear as one of the rationales in support of bilingual approaches for deaf children. Mayer and Wells (1996), however, asserted that this reasoning is inappropriate on two counts: (a) ASL does not have a written form and (b) deaf learners of English have no access to the auditory-oral channel, thus depriving them of the inner speech support that hearing learners of the written mode obtain from their growing mastery of the spoken form.

Mayer and Wells (1996) offered thorough theoretical support for their position, drawing on the work of Vygotsky and Halliday, by showing how literacy acquisition is theoretically different for deaf learners. They maintained that the link between ASL inner speech and written English is doubly interrupted because ASL is different from written English both in mode and language. For the most part, Mayer and Wells employed the Vygotskian definition of inner speech, namely, the representation of thought by words, as opposed to the more concrete notion of vocal speech without sound. The importance of inner speech in the relation between social speech and written language is crystallized in the following statement: "While the development of external (i.e., social) speech precedes the development of inner speech, written speech emerges only after the development of the latter. Written speech presupposes the existence of inner speech" (Vygotsky, 1987, p. 203; quoted in Mayer and Wells, 1996, p. 95).

With their reasoning that, for deaf persons, the connection between inner speech and written speech is obstructed by variations in both mode and language, Mayer and Wells (1996) challenged the appropriateness of Cummins's (1981/1989) underlying proficiency model as a rationale for bilingual programs for deaf students. They maintained that deaf children, by virtue of their very deafness, lack access to the "bridge" of spoken English that enables hearing children to move through the various stages from initial first language learning, through the acquisition of inner speech, to written and then academic language. At the same time, the authors recognized that ASL should "play a major role in the education of deaf children" (p. 94).

It should be noted that Mayer and Wells (1996) refuted what might be termed the "strong" version of the argument for considering the common underlying proficiency of ASL and English. Specifically they "are challenging claims that ASL, *when used alone,* can bridge the gap between inner sign and written English" (p. 105, italics added). They refuted the arguments in defense of interdependence between ASL and English offered by Rodda, Cumming, and Fewer (1993), who provided perhaps the closest published expression of the extreme view Mayer and Wells (1996) disputed.

Rodda et al. (1993) claimed that ASL "can be used as an intralanguage to facilitate the acquisition of a second language" (p. 346). They maintained that when ASL is established through interpersonal communication to provide Vygotskian inner speech in a child, "it is in theory and a few cases in practice, possible for deaf students to achieve fluency in both languages" (p. 346). It is not absolutely clear that this hypothesis embodies the notion of ASL "used alone" as the bridge to English that Mayer and Wells (1996) attacked, but it is surely close. A slightly weaker version of the assertion of a common underlying proficiency between ASL and English, although recognizing the absence of transfer in reading and writing skills, might focus on the enhanced cognitive flexibility and metalinguistic abilities that facilitate the acquisition of English literacy. Mayer and Wells conceded the possibility of such transfer, disputing only the strictly linguistic interdependence. Rodda et al. (1993), however, did not restrict their argument to linguistic interdependence.

If it is recognized that ASL should not only play an important role in deaf education, but that it also, for many deaf children, is the appropriate first language that may indeed provide for the transfer of broad cognitive and conceptual skills, then maybe the question of the strict applicability of Cummins's (1981, 1989) model is moot. Furthermore, if a link between ASL skill and English literacy acquisition is empirically verified, whether or not it is direct or mediated by some other signed version of English, then deaf education would be better served by considering how best to capitalize on this relation than on its goodness of fit with existing bilingual theory. Without empirical evidence, however, the theoretical debate may continue indefinitely.

The data we report in this chapter, and the other studies we cite in our concluding remarks, allow us, we feel, to move one step beyond the theoretical argument outlined earlier, and thus take us that much closer in our efforts to improve instructional practices for deaf children.

THE STUDY

The purpose of our research project, funded for 4 years by a field-initiated grant from the U.S. Department of Education, Office of Special Education, was to examine the relation between ASL and English literacy skills among children aged 8 to 15 at a school for the deaf in California. In the absence of any research on the effectiveness of bilingual programs for deaf students, we felt a study that looked closely at this relation would inform those who were interested either in initiating or vetoing the establishment of educational programs for deaf students that incorporated ASL in some manner. A strong relation between ASL and English literacy development would seem to be the minimum foundation on which to develop arguments in favor of a bilingual ASL–English educational approach, whereas the lack of a positive relation would suggest that such a program might not be indicated.

We chose a residential school setting as being the most appropriate for this investigation because of the relatively large proportion of children from ASL-using deaf families, the widespread social use of ASL by students from both hearing and deaf homes, the presence of deaf teachers, and the strong community and school interest in the concept of bilingual educational approaches for deaf children. We felt that if an educational approach incorporating ASL were to be justified by the research, then it would be most suited to initial application in a residential school for the deaf, given the existing widespread social use of ASL.

We recruited all students from the population of 8- to 15 year-olds, excluding only those whose parents did not sign permission waivers, those with special education needs, and those with aided hearing levels of 70 decibels or better. Children younger than 8 years would have been unlikely to produce the writing samples required in our tests, whereas students older than 15 might have graduated before the 3 years of the study were over. Using school records, we determined the hearing status of the parents or guardians. Given the existing research that shows differences in academic performance between deaf students with hearing parents and deaf students with deaf parents, we considered information on parental hearing status to be critical. We ended up with a sample of 155 for whom these data were available; 40 with deaf mothers and 115 with hearing mothers (see Table 8.1). We divided them into two age groups: 8 to 11 (56 students) and 12 to 15 (99 students).

The ASL and English literacy abilities of each student were tested by one hearing and two deaf researchers, all fluent in ASL and English. Nonverbal IQ was also tested using the Matrix Analogies Test (Naglieri, 1985). ASL was measured using a specially devised test of comprehension and production called the Test of ASL or TASL (Prinz & Strong, 1994). The TASL was developed and piloted over the course of a year with the

TABLE 8.1
Distribution of Participants According to Age Group and Mother's Hearing Status

Mother's Hearing Status	8–11	12–15	Total
Deaf	14	26	40
Hearing	42	73	115
Total	56	99	155

input of five deaf linguists[1] and performance data from more than 30 participants aged 8 to adult. The test includes four comprehension and two production subtests. Story comprehension was measured by having students view a videotaped ASL story interlaced with comprehension questions. Classifier comprehension was assessed by having students select the best signed representation of a given picture from four alternatives. Comprehension of temporal concepts was evaluated by having students identify the correct calendar representation of given signed time markers. Visual–spatial ability was tested by showing students a signed portrayal of objects in relation to one another and having them select the representative picture. Production of classifiers was achieved by showing students a cartoon and having them sign elements of the action to the camera. Narrative production was measured by having students sign the story shown in a wordless picture book.

English reading and writing was measured using adapted subtests of the Woodcock Johnson Psychoeducational Test Battery, Revised Version, and the Test of Written Language (TOWL). We wanted a writing sample analogous to the ASL narrative that we scored using the TOWL guidelines, and we used the Woodcock items that were appropriate for the whole age group and that required no signing or speaking in their administration.[2]

Two research questions were initially addressed: (a) What is the relation between ASL competence and English literacy among deaf students aged 8 to 15? (b) Do deaf children of deaf parents outperform deaf children of hearing parents in ASL skills and English literacy? The second question was posed as a replication of earlier research (Meadow, 1968; Quigley & Frisina,1961; Stevenson, 1964; Stuckless & Birch, 1966) that had shown how deaf children of deaf parents outperform deaf children of hearing parents academically, at least in the early years. If the data allowed, we would then address the question of whether ASL skill might explain this

---

[1] Ben Bahan, Lon Kuntze, Ella Lentz, Ted Supalla, and Clayton Valli.

[2] For a more detailed description of the measures, procedures, and data analysis, see Strong and Prinz (1997).

discrepancy, a hypothesis that has been offered to account for the earlier findings but was hitherto untested.

The data were analyzed in response to the first question in two stages. First, Pearson correlation coefficients were calculated for the relation between the ASL and English literacy scores for the whole sample and for subgroups according to age and maternal hearing status, because we wanted to be able to discuss findings separately for older and younger students and for students from deaf and hearing families, as these factors may be expected to affect language outcomes differentially. Second, participants were divided into three ASL ability levels and Analysis of Covariance (ANCOVA) was performed to compare the English literacy performance among the three groups, controlling for age and IQ (see Table 8.2).

Results revealed statistically significant correlations between ASL and English literacy for the sample as a whole and for all subgroups except for the older students with deaf mothers. In this group, students clustered at the medium and high ASL levels, allowing little variance in scores. ANCOVA results showed significant differences in English literacy skill according to ASL ability level for the sample as a whole and for the age groups considered separately. Post hoc analysis showed that the high ASL group outperformed the medium and low groups, and medium ASL groups outperformed the low ASL groups among the older students.

To address the second research question, two more sets of ANCOVAs were run, with English literacy and ASL scores as the dependent variables, maternal hearing status as the independent variable, and IQ and age as covariates (see Table 8.3). Results revealed that students with deaf mothers significantly outperformed students with hearing mothers in both ASL and English literacy measured together and by age group. This finding, which

TABLE 8.2
Distribution of Participants by Age Group, Maternal Hearing Status, and ASL Level

| ASL Level | 8–11 | | | 12–15 | | | Total |
	DM	HM	MD	DM	HM	MD	
Low	03	21		01	24	02	51
Medium	05	11		05	30	01	52
High	05	09	01	19	14	01	49
Total	13	41	01	25	68	04	152

Note. Totals vary because of missing data. DM = deaf mother; HM = hearing mother; MD = missing data.

TABLE 8.3
Pearson Correlation Coefficients for Total ASL Scores With Total English Literacy Scores Among
All Participants and Subgroups According to Age and Maternal Hearing Status

Group	N	Pearson r	Probability
All participants	145	.580	.000
Age 8–11	52	.663	000
Age 12–15	93	.500	000
DM	36	.603	.000
HM	104	507	.000
8–11, DM	13	.742	.000
8–11, HM	38	.660	.000
12–15, DM	23	.219	ns
12–15, HM	66	.391	.001

Note. Totals vary because of missing data DM = deaf mother; HM = hearing mother;
ns = nonsignificant.

is consistent with earlier research, enabled us to address one further question: If ASL level is held constant, do students with deaf mothers still outperform students with hearing mothers in English literacy? Comparisons of the two groups (deaf and hearing mothers) on English literacy scores within ASL ability level revealed a significant difference only at the low ASL level. In other words, the scores in English literacy of students with deaf mothers are no longer superior to those of students with hearing mothers at the medium and high levels of ASL ability. This supports the hypothesis that differences in academic performance between students with deaf and hearing parents discovered in previous research may indeed be largely attributable to a fluency in ASL, a notion that is consistent with the Cummins (1981, 1989) theory of cognitive and linguistic interdependence. At low levels of ASL skill, children benefit from having a deaf mother, an advantage possibly derived from factors such as emotional stability, good parent–child communication (other than through ASL), and parental acceptance.

DISCUSSION

This study produced three main findings: (a) ASL skill is significantly related to English literacy; (b) children of deaf mothers outperform children with hearing mothers in both ASL and English literacy; and (c) within the two higher levels of ASL ability, students with deaf mothers performed no better in English literacy than students with hearing mothers.

The strong relation between ASL ability and English literacy is open to three possible interpretations. First, ASL skill may lead to greater English proficiency; second, English literacy ability may influence ASL acquisition; finally, some other variable may affect the acquisition of both ASL and English literacy. We suggest that the first of these explanations is the most plausible, given a setting where ASL is the social medium of communication and the fact that children from hearing families, who were more likely to be exposed to English than ASL, performed less well in the English literacy tests than the children from deaf families who more often learned ASL at home. However, the possibility that another factor, such as good parent–child communication (as opposed to a specific language) or a heightened metalinguistic awareness (i.e., an ability to speculate on language itself), might have influenced the acquisition of both ASL and English literacy is by no means ruled out by our data. Work by Schlesinger (1988) and Schlesinger and Acree (1984) pointed to the influence of early mother–child interaction on later reading levels of deaf children, and a study by Lou, Strong, and DeMatteo (1991) indicated the possible importance of consistent linguistic input, regardless of language type, on various academic and cognitive outcomes. Strong and DeMatteo (1990) and Hoffmeister (chap. 9, this volume) suggest that metalinguistic skills as reflected either in the ability to discriminate between ASL and signed English or to identify certain aspects of ASL (Hoffmeister focuses on synonyms and antonyms, arguably marginal as examples of metalinguistic skills) may be important steps in becoming bilingual in ASL and English. In any event, the data provide yet another indication that the positive correlation between ASL and English literacy is not limited to deaf children with deaf parents.

A critical test for the soundness of any research findings is the extent to which they are replicated in other studies. Probably because of the lack of suitable measures of ASL and the disinterest in or active opposition to the use of ASL in schools, no studies have attempted to assess the relation between ASL skill and English literacy in deaf children until recently, and these are published in the current volume. The emergence of this research focus reflects an increased interest in bilingual educational approaches together with some federal funding from the Department of Education.

Hoffmeister, de Villiers, Engen, and Topol (1997) examined the reading comprehension of 50 deaf students aged 8 to 16 from four schools, as measured by the Stanford Achievement Test–Hearing Impaired (SAT–HI) normed for deaf children. Using an ASL test battery (Supalla, 1989) and synonym–antonym tasks (Hoffmeister, 1996) to assess ASL production and comprehension skills, Hoffmeister et al. (1997) found statistically significant correlations between ASL and reading comprehension. They also administered the Rhode Island Test of Language Structure (RITLS) to assess knowledge of English syntax. Stimulus items for this test are in signed and spoken English. Scores on the RITLS also correlated significantly with ASL and with reading comprehension. Subsequent regression analyses showed the RITLS to be the strongest predictor of reading comprehension skill, with the ASL synonym–antonym test entering the equation second.

Hoffmeister et al. (1997) also addressed the question of parental hearing status with regard to ASL ability and reading achievement. They decided, however, to divide the students into two groups by ASL exposure, combining school residency with parental hearing status. The high-exposure group included children with at least one deaf parent and children who resided at schools for the deaf; the low-exposure group consisted on nonresident children with hearing parents. In their study, the high-exposure group had significantly higher scores in both ASL and reading achievement.

With regard to the relation between ASL and English reading, Hoffmeister et al. (1997) found the same significant positive correlation we report in our study, albeit with a smaller sample. In their introduction, the authors suggested that lack of assessment of "through-the-air" English skills reduces the impact of our results, because skills in English signing may mediate the relation between ASL and English literacy. It is our opinion that knowledge of English syntax and English literacy skills are, by definition, closely related, a relation confirmed by their own findings. In other words, one cannot successfully read and understand a language if one is unfamiliar with its syntax. We are, however, interested in the potential relation between what might be called "English-based signing" skill and English literacy. The definition of English-based signing, of course, needs careful refining. Loosely, it refers to Woodward's (1973) concept of Pidgin Sign English, having neither the syntax of ASL nor that of English. We would like to examine this potential relation in future studies, but feel it is critical to distinguish between sign varieties that encode all English morphemes and those that do not, to avoid the confounding of skills shared by both the predictor and outcome variables.

Padden and Ramsey (1996) studied 135 deaf and hard-of-hearing students, 83 in a residential school and 52 in a local school district program. The authors examined a number of quantitative and qualitative questions, including, for a subsample of the participants, the relation between ASL ability and SAT–HI scores in reading. ASL was measured with three tests: an imitation task, a verb-agreement production test, and a sentence-order comprehension test. The first two tests correlated significantly with SAT–HI reading scores for both the residential and public school students. This study, as Padden and Ramsey (chap. 10, this volume) reports, replicates the association between ASL and reading. It should be pointed out that the residential students were from the same school as that sampled by the current authors. Thus, strictly speaking, replication applies only to the findings for their public school students.

Padden and Ramsey (1996) also examined fingerspelling comprehension and found that it was significantly correlated with the same two measures of ASL and also with SAT reading. They pointed out that students with more exposure to ASL are likely to have more exposure to fingerspelling, a perhaps important built-in link with English and another indicator that it might be fruitful to look at English-based signing skills separately from ASL signing ability.

A third study, completed recently by Singleton, Supalla, and their colleagues (Singleton & Supalla, 1996), looked at the relation between ASL and English ability from a number of different perspectives. Among other approaches, these researchers examined the effects of training parents in ASL on their children's language development. We look forward to the publication of their results, which, anecdotally (J. Singleton, personal communication, 1997), also show evidence of a positive (although not statistically significant) relation between ASL skill and English literacy.

Our study and the others cited here all provide consistent and strong evidence of a correlation between ASL skill and English literacy ability. Empirical data such as these are critical for bolstering the theoretical justifications that have hitherto been put forward in support of a bilingual approach for deaf children, the common underlying proficiency between ASL and English, and for the contention that ASL knowledge is the key to explaining academic differences between children from deaf and hearing families. Further information is necessary, however, on the precise nature of this relation between ASL and English, and the possible role of English-based signing or other factors that may act as a bridge in this relation.

REFERENCES

Cummins, J. (1981). The role of primary language development in promoting educational success for language minority students. In *Schooling and language minority students: A theoretical framework* (pp. 3–50). Los Angeles: California State University, Evaluation, Dissemination, and Assessment Center.

Cummins, J. (1989). *Empowering minority students*. Sacramento: California Association for Bilingual Education.

Hoffmeister, R. (1996, September). *A piece of the puzzle: ASL and reading comprehension in deaf children*. Paper presented at the Theoretical Issues in Sign Language Research Conference, Montreal, Canada.

Hoffmeister, R., de Villiers, P., Engen, E., & Topol, D. (1997). English reading achievement and ASL skills in deaf students. In E. Hughes, M. Hughes, & A. Greenhill (Eds.), *Proceedings of the 21st Annual Boston University Conference on Language Development* (pp. 307–318). Brookline, MA: Cascadilla Press.

Lou, M., Strong, M., & DeMatteo, A. (1991). The relationship of educational background to cognitive and language development among deaf adolescents. In D. Martin (Ed.), *Advances in cognition, education, and deafness* (pp. 118–126). Washington, DC: Gallaudet University Press.

Mashie, S. (1995). *Educating deaf children bilingually.* Washington, DC: Gallaudet University, Pre-College Programs.

Mayer, C., & Wells, G. (1996). Can the linguistic interdependence theory support a bilingual-bicultural model of literacy education for deaf students? *Journal of Deaf Studies and Deaf Education, 1*(2), 93–107.

Meadow, K. (1968). Early manual communication in relation to the deaf child's intellectual, social, and communicative functioning. *American Annals of the Deaf, 113,* 29–41.

Naglieri, J. (1985). *Matrix Analogies Test—Short Form (MAT).* San Antonio, TX: The Psychological Corporation.

Padden, C., & Ramsey, C. (1996). *Deaf students as readers and writers A mixed mode research approach* (Final report to the US Department of Education). University of California, San Diego.

Prinz, P., & Strong, M. (1994). *A test of ASL.* Unpublished manuscript, San Francisco State University, California Research Institute.

Quigley, S., & Frisina, R. (1961). *Institutionalization and psychoeducational development of deaf children* (CCEC Research Monograph, Series A, No. 3). Washington, DC: Council for Exceptional Children.

Rodda, M., Cumming, C., & Fewer, D. (1993). Memory, learning, and language: Implications for deaf education. In M. Marschark & M. D. Clark (Eds.), *Psychological perspectives on deafness* (pp. 339–352). Hillsdale, NJ: Lawrence Erlbaum Associates.

Schlesinger, H. (1988). Questions and answers in the development of deaf children. In M. Strong (Ed.), *Language learning and deafness* (pp. 261–291). Cambridge, England: Cambridge University Press.

Schlesinger, H., & Acree, M. (1984). Antecedents of achievement and adjustment in deaf adolescents: A longitudinal study of deaf children. In G. B. Anderson & D. Watson (Eds.), *The habilitation and rehabilitation of deaf adolescents* (pp. 48–61). Washington, DC: The National Academy of Gallaudet College.

Singleton, J., & Supalla, S. (1996, September). *The effects of sign language fluency upon literacy development.* Plenary address at the Fifth International Conference on Theoretical Issues in Sign Language Research, Montreal.

Stevenson, E. (1964). A study of the educational achievement of deaf children of deaf parents. *California News, 80,* 143.

Strong, M. (1995). A review of bilingual/bicultural programs for deaf children in North America. *American Annals of the Deaf, 140*(2), 84–94.

Strong, M., & DeMatteo, A. (1990). The effects of metalinguistic awareness on an experimental bilingual program for deaf children. *Linguistics and Education, 2*(4), 345–364.

Strong, M., & Prinz, P. (1997). A study of the relationship between American Sign Language and English literacy. *Journal of Deaf Studies and Deaf Education, 2*(1), 37–46.

Stuckless, R., & Birch, J. (1966). The influence of early manual communication on the linguistic development of deaf children. *American Annals of the Deaf, 106,* 436–480.

Supalla, T. (1989, November). *Test battery for ASL morphology and syntax.* Presentation to the Fourteenth Annual Boston University Conference on Language Development, Boston, MA.

Vygotsky, L. S. (1987). Thought and word (N. Minick, Trans.). In R. W. Rieber & A. S. Carton (Eds.), *The collected works of L. S. Vygotsky· Volume 1* (pp. 243–285). New York: Plenum. First published 1934 (in Russian).

Woodward, J. (1973). Some characteristics of Pidgin Sign English. *Sign Language Studies, 3,* 39–46.

Chapter 9

A Piece of the Puzzle: ASL and Reading Comprehension in Deaf Children

Robert J. Hoffmeister
Boston University

This chapter addresses the role of language knowledge in Deaf children's acquisition of literacy skills. Literacy, as defined here, includes not only reading skills but also skills required to become a literate user of American Sign Language (ASL). Literacy skills in ASL have only recently begun to be identified (Bahan & Supalla, 1996). Within the education of Deaf children, language and literacy skills in ASL have not been recognized as having the potential to impact the acquisition of English literacy skills. Yet, ASL is the most widely used language among Deaf adults in the United States and Canada (Lane, Hoffmeister, & Bahan, 1996). However, because ASL has no agreed-on or shared written form, it has not been considered useful in the classroom.

ASL is a language that is visually based. Deaf persons acquire, use, and gain language information using vision. The reception of spoken language for most Deaf individuals is extremely limited, which restricts the learning of English via the auditory channel. For many Deaf individuals, this restriction has resulted in great difficulty mastering reading, which is based on English. The frequently quoted statement that the average Deaf high school graduate is able to read at the fourth-grade level underscores the difficulty a Deaf person can have in learning how to read English (Holt, Traxler, & Allen, 1997). Some data show that only 3% to 5% of the Deaf population are able to achieve parity with their hearing peers in English reading skills (Allen, 1992). However, there are many Deaf individuals who are able to attain excellent mastery of reading English even without oral knowledge of English. Many of these Deaf individuals are well versed in both ASL and English (Mayberry, 1992; Mayberry & Chamberlain, 1994). These two facts make for a novel type of bilingualism that has yet to be fully investigated.

The notion of the Deaf child as a bilingual learner is not a recent one. Among individuals who are bilingual in two spoken languages, the spoken form of the second language is typically (but not always) acquired prior to learning to read the second language. Of interest to the present discussion are studies of hearing bilinguals that find knowledge of the first language to facilitate literacy development in the second language (Cummins, 1991; Krashen, 1996). The question that underlies the present study is whether this relation holds for ASL and English, given that the typical Deaf bilingual does not know a written form of ASL or a spoken form of English.

Complicating this situation are two important facts about the lives of Deaf individuals. First, most Deaf individuals are born to hearing parents (90% or more). Second, the use of ASL as a model for the first language is rare. The major issue of language access has been controversial in the education of Deaf children for more than 130 years (Ewoldt, Israelite, & Hoffmeister, 1989). During the past 30 years, Deaf children have been exposed to some form of signed language not only in school but at home as well. This has resulted in many Deaf children being exposed to signs at a very early age. Exposure to signing has provided access to a signed form from which the Deaf child is able to abstract signed language rules and then use these rules to gain information from the environment (Hoffmeister, 1996; Hoffmeister, Philip, Costello, & Grass, 1997). However, this has not solved the problem of access to spoken and heard English, which is the natural way of learning English. The learning of English becomes a school-related task for Deaf children. They must learn to read English and essentially learn English at the same time.

This leads to the question of the present study: What is the relation between ASL and learning to read English? In essence, there are three main hypotheses that underlie discussions about ASL, bilingualism, and English literacy: (a) ASL interferes with the development of English literacy; (b) ASL does not affect (i.e., has no correlation to) the development of English literacy (Mayer & Wells, 1997; Moores & Sweet, 1990); and (c) ASL correlates to the development of English literacy. The present study tests these hypotheses, which are explained next, followed by a description of the kind of language commonly used in classrooms—the MCE systems— and how they are related to ASL in many unacknowledged ways.

HYPOTHESES ABOUT THE RELATION OF ASL TO ENGLISH LITERACY

ASL as Interfering With English Literacy

In the early 1970s, many previously "oral-only" programs for Deaf children changed their educational practice and began to introduce signs into schools. This change was due to a number of research studies that demonstrated the efficacy of using signs when communicating with Deaf children as compared to oral-only communication (see Moores, 1996, for a review). However, because of the controversy surrounding the use of signed languages in schools and programs for Deaf children in the United States and Canada, the use of the natural language of Deaf people—ASL—was avoided. Many educators believed that the natural signed language of the Deaf community was not a viable means of learning how to read. In fact, many educators believed that ASL, because of its different structure, would interfere with learning to read English (Nover, 1997). The achievement of English literacy was believed possible only if the Deaf child acquired a representation of the spoken language in a visual form. In an attempt to provide a visual representation of a spoken language as input to Deaf children, "signs" were borrowed from ASL for use within educational settings (for reviews, see Hoffmeister, 1996; Hoffmeister & Bahan, 1991; Lane, 1992; Stedt & Moores, 1990). As a result, a number of manual systems were artificially created for the sole pedagogical purpose of trying to teach Deaf children to read English. These artificial signed forms are referred to here as Manually Coded English (MCE; Bornstein, Hamilton, Saulnier, & Roy, 1975; Bornstein & Saulnier, 1981; Bornstein, Saulnier, & Hamilton, 1980; Gustason, Pfetzing, & Zawolkow, 1982).

Little research has investigated the efficacy of the MCE forms as compared to the learning of a natural language in Deaf children learning to read (Hoffmeister, 1996). The degree to which Deaf children acquire English when an MCE system based on spoken English is used in the classroom has not been investigated at length (but see Schick & Moeller, 1992; Supalla, 1991).

ASL continues to be avoided by many educators. It is generally believed the use of a visual model based on spoken English will result in the acquisition of English by Deaf children and that using ASL will interfere with learning to read (Lane, 1992). In place of ASL, the MCE systems have become the preferred communication mode used by hearing teachers in schools and programs for Deaf children. Only a small number of programs have decided to use ASL as the language of instruction in bilingually structured educational settings for Deaf children (Strong, 1995).

ASL as Having No Relation to English Literacy

A second commonly held hypothesis is that ASL knowledge has no effect on reading and writing development. As an extension of this hypothesis, some educators argue that ASL should be limited to conversational use by Deaf children. This practice ensures that the input models for Deaf children are removed from the classroom. Again, however, there is little research investigating the relation between ASL knowledge and the ability to read and write English in Deaf children.

Mayer and Wells (1996) presented a detailed argument against the potential of ASL for supporting the learning of English literacy skills. They argued that the bilingual model as presented by Cummins (1991) is inappropriate when viewed from three theoretical frameworks. First, in order for the first language to support the learning of a second language, there must be the development of a *social speech* system, an *inner speech*, in addition to some way for these to directly relate to written text. This proposal is based on the notion that without some decoding process based on the mapping of speech onto the printed page, the possibility of learning to read and write is close to zero. The fact that ASL is so different from spoken language precludes the possibility of transferring somewhat similar skills learned in ASL to a spoken language. They claimed that the differences between ASL and English—differences in modality, phonemic and morphemic rules, constituent ordering, and meaning representation—constitute a barrier rather than a bridge between the two languages. These differences, then, are hypothesized to prevent the Deaf child from engaging in sound-to-print mapping, one-to-one mapping of meaning to print, and mapping of word order in ASL. Hence, ASL provides no support for learning to read and write English (Mayer & Wells, 1996).

Mayer and Wells (1996) offered no empirical support for their claim. There is, however, one study of the relation of ASL to English literacy skills in Deaf children that found no relation between the two. Moores and Sweet (1990) rated conversational ASL skills to measure ASL knowledge in a large group of Deaf children. ASL skills in conversation with a Deaf examiner were rated on a scale ranging from 1 to 4 (where 1 is poor and 4 is fluent). Moores and Sweet found no correlation between scores on the ASL rating scale and a number of detailed measures of English, such as the Test of Syntactic Ability and the Peabody Individual Achievement Test. The lack of a correlation led to the conclusion that ASL skill has no influence on English reading skills in Deaf children. However, the ASL measure used in the study was only a gross measure of ASL competency and not a detailed investigation of ASL linguistic knowledge, as was the case for the measures of English literacy.

ASL Is Related to English Literacy

The average Deaf child in the United States and Canada is exposed to at least two languages throughout his or her life, English and ASL. However, there is educational support for formal exposure to English, whereas ASL must be learned under a huge range of linguistically impoverished, and sometimes negative, circumstances. Currently, the only Deaf children who have consistent exposure to ASL or close variants of ASL are those with Deaf parents. In rare cases, some hearing parents learn to use ASL with their young Deaf children and thus supply their Deaf child with the input necessary to acquire ASL in a typical language acquisition situation.

It is primarily in Deaf children of Deaf parents (DCDP) that we have a parallel with hearing, bilingual children. Even with more limited access to the second language, DCDP are able to tap into what Wong-Fillmore (1991) proposed as a model of bilingual language learning. Her bilingual model requires exposure and interaction in a social setting with appropriate linguistic input and information that supports cognitive processes.

Almost every research study that has included a cohort of DCDP has found DCDP to perform significantly better than Deaf children of hearing parents (DCHP) on most measures of language and academic achievement (see Moores, 1996, for a comprehensive review of this issue). Yet, it is rarely acknowledged that the input language to DCDP is in most cases ASL, or a close variant of ASL. Only rarely is ASL learned from parents or adults unless those parents and adults are Deaf. Thus, a major factor in the studies that have included a cohort of DCDP is the amount and kind of visual language input. This research aptly demonstrates that DCDP function well in school (Ewoldt et al., 1989). They function well in school because they arrive with an intact language—ASL—with which they can learn English. As they become better readers, these children are able to obtain more information from print and hence add to their store of knowledge. For these children, it is unnecessary to learn a language, learn to communicate using the language, and obtain content information from that language, all at the same time.

Lichtenstein (1998), among others, proposed that working memory along with language knowledge is important in learning to read. Deaf children who come to the reading task knowing ASL may have the memory capacity to rapidly encode print that may be based on the language they have already acquired. Having learned ASL, the focus of these children's reading process can be on obtaining meaning rather than learning a language through print. These children may be able to chunk information rather than having to decode every piece of information, as has been observed in Deaf children who have not been exposed to ASL (Bebko, 1997). Thus, having a first language allows the child to focus on learning the second language from a position of strength. Knowledge of ASL may allow the child to develop strategies for learning the rules of the second language.

THE ASL–READING QUESTION FROM THE STANDPOINT OF CLASSROOM LANGUAGE

A major feature of the MCE systems in use today is that they are a combination of ASL lexical forms, English word order, and artificially created visual lexical units. The artificial lexical units typically represent the many bound morphemes of English, such as the plural -s, the derivational forms of nouns, like -ness, -ment, and so forth. Artificial lexical units also represent many English terms that do not have a one-to-one correspondence with ASL lexical items, such as English function words, *the, a, an,* pronouns, and the verb *to be.* The use of this type of input is based on the premise that if Deaf children are exposed to this visual modification of ASL and English, they will then (a) learn English and (b) learn to read English.

One unanswered question about classroom use of the MCE systems is whether the purpose of MCE input is to provide a model for MCE *output* by Deaf children, and if so, in what mode. Most reports on the value of MCE restrict discussion to the Deaf child's output in print-related forms (i.e., reading and writing) and not to output in an MCE form. The question is whether Deaf children exposed to MCE do, in fact, internalize the rules of spoken English and reproduce fluent English via an MCE code as their adult, hearing MCE models are expected to do (Schick & Moeller, 1992).

Because the MCE input model contains a great many ASL forms along with use of visual space, rather than auditorially based sequencing, the language being acquired by the Deaf child may be derived from the visual input rules of ASL instead of the auditory input rules of English. Hence, despite being exposed to MCE, the Deaf child is learning a visual language, using the processing mechanisms of visual language, and deriving visual language rules (Hoffmeister, 1990, 1992, 1994, 1996; Singleton, 1989; Supalla, 1991).

DCHP who are exposed to the MCE systems in classrooms and exposed to the language of their peers may, in fact, be learning a "signed" language, but it may not be English (Hoffmeister, 1992, 1994, 1996; Supalla, 1991). The problem for these children in learning to read may also be different from the DCDP, who can be conceived of as becoming bilingual, with ASL as their first language. However, it is not clear how DCHP fit into the bilingual framework. A significant amount of MCE systems' sign forms are borrowed from ASL. Some estimates are as high as 88% (Woodward, 1990). This creates a conflicting input problem for Deaf children. They are, in effect, using a code to represent English-like structures through the air, using handshapes, movements, and locations in visual patterns. For the child, the *spatial* nature of the input suggests that there are visual patterns that are consistent and regular. However, the *sequential* nature of the input suggests that there are patterns based on audition.

The conflict for the Deaf child is determining which patterns provide the most predictable set of rules: the spatial patterns emphasizing combinations of form, space, and movement or the sequential patterns that emphasize individual units in ordered sets. Given the amount of ASL visual forms in the MCE systems, the most prevalent and predictable patterns would tend to favor a visual organization, which moves the child more toward an ASL type of language (see Hoffmeister, 1994, 1996 for a detailed discussion of the processing of MCE). This is a major problem for most research investigating the nature of language in Deaf children with hearing parents. Thus, one important question that underlies the following studies is how Deaf children whose language input is primarily in the form of MCE perform on measures of ASL.

Research Questions

The questions addressed in the present research are whether (a) ASL knowledge is related to reading comprehension in Deaf children and (b) whether children with primary exposure to MCE also develop knowledge of ASL. It is my contention that measures of ASL have not been detailed enough to observe the facilitating relation between knowledge of a first language—in this case, ASL—and school achievement in a second language—namely English—in Deaf children. I predict that such a relation exists, given previous research with hearing bilingual children (Cummins, 1984, 1991; see Cummins & Swain, 1986, for a review).

In addition to the question of how ASL can be measured, language exposure is a critical factor in the language learning of all Deaf children. The age at which Deaf children begin to receive the visual language affects their level of knowledge, not only of English but also of ASL (Mayberry, 1994; Mayberry & Eichen, 1991).

In the present study, we investigate the reading skills of two groups of Deaf children. One group of children received no formal exposure to ASL except for interactions with DCDP. A few of these children experienced these interactions because they reside in dorms. The remaining Deaf students would not be expected to know very much about ASL. However, because they interact with each other via visual language, coupled with the fact that there is so much ASL in the MCE input, suggests that these Deaf students might be acquiring a somewhat different visual language than their hearing teachers, school administrators, and parents would predict. The second group were DCDP who came to school and the reading task with a developed first language, namely, ASL.

These questions are investigated in two studies. In the first study, we develop and assess measures of ASL comprehension. In the second study, we measure MCE and ASL comprehension and explore their possible relations to reading comprehension.

STUDY I: ASL KNOWLEDGE

Subjects

Educational Settings. A total of 78 students participated in the first study; 40 participants attended two large residential schools and 38 attended two day-school programs. One residential school was located in New England

and the other in the Midwest, with enrollments of 250 and 400 students, respectively. Each of the day schools had enrollments of more than 125 students. Within the residential schools, the students were both dormitory and commuter students. Despite spending less time at the school, the commuter students at the residential schools had more opportunities for exposure to signed language than did students at the day schools. These were after-school activities at the residential schools coupled with the schools' close relationships with the Deaf Community. Many commuter students explained to us that they spent time in the dorms (i.e., stayed overnight with their friends, participated in snack bar activities in the evening, etc.).

By contrast, the students at the day schools had a more limited exposure to a signed language. There were very few after-school activities and many students were bused in from great distances. Although the day schools provided activities in collaboration with local Deaf Communities, they were few in number compared to the number of events at the residential schools. Hence, the day-school students were limited to group activities for their exposure to conversational signing. Hearing children have the advantage of peer interaction outside of school. Deaf children, unless they have Deaf siblings—26.2% in our sample—do not have this opportunity to converse with peers in a signed language. Their exposure to a signed language is limited to conversational partners, especially with respect to the adults in their lives.

Exposure to a signed language for the majority of day students who had hearing parents, 78% of this sample, was limited to the school day. The small amount of peer interaction was restricted to recess, lunch, and other short sanctioned periods during the school day. There was very little opportunity for extended peer interaction until the student was older and had a driver's license.

The residential schools had a higher number of Deaf teachers. In our sample, there were at least three deaf teachers who interacted with the students on a daily basis. There were no deaf teachers in classrooms with the day students; however, there was a Deaf teacher who "rotated" among the classrooms within the schools.

ASL Exposure. Seventeen of the students had exposure to Deaf adults from birth. In interview reports, all of these students stated that their parents signed with them. The older students explained that they thought their parents used both ASL and Pidgin Signed English (PSE). The younger students were not cognizant of the differences and reported a combination of MCE, ASL, and PSE.

The 61 students with hearing parents had exposure to some form of a signed language that ranged from "school only" to parents who signed "pretty good." The older students who thought their parents were good signers reported that they used various forms of MCE. None of the hearing parents were reported to be using ASL. Many of the hearing parents were in the process of learning to sign when their deaf child was very young. For many of these children, initial exposure to a signed language was limited before entering school but expanded rapidly after school enrollment.

Table 9.1 shows the makeup of the total sample of 78 students who were between the ages of 8 and 15. Sixty-one students had hearing parents and 17 students had deaf parents; 28 students were male and 33 were female. The mean age of the DCHP was 11.5 years and the mean age of the DCDP was 12.0. The DCHP had an average hearing loss of 100.9 dB and the DCDP had a mean hearing loss of 95.5 dB.

The etiologic characteristics of the students' hearing losses are shown in Table 9.2. Approximately 25% of these students had genetic deafness.

TABLE 9.1
Student Characteristics in Study 1

Variable	Hearing Parents	SD	Deaf Parents	SD
N	61		17	46
Age (M)	11 5 (8–15)	(2 03)	12 0 (8–15 8)	(3 0)
Hearing loss	100 9	(12.71)	95.5	(12 4)
Males	46 2% (n = 28)		53% (n = 9)	
Females	53.8% (n = 33)		47% (n = 8)	

TABLE 9.2
Etiology of Students' Hearing Loss

Etiology	% of Sample
Genetic	24.4
Premature	3.8
Anoxia	2.6
RH	2.6
Meningitis	11.5
Rubella	2.6
Other	9
Unknown	43.9

Our student sample had a slightly higher percentage of genetic deafness than is reported for the population at large but otherwise represents the typical categories of hearing loss compared to published reports (Moores, 1996; Vernon & Andrews, 1990).

ASL Tasks

Stimuli Design. We used three tasks to measure ASL knowledge: ASL synonyms, antonyms, and plurals–quantifiers. Each stimulus item consisted of a single lexical item that was controlled for phonological and semantic complexity in addition to level of use. Some stimulus items reflected frequent use within the ASL of the Deaf Community whereas other items reflected infrequent use; these latter items would be known only by students with a sophisticated knowledge of ASL.

We did not include fingerspelled items as stimuli because fingerspelling displays different developmental and linguistic processing patterns from those of signs (Mayberry & Waters, 1991). Fingerspelling is also related to spoken and printed English (Bochner & Albertini, 1988; Padden, 1991). Our goal in the design of these ASL tasks was to reduce as much as possible any influence from spoken, signed, or printed English.

Response Alternatives. We created four response alternatives for each stimulus item. The response alternatives represented the correct response, a phonological foil, a semantic foil, and a nonsense foil, respectively. In pilot work, we used all our possible stimulus items on adult community members with varying ASL backgrounds. Only those items that were known by 90% or more of the adult Deaf Community members were chosen for use in our experimental tasks.

Testing Paradigm. Another goal in the design of our ASL tasks was to minimize memory load so it would not confound linguistic performance. Deaf signers are able to recall signs in the same fashion as hearing speakers recall spoken words even though the modality is different (Bellugi, Klima, & Siple, 1975). When Deaf signers recall signs, many of their errors are related to the phonology of the signs themselves. These phonological intrusion errors demonstrate that signers use a phonological recoding process similar to hearing speakers (Bellugi et al., 1975). However, Mayberry and Fischer (1989) and Mayberry and Eichen (1991) found that the errors of nonnative signers were phonologically related to the target signs, whereas native signers' errors were semantically related to the target on ASL processing tasks such as sign shadowing and sign recall. They hypothesized that because nonnative signers must attend to surface information, more processing space is taken up in remembering this surface information, thereby reducing processing resources for meaning.

To minimize memory constraints, we used a recognition paradigm. We designed a response booklet using still frames of each of the videotaped ASL stimuli with no printed English. This allowed the students to scrutinize each alternative response along with the stimulus item, thereby removing the necessity to hold some portion of stimulus sign form in memory while making a response. Each page of the booklet showed five pictures that corresponded directly to the video presentation. The pictures were still frames of signs shown on the videotape. Each signed stimulus and each signed response was represented on paper in the following manner:

$$\Delta_1 \qquad ¥_2$$

$$\Sigma$$

$$£_3 \qquad \Sigma_4$$

Σ represents the stimulus item and the remaining symbols represent the four alternative responses. After viewing the video, the student responded by circling the correct printed still frame (1, 2, 3, or 4) in the response booklet.

Testing Format. The synonyms, antonyms, and plurals–quantifiers tasks were receptive language tasks presented on videotape. The testing procedure consisted of four parts: an introduction; two demonstration examples followed by two practice items; and two blocks of 15 synonyms, 14 antonyms, and 21 plural stimulus items. All instructions were given in ASL.

In the introduction, a native signer presented an ASL narrative explaining what the task consisted of, what response was required (choosing the best response that matched the stimulus item), and how to respond using the test booklet. The instructions included a simulation of someone performing the task using a videotaped presentation and the test booklet. The stimuli and response items were presented sequentially. The stimulus item was presented first, followed by a video fade, followed by a sequence of the four response alternatives.

Testing Procedure. Testing was completed in a group format. Most of the groups corresponded to the class size at the particular time of the test. On one occasion, two classes were grouped together. Because all the information was on the video, the test facilitators' only role was to answer questions when the students asked for clarification. Each test took approximately 30 minutes for the students to complete. Because we were attempting to reduce memory constraints, all requests for repeating the stimulus and response items were honored.

TABLE 9.3
Students' Performance on the ASL Tasks

	Hearing Parents		Deaf Parents	
Task	M %	SD	M %	SD
Antonyms	44.98	22.89	64.73	25 7
Synonyms	43.59	25 80	68.75	31.4
Plurals	49.33	14.90	60 11	14.00

Scoring and Analyses. Frequencies of all responses were determined both within and across participants. Because the test included items that tended to be used infrequently in ASL compared to items that occurred more frequently, higher scores represented more advanced ASL knowledge.

Results

Table 9.3 shows the performance of the students with hearing and Deaf parents on the ASL tasks. A two-way analysis of variance (group by ASL task) showed that DCDP scored significantly higher than the DCHP on the synonyms task, $F(1, 76) = 7.57$, $p < .01$, and on the antonyms task, $F(1, 76) = 9.05$, $p < .001$, but not on the plurals–quantifiers task. These results demonstrate that the students with hearing parents know ASL, although not as well as the students with Deaf parents.

To determine if the ASL test was sensitive to developmental improvement that might be associated with age, the students' performance was analyzed with a Pearson correlation coefficient. The results revealed significant correlations between age and performance on the ASL tasks for all the students, both with hearing and Deaf parents: antonyms ($r = +.69$, $p < .01$ and $r = +.63$, $p < .05$, respectively); synonyms ($r = +.68$, $p < .001$ and $r = +.63$, $p < .05$, respectively); and plurals–quantifiers ($r = +.44$, $p < .01$ and $r = +.51$, $p < .05$, respectively). These results show that as Deaf children become older, they become more knowledgeable about ASL lexical items, classifiers, and use of space, even if the language of their classroom is not ASL.

STUDY II: SIGNED LANGUAGE KNOWLEDGE AND READING

The purpose of the second study was to determine if there are relations between exposure to ASL and performance on tests of MCE and reading skill.

Subjects

General Sample Characteristics.   A total of 50 students who participated in the previous study were tested with a battery of tests of signed language and reading; 36 students had hearing parents and 14 had Deaf parents. All students were prelingually deaf (prior to 18 months), had a minimum 70 dB hearing loss, a nonverbal IQ in the normal range, and ranged in age from 8 to 16. Half the students were girls and half were boys (see Table 9.4).

ASL Exposure Groups.   The 50 were divided into two groups—those with intensive ASL exposure (*n* = 21) and those with limited ASL exposure (*n* = 29). Of those children with intensive ASL exposure, 14 had a Deaf mother and 7 had hearing parents, but these children were resident in the dormitories. The children with limited ASL exposure had hearing parents and commuted to school. The first group received more intensive exposure to ASL from interactions with their Deaf parents, native signing peers and siblings, Deaf dormitory counselors, each other, and the many Deaf adults that tend to be associated with Deaf families and residential school activities. By contrast, the second group received less intensive exposure to ASL because they were commuter students and thus had less contact with Deaf adults and few of their hearing parents knew ASL. Their ASL or signed interaction was mostly restricted to time in school, and the language of their classroom would have been MCE.

Reading and Signed Language Tasks

Reading Comprehension.   Reading comprehension was assessed using a version of the Stanford Achievement Test (SAT–HI) normed for Deaf children. In my opinion, this reading test has considerable limitations as an

TABLE 9.4
Performance on Language Tasks by Groups With Intensive and Limited ASL Exposure

	Intensive ASL *(n = 21)*	*Limited ASL* *(n = 29)*	*Significance Level*
Age	12 3	12 1	*ns*
Hearing loss	97.9 dB	101.0 dB	*ns*
ASL—Synonyms	69 5%	43.9%	*p* < .001
ASL—Antonyms	65.0%	48 0%	*p* < .01
ASL—Plurals	60.3%	53.9%	*p* < 05
MCE—RITLS	84.6%	74.9%	*p* < .05
Reading—SAT	592	548	*p* < 05

Note MCE = manually coded English, RITLS = Rhode Island Test of Language Structure; SAT = Stanford Achievement Test.

in-depth assessment of literacy skills because it only measures a particular kind of unscaffolded, decontextualized reading of unfamiliar materials in sentences or short passages (Topol, 1994). However, performance on the SAT–HI correlates with a number of other similarly decontextualized academic skills in the classroom, and it has been used in much of the research on reading achievement in Deaf children.

MCE Comprehension. The student's comprehension of English syntactic structures expressed via an MCE system was measured with the Rhode Island Test of Language Structure (RITLS; Engen & Engen, 1983). This test uses a picture-choice paradigm of single sentences produced simultaneously in MCE and spoken English. The participants completed all 100 items of the RITLS. However, for the present study, a complex sentence score was created based on percent correct of five exemplars each of seven different complex structures in English ($n = 35$). These complex sentences were as follows: (1) sentence-initial and sentence-final adverbial clauses; (2 & 3) medial and final relative clauses; (4) subject complement sentences with noninitial subjects (as in cleft sentences); and (5) reversible passives. These complex sentence types with embedded and noncanonical word or clause order have been found to be particularly difficult for Deaf children learning English (Engen & Engen, 1983; Quigley & Paul, 1994). This task was presented using personnel from each of the educational programs that the students attended. The purpose of this procedure was to ensure that the tester and students used the same MCE format.[1]

ASL Tasks. ASL knowledge was tested with the ASL tasks previously described in Study I.

Results

The performance similarities and differences between the two ASL exposure groups were analyzed with a series of *t* tests. Although the groups did not differ in mean age or level of hearing loss, they did differ in their ASL performance, as shown in Table 9.4. As would be expected, the students with intensive ASL exposure scored higher on the ASL tasks than those with more limited exposure. In addition, however, the students with more intensive ASL exposure also scored at higher levels than those with limited exposure on the MCE comprehension measure. These results show that intensive exposure to ASL does not interfere with MCE development. To

---

[1]MCE is presented with spoken English in "sim-com" and is primarily what Deaf children have been exposed to over time in their classrooms staffed by hearing teachers. Our goal was to present the MCE tasks to the students within the mode and form with which they were most familiar.

TABLE 9.5
Correlations Among Language Measures
for Students With Intensive and Limited ASL (Combined) With Age Partialed Out

Task	Reading	ASL–SYN	ASL–ANT	ASL–PLU	MCE–RITLS
Reading	1				
ASL–SYN	0 51**	1			
ASL–ANT	0.54**	0.66**	1		
ASL–PLU	0.53**	0.45**	0.59**	1	
MCE–RITLS	0.38*	0.38*	0.36*	0.44*	1

Note ASL–SYN = American Sign Language–Synonym. ANT = antonyms, PLU = plurals, and RITLS = Rhode Island Test of Language Structure.

the contrary, the more intensive exposure to ASL was accompanied by higher mean scores on the measures of MCE comprehension as well as on the SAT reading comprehension test.

The relations among the students' performance and the language measures were analyzed next with multiple correlation with the effects of age partialed out. As Table 9.5 shows, performance on all the language measures was significantly and positively intercorrelated. Performance on the ASL tasks was significantly and positively correlated with performance on the SAT reading task and the MCE task (the RITLS), and vice versa. These results support the hypothesis that ASL knowledge is related to reading and not the hypothesis that it interferes with reading. Deaf students who perform well on measures of ASL also perform well on measures of MCE and reading.

DISCUSSION

The results of the first study demonstrate that Deaf students, including those with limited exposure to ASL, have derived rules that are related to a visual language, namely ASL. The ability of the Deaf students to "know" synonyms, antonyms, and plurals–quantifiers in ASL reflects their internal representation of ASL. In addition, as the students became older, their scores increased. This suggests that Deaf children who are not exposed to ASL on a regular basis develop a fairly solid understanding and use of ASL. Their performance on the ASL tasks demonstrates that they have induced some rules of ASL and apparently have some sophisticated linguistic processing skills in ASL. These ASL skills may have come from interaction with Deaf peers and a small number of Deaf adults as well as from the substantial overlap between ASL and MCE as described in this chapter.

The results of the second study showed that Deaf students with intensive exposure to ASL perform at higher levels on measures of ASL knowlege than students with more limited exposure to ASL. In addition, however, the Deaf students with intensive ASL exposure outperformed their peers with more limited ASL exposure on measures of MCE comprehension and reading comprehension. Rather than interfering with language development, intensive language exposure in the form of ASL enhanced language functioning, as reflected in the MCE and reading measures. It is important to note that intensive ASL exposure was confounded here with the total amount of language exposure that the students in the two groups received. Students with intensive ASL also received more intensive language exposure overall. The fact that this exposure was in ASL in no way impeded their development of reading and MCE skills. To the contrary, it enhanced it.

How does ASL knowledge relate to English reading comprehension? Some researchers propose it cannot support reading development at all because ASL is so different from English. However, Deaf students who have a first language of ASL, which they learned from Deaf parents, have been consistently reported in the literature to achieve higher academic achievement levels than those who do not have ASL as a first language (Ewoldt et al., 1989). The results of the present study also substantiate this well-documented finding. The Deaf students with intensive ASL exposure scored at higher levels on the ASL tasks than those with limited exposure. In addition, performance on the ASL tasks correlated with the SAT reading task independent of age. This finding does not support the hypothesis that ASL interferes with reading development. Moreover, the finding that performance on the ASL tasks positively correlates with the SAT reading comprehension test for the entire participant sample futher supports the hypothesis that ASL knowledge is related to reading development. There is no evidence to support the hypothesis that the relation between ASL knowledge and reading skill is nil.

This brings us back to the finding that the students' MCE comprehension correlated with performance on the SAT reading task. How does this finding relate to the finding that ASL knowledge correlated with reading development? As previously described, the MCE systems borrow heavily from ASL. Most of the descriptive studies that estimate the extent of MCE system borrowing from ASL have focused exclusively on lexical borrowing. If, however, we consider the fact that there is a great deal of other visual information in MCE, such as movement and spatial location, we might better understand how knowledge of ASL might relate to comprehension and production of sentences in MCE systems.

First, MCE sentences do follow the word order of English, with one sign occurring after another. However, inspection of the test items given the children shows that there are a number of MCE sentences that, although signed in MCE, are similar to structures of ASL. For example, consider the following two complex English sentences given in MCE on the comprehension task:

#65. What hit the boy was the ball

#71. It is the boy who the dog is following.

In item #65, the sequence of signs is reflective of what is called a rhetorical question type of structure in ASL. The sign sequence "WHAT HIT BOY, BALL," with eyebrows raised over the first three signs, then with a pause, and eyebrows dropping over the last sign, would be seen as a rhetorical question in ASL. This is interpreted as the "The ball hit the boy," which is equivalent to the MCE–English interpretation of item #65 and constitutes the correct response on the RITLS task. Thus, knowing complex ASL sentence structure in this case could readily facilitate learning complex MCE–English structure. Knowing complex ASL sentence structure could also support the understanding of the type of sentence given in #71. Many of the relative clause examples in the RITLS task, when signed in MCE, could be related to a rhetorical question type of sentence in ASL.

In item #71, a second type of potential ASL transfer to English can be seen in the formation of the sign for the verb *following*. The sign for this MCE verb is typically derived from the ASL verb CHASE. In the formation of this verb in MCE, one hand is placed in front of the other hand, thereby representing the spatial relation between two objects. In logical form, the "boy" is mentioned first in the sentence and the "dog" is mentioned second. When the MCE verb form meaning "is following" is produced, one hand will be placed in space before the other. Any Deaf child with even minimal knowledge of ASL will be able to understand this relation and score correctly on this item or items similar in structure. Indeed, those Deaf children who have greater knowledge of ASL could clearly transfer their understanding of syntactic structure from one language to another, especially because the "form" of the English is also signed MCE.

Clearly, the amount of ASL information contained in MCE signed forms needs to be more closely examined. If Deaf children are abstracting visual principles from the MCE systems that result in an ASL-like language or interlanguage, is MCE limiting the student from developing a full language, either in English or ASL? For the Deaf students in the present study, learning English means learning how to read.

Bialystok (1991) suggested that the stages of learning to read include (a) an oral or conversational stage, (b) a literate stage—learning to read, and

(c) a metalinguistic stage—the ability to manipulate language. The oral or conversational stage consists of learning a language in one's environment. The literate stage is learning to use the language one has learned in a different format and representation (print); and the final stage is the metalinguistic stage or learning how to focus and discuss language as an object.

Bialystok (1991) further proposed that the child must learn to analyze the linguistic input in order to understand, internalize, and integrate their language into their cognitive system, and then the child must gain control over the processes of linguistic knowledge. Control over the stages of language processes incorporates different functions from the ability to carry on a conversation (the analysis and internalization of rules). As the child is exposed to variations in the strategies for applying his or her current skills to the purpose of learning new skills, both analysis and control processes may show advancing skills. Most important is that within each stage—conversational, literate, and metalinguistic—the child may be functioning at different skill levels.

The functioning level of bilingual children within each stage of literacy development will be influenced by their fluency level in both languages. This is especially so if the literacy and metalinguistic skills are being developed in the second language (Bialystok, 1991; Cummins, 1984, 1991; Cummins & Swain, 1986). For Deaf children, these issues in bilingual learning are paramount.

The relation of ASL knowledge, control over ASL linguistic processes, and the effect of ASL on learning to read and write English has been reported to be nonexistent (Moores & Sweet, 1990). However, these researchers used inadequate measures of ASL knowledge. In terms of the Bialystok (1991) model of reading development and bilingualism, the ASL measures used in the Moores and Sweet (1990) study focused only on conversational skills. Conversational skills, although important, play a relatively minor role in school language. The ASL measures in the present study tapped sophisticated knowledge of ASL lexical and morphological rules, thereby tapping language skills that are more related to the language of schooling and reading. Thus, when the level of the ASL skill measured is sophisticated, it relates to reading skills.

The highly significant relation found in the present study between ASL knowledge and MCE and reading skill supports a bilingual model for education of the Deaf child. The fact that the Deaf students in our study were able to perform our ASL tasks without any formal training in ASL crucially substantiates the notion that the Deaf reader is bilingual. It is clear from the results of these studies that Deaf students can and do transfer skills from one language to another. A piece of the puzzle to understanding Deaf children's attempts to become good readers of English clearly lies in access to high levels of a visual language, namely ASL.

ACKNOWLEDGMENTS

I thank Ben Bahan, Kristin DePerri, Janey Greenwald, Aurora Wilber, Peter deVilliers, and Brenda Schick for their helpful and expert advice on this chapter. I am deeply indebted to Rachel Mayberry. Charlene Chamberlain, and Jill Morford for their discussions and numerous reviews of this chapter. They have gone above and beyond what was expected. The data reported here are part of a larger project that investigated the learning of English and ASL by Deaf children, funded by USDOE NIDRR, grant number H133A80070 to P. DeVilliers, P. Blackwell, and R. Hoffmeister.

REFERENCES

Allen, T. (1992). Subgroup differences in educational placement for Deaf and hard of hearing students. *American Annals of the Deaf, 137*(5), 381–388.

Bahan, B., & Supalla, S. (1995). Line segmentation and narrative structure: A study of eyegaze behavior in American Sign Language. In K. Emmorey & J. Reilly (Eds.), *Language, gesture, and space* (pp. 171–194). Hillsdale, NJ: Lawrence Erlbaum Associates.

Bellugi, U., Klima, E., & Siple, P. (1975). Remembering in sign. *Cognition, 3*, 93–125.

Bebko, J. (1997) Learning, language, memory and reading: The role of automatization and its impact on complex cognitive activities. *Journal of Deaf Studies and Deaf Education, 3*, 4–14.

Bialystok, E. (1991). Metalinguistic dimensions of bilingual language proficiency. In E. Bialystok (Ed.), *Language processing in bilingual children* (pp. 113–140). New York: Cambridge University Press.

Bochner, J., & Albertini, J. (1988). Language varieties in the Deaf population and their acquisition by children and adults. In M. Strong (Ed.), *Language learning and deafness* (pp. 20–54). New York: Cambridge University Press.

Bornstein, H., Hamilton, L., Saulnier, K., & Roy, H. (1975). *The signed English dictionary for preschool and elementary levels.* Washington, DC: Gallaudet College Press.

Bornstein, H., & Saulnier, K. (1981). Signed English: A brief follow up to the first evaluation. *American Annals of the Deaf, 127*, 69–72.

Bornstein, H., Saulnier, K., & Hamilton, L. (1980). Signed English: A first evaluation. *American Annals of the Deaf, 125*, 467–481.

Cummins, J. (1984). *Bilingualism and special education: Issues in assessment and pedagogy.* San Diego, CA: College Hill Press.

Cummins, J. (1991). Interdependence of first-and second-language proficiency in bilingual children. In E. Bialystok (Ed.), *Language processing in bilingual children* (pp. 70–89). New York: Cambridge University Press.

Cummins, J., & Swain, M. (1986). *Bilingualism and education.* New York: Longman.

Engen, E., & Engen, T. (1983). *The Rhode Island test of language structure* Austin, TX: Pro-Ed.

Ewoldt, C., Israelite, N. & Hoffmeister, R. (1989). *A review of the literature on the effective use of native sign language on the acquisition of a majority language by hearing impaired students A final report to Minister of Education, Ontario.* Faculty of Education, York University and Center for the Study of Communication and Deafness, Boston University. (Monograph)

Gustason, G., Pfetzing, D., & Zawolkow, E. (1982). *Signing exact English.* Los Angeles: Modern Signs Press.

Hoffmeister, R. (1990). ASL and Its implications for education. In H. Bornstein (Ed.), *Manual communication in America* (pp. 81–107). Washington, DC: Gallaudet University Press.

Hoffmeister, R. (1992). Why MCE won't work: ASL forms inside signed English (Working Paper #16). Boston: Boston University, Center for the Study of Communication and Deafness.

Hoffmeister, R. (1994). Metalinguistic skills in Deaf children: Knowledge of synonyms and antonyms in ASL. In J. Mann (Ed.), *Proceedings of the Post Milan: ASL and English Literacy Conference* (pp. 151–175). Washington, DC: Gallaudet University Press.

Hoffmeister, R. (1996). What Deaf kids know about ASL even though they 'see' MCE! In *Deaf studies IV: conference proceedings* (pp. 273–308). Washington, DC, Gallaudet University.

Hoffmeister, R., & Bahan, B. (1991, February). *The relationship between American Sign Language, signed English and sim-com in the language development of Deaf children or why MCE won't work* Paper presented at ACEDHH's Annual Conference, Jekyll Island, GA.

Hoffmeister, R., Philip, M., Costello, P., & Grass, W. (1997). Evaluating American Sign Language in Deaf children: ASL influences on reading with a focus on classifiers, plurals, verbs of motion and location. In J. Mann (Ed.), *Proceedings of Deaf Studies V Conference*, Washington, DC: Gallaudet University.

Holt, J. A., Traxler, C. B., & Allen, T. E. (1997). *Interpreting the scores A user's guide to the 9th edition of the Stanford Achievement Test for educators of deaf and hard of hearing students* (Tech. Rep. 97-1). Washington, DC: Gallaudet University, Gallaudet Research Institute.

Krashen, S. E. (1996). *Under attack The case against bilingual education.* Culver City, CA: Language Education Associates.

Lane, H. (1992). *The mask of benevolence.* New York. Knopf.

Lane, H., Hoffmeister, R., & Bahan, B. (1996). *A journey into the Deaf world* San Diego, CA: Dawn Sign Press.

Lichtenstein, E. (1998) Reading in Deaf children. *Journal of Deaf Studies, 3*(2), 1–55.

Mayberry, R. I. (1992). The cognitive development of deaf children: Recent insights. In I. Rapin & S. Segalowitz (Eds.), *Child neuropsychology, Volume 7 The handbook of Neuropsychology* (pp. 51–68). Amsterdam: Elsevier.

Mayberry, R. I. (1994). The importance of childhood to language acquisition: Insights from American Sign Language. In J. C. Goodman & H. C. Nusbaum (Eds.), *The development of speech perception The transition from speech sounds to words* (pp. 57–90) Cambridge, MA: MIT Press.

Mayberry, R., & Chamberlain, C. (1994, November). *How ya gonna read da language if ya dun speak it? Reading development in relation to sign language comprehension* Paper presented at the Boston University Conference on Language Development, Boston.

Mayberry, R., & Eichen, E. (1991). The long-lasting advantage of learning sign language in childhood: Another look at the critical period for language acquisition. *Journal of Memory and Language, 30,* 486–512.

Mayberry, R., & Fischer, S. (1989). Looking through phonological shape to lexical meaning: The bottleneck of non-native sign language processing. *Memory & Cognition, 17,* 740–754.

Mayberry, R., & Waters, G. (1991). Children's memory for sign and finger-spelling in relation to production rate and sign language input. In P. Siple & S. Fischer (Eds.), *Theoretical issues in sign language research, Volume 2 Psychology* (pp. 221–229). Chicago: University of Chicago Press.

Mayer, C., & Wells, G. (1996). Can the linguistic interdependence theory support a bilingual-bicultural model of literacy education for deaf students? *Journal of Deaf Studies and Deaf Education, 1,* 93–107.

Moores, D. (1996). *Educating the Deaf Psychology, principles and practice* (4th ed.). Boston: Houghton Mifflin.

Moores, D., & Sweet, C. (1990). Factors predictive of school achievement. In D. Moores & K. Meadow-Orlans (Eds.), *Educational and developmental aspects of deafness* (pp. 154–201). Washington, DC: Gallaudet University Press.

Nover, S. (1997, June). *Language policy and Deaf education· Historical views* Paper presented at the Bi-Annual Conference of American Instructors of the Deaf, Hartford, CT.

Quigley, S., & Paul, P. (1994). *Language and deafness* (2nd ed.). San Diego, CA: Singular Publishing Group.

Padden, C. (1991). The acquisition of fingerspelling by deaf children. In P. Siple & S. Fischer (Eds.), *Theoretical issues in sign language research: Volume 2: Psychology* (pp. 191–210). Chicago: University of Chicago Press.

Pattison, R. (1982). *On literacy*. New York: Oxford University Press.

Schick, B., & Moeller, M. P. (1992). What is learnable in manually coded English sign systems? *Applied Psycholinguistics, 13*, 313–340.

Singleton, J. (1989). *Restructuring of language from impoverished input: Evidence for linguistic compensation*. Unpublished doctoral dissertation, University of Illinois at Urbana-Champaign.

Stedt, J., & Moores, D. (1990). Manual codes on English and American Sign Language: Historical perspectives and current realities. In H. Bornstein (Ed.), *Manual communication: Implications for education* (pp. 1–20). Washington, DC: Gallaudet University Press.

Strong, M. (1995). A review of bilingual/bicultural programs for deaf children in North America. *American Annals of the Deaf, U140*, 84–94.

Supalla, S. (1991). Manually Coded English: The modality question in signed language development. In P. Siple & S. Fischer (Eds.), *Theoretical issues in sign language research, Volume 2: Psychology* (pp. 85–109). Silver Spring, MD: TJ Publishers.

Topol, D. (1994). *A text-based approach to reading assessment for Deaf readers*. Unpublished manuscript, Rhode Island School for the Deaf, Providence, RI.

Vernon, M., & Andrews, J. (1990). *The psychology of deafness*. New York: Longman.

Wong-Fillmore, L. (1991) Second-language learning in children: A model of language learning in social context. In E. Bialystok (Ed.), *Language processing in bilingual children* (pp. 49–69). New York: Cambridge University Press.

Woodward, J. (1990) Sign English in the education of Deaf students. In H. Bornstein (Ed.), *Manual communication in America* (pp. 67–80). Washington, DC: Gallaudet University Press.

Chapter 10

American Sign Language and Reading Ability in Deaf Children

Carol Padden
University of California, San Diego

Claire Ramsey
University of Nebraska, Lincoln

The intent of this chapter is to examine bases of reading ability in signing deaf children. If learning to read is viewed as the task of learning the relation between spoken language and its representation in print (Adams, 1990; Liberman, Shankweiler, Liberman, Fowler, & Fischer, 1977), then the task of learning to read in the case of signing deaf children must be doubly complicated. First, of course, is their lack of direct access to spoken language. They do not hear, and presumably do not use, at least not efficiently, sounding out processes that might help them learn to read. Second, the form and structure of the signed language they use is unrelated to either spoken English or its written form. If signed language competence has a relation with reading, it is not obvious why it should. Indeed, most of the literature on reading development and achievement in deaf children does not include deaf children's signed language competence as a variable (e.g., Conrad, 1979; Campbell, 1992; Hayes & Arnold, 1992; Holt, 1994).

Recently, there have been suggestions that American Sign Language (ASL) skills might play a role in reading (Kuntze, 1994; Paul, Bernhardt & Gramly, 1992), in part because of studies showing that deaf children with deaf parents perform well on reading achievement tests when compared to deaf children of different backgrounds (Mayberry, 1989; Moores & Sweet, 1990; Prinz & Strong, 1998; Singleton et al., 1998). One could argue, however, that the relation between signed language and reading is simply fortuitous. A child's skill in ASL provides a linguistic foundation from which development of another language skill such as reading can take place. Possibly also, experience with ASL forms a symbolic base from which children can learn meaning of words in print. This is essentially the claim that Paul et al. (1992) made: Children who comprehend written text and the message of the text are better equipped to carry out the decoding that is basic to reading ability. Paul et al. also referred to the influence of a community of deaf adults who read as enabling deaf children to imagine themselves as readers. These are important, even essential, elements to reading development, but the question of whether ASL specifically is implicated in reading and writing ability has yet to be addressed.

For the last 3 years, our research group has been involved in a project to study reading achievement in deaf children.[1] Like others who have studied this population, we are intrigued by the unusual challenges deaf children face. Whereas others have studied oral deaf readers (Waters & Doehring, 1990), or hard-of-hearing readers (Arnold & Mason, 1992) and explored to what extent their experience with spoken language aids reading development, our focus is on a population of deaf children whose early experiences instrumentally involve signed language. These are children who grow up using sign language either at home or at school. They are also more likely to have greater degrees of hearing loss; as a consequence, they face a daunting challenge in learning to read (Conrad, 1979; Karchmer, Milone & Wolk, 1979).

The investigation we describe here has three components: (a) a detailed demographic assessment of individual and social variables of deaf students participating in our study, (b) results of a language battery testing interrelation between reading ability and specific language skills, and (c) a descriptive study of classroom instructional techniques involving signing and written English and their role in reading development. The latter component follows from a basic premise we hold, namely, that reading development is unique among the language skills in that it is not natural. It requires presence of language and cognitive ability but is intimately linked to contexts of instruction. Even with good language skills, very few children can teach themselves to read; instead they need guidance by skilled adults. The three components of our research are joined by a design that measures component skills of children who are trying to learn to read with the aid of others and to a large extent within school settings.

The deaf children who participated in our study came from school settings most typical for children of this type of hearing loss (Holt, 1994)—a residential school that employs ASL-based approaches to teaching and a

[1]This research was funded by grant H023T30006 from the U.S. Department of Education to Carol Padden and Claire Ramsey, Co-Principal Investigators. The work contributing to this chapter was carried out by a dedicated research group that included Sharon Allen, Tom Humphries, Eric Johnson, Francine MacDougall, Jamie Sklolnik, Susan Sterne, and Rochelle Tractenberg.

public school special program that uses a *total communication* approach.[2] In the latter environment, there is some presence of ASL, used by deaf teachers and competent hearing signers, but it is not officially targeted as a language of instruction. In the former, the school actively seeks to incorporate ASL in the curriculum, and teachers are invited to engage in innovative curriculum development that includes training in ASL. This variation in emphasis on ASL by school setting not only gives us access to children of different backgrounds within a narrow range of overall deaf and hard-of-hearing population, but also allows us to examine the impact of different instructional environments on reading development. Further, because we wanted to study reading instruction, we selected deaf children who were taught in reading classes specifically designed for them. We did not include children who were mostly or entirely integrated into classrooms with hearing children. This investigation focuses primarily on deaf children who use signed language with each other and with their teachers and who attend special classes with other deaf children.

The results of our language battery show that knowledge of specific ASL structures correlates with reading achievement. Young deaf children who perform better on reading tests are those who are also competent in what we call *associative skills,* or have the ability to write down words that are fingerspelled to them, and are able to translate initialized signs. We find that these skills are more likely to be found among deaf children who have grown up with ASL, as with those who have deaf parents, but they are also used by other children who perform well on tests of ASL ability.

When we examine the better readers' demographic backgrounds, we find that they share certain characteristics. Among the significant correlations we find with higher reading scores are having deaf parents, early detection of deafness, and an absence of handicaps. Because the children we studied had similar degrees of hearing loss, which was generally severe to profound deafness, and had similar etiologies, or causes of deafness, which was either deafness from birth or shortly after, the age at which they became deaf was not significantly correlated with reading achievement. Instead, the age at which their deafness was detected and reported in school records turned out to be significant. We believe this variable measures when families start to reorganize their communicative resources and plan alternative schooling for their children.

From our videotapes of classroom teaching techniques, we found examples of how young deaf children become aware of associations between ASL and written text. Using these data, we argue that associative skills such

---

[2]Because most states support only one residential school, we do not identify the state or the region in which the schools are located to ensure the privacy of the students, teachers, and school administrators in our study.

as those we uncover in our language battery need to be discovered and cultivated by a process of language and reading instruction that teaches children to link ASL morphology to English orthography. We do not view these skills as "naturally" acquired in the same sense that ASL competence is; instead, they must be fashioned by way of instruction.

Our findings lead us to some central issues about the process of learning to read, as summarized in Adams (1990). For young hearing readers, those who can learn to associate sound elements with orthographic representation are more likely to succeed at reading. The better readers in our study have made an alternative discovery in which they form associations between elements of a signed language and elements of a written language as they acquire the ability to read. In addition to the question of whether and how these associations promote reading development is the equally interesting question of how these associations come about. We suggest that these associations are not fortuitous or idiosyncratic discoveries by individual children, but result from systematic exposure to a culture of signers and adult deaf readers who directly and indirectly teach young signers how to make sense of written English text. Our findings emphasize that whereas reading is an individual accomplishment, it is fundamentally a cultural achievement in which forces of society and institutions combine to support a notable alternative route to reading.

STUDY 1: DEMOGRAPHIC AND BACKGROUND ASSESSMENT

Student Characteristics

Mertens (1990) found that most survey research on deaf children concentrates on individual characteristics such as onset of hearing loss, degree of hearing loss, age, and individual performance on specific tests, often to the exclusion of a wide range of variables that measure institutional and social characteristics. Accordingly, we developed a list of characteristics for student backgrounds that measure not only enduring individual characteristics but social characteristics as well, such as hearing status of parents, ethnicity, age of first educational contact, and age when the child's deafness was detected. We also included a measure of when the child began attending school and the length of time the child remained in one type of program. The latter variable, termed *tenure,* was designed to examine the effect over time of a particular school setting on the child's reading achievement.

Because we were interested primarily in reading development during the crucial first levels of school, we solicited participation only from elementary and middle school students. Their parents were mailed letters explaining the project, including what information would be gathered and what tests would be given to their children. Parents of 135 students returned consent forms, 83 in the residential school and 52 in the public school.[3] With their consent, we gained access to their children's files for the purpose of coding for a set of background characteristics. Also from the files, we obtained the students' most recent Stanford Achievement Test (SAT)– Hearing Impaired[4] scores, including their SAT–Reading comprehension (SAT–R) and the SAT–Math computation (SAT–M) scores. Of the 135 students in our survey, 98 had valid reading comprehension scores and 73 had math computation scores.

The first fact to emerge from our data is that we did not have similar groups of children at the two school settings. The proportion of students with deaf parents in the residential setting participating in our study was nearly five times higher than that in the public setting. The ethnic status of the students in the public setting indicated a much higher degree of heterogeneity than in the residential setting. Deaf children at the public school who participated in our study were nearly twice as likely to have a physical handicap such as impaired vision or mobility compared to those who participated at the residential school.

At least one influence on this pattern of enrollment is educational policy that promotes philosophical choices by parents. Since the 1970s, when public schooling of deaf children became more widely available and residential schools were no longer the dominant (or only) educational option for families, parents needed to decide which school setting to choose for their deaf child (Ramsey, 1997). In our population, deaf parents were far more likely to select the residential school in part because, as many of them told us, they had attended similar schools as children and they continued to believe that such schools best accomodate their ideas about language environments for their children. The residential school we used for our study reported that approximately 12% of their school population, from preschool to Grade 12, are children with deaf parents. The public school district, in contrast, had less than 1% children with deaf parents

---

[3]The greater representation of residential school students in the study reflects the differential enrollment levels at the two schools. The residential school reports an enrollment of 206 students in the elementary and middle schools compared to 88 students in the public school at the same levels. To evaluate interrelations between reading development, classroom instruction practices, and signing ability, consent forms were not distributed to parents of students who were fully mainstreamed or students with severe emotional or cognitive handicaps because these are students who do not participate in regularly scheduled classes of reading instruction with other deaf students.

[4]The tests that were administered to the students in our study were normed for hearing-impaired students. Although the tests themselves are identical to those given to hearing children, the screening procedure to determine which level of test to give to the deaf child is based on guidelines developed specifically for deaf and hard-of-hearing children.

TABLE 10.1
Demographic Comparisons Across School Settings

Variable	Public School (N = 52)	Residential School (N = 83)
Handicaps	19%	10%
One or more deaf parents	8%	39%
Ethnicity (% White)	33%	70%
Mean age of first educational contact	3.125 years	2.34 years
Mean age of detection of deafness	2 2 years	1 year
Mean tenure in program	3.5 years	3.2 years
Mean degree of hearing loss[a]	3.06	3 45
Mean SAT–HI Reading Comprehension score[b]	534.42	567 23

Note SAT–HI = Stanford Achievement Test–Hearing Impaired.
[a]Pure tone audiometry on ascending scale of 1 to 4, with 4 = profound deafness.
[b]Scaled score

across all levels of schooling. In our study population, we had a higher proportion of children with deaf parents (20% of our total group of 135 students), almost all of whom had children at the residential school.[5]

The presence of deaf children of deaf parents in our population influenced school group means by nearly every characteristic. Deaf parents are more likely than hearing parents to recognize deafness in their child at an early age and to locate schooling for their deaf child at an earlier stage, pushing means for both of these characteristics at younger ages for children at this school setting. Of our population of deaf children of deaf parents at the residential school, 78% are White, reflecting demographic studies showing that the condition of congenital deafness is more prevalent within the White population in the United States than among other ethnic groups (Holt & Hotto, 1994).

In contrast, the public school's location near an urban center as well as its accessibility to families who recently emigrated to the United States result in a larger diversity of ethnicity among its students. As for why the public school had more children with handicaps and illnesses, it may be that parents want them to remain closer to home, where medical care is more convenient. As discussed next, we found many of these characteristics to interact with reading achievement (Table 10.1).

A key point here is that any attempt to measure the effect of school setting on reading achievement requires analyses that recognize that popu-

---

[5]Possibly, the higher participation rate of deaf parents in our study was due to our description of the goals of the study as exploring factors of "sign language and reading," a topic of specific interest to middle-class deaf parents.

lations in the two types of school settings are not randomly distributed in terms of characteristics. This is not a surprising discovery, but it also bears noting that although school populations may vary in terms of characteristics such as ethnicity and family income, they also vary in terms of the proportion of children with deaf parents and by consequence, the average age of detection of deafness among their students. Average age of detection in turn influences the average age of enrollment in an educational program suitable for deaf children. Few demographic studies include these characteristics, although as we discuss next, they interact with reading achievement. Our study suggests that although in principle, all options of schooling are available to families with deaf children, educational policy of the last 30 years has led to quite different distributions of students across different schools.

Reading Achievement

Of the 98 students with valid reading comprehension scores (across both school settings), we found three factors to correlate significantly with reading achievement: deaf parents, age of detection, and length of time the child has been in school (tenure). One factor negatively correlated with reading achievement: the presence of handicaps. The need for variables that measure social characteristics was borne out by our discovery that age of detection of deafness correlated with reading achievement. The longer the parents waited before confirming deafness, the greater the negative impact on reading achievement. These variables taken together point to the strong influence of early language experience and school experience on reading achievement among profoundly deaf children. As might be expected, the presence of handicaps complicates the linguistic and cognitive profile of the child, leading to overall difficulty in reading development (Table 10.2).

Returning once more to the issue of school setting, we found that if reading achievement scores are compared across school settings, average scores at the residential school are significantly higher than those at the public school, but if children with deaf parents are removed from the comparison, neither school has an advantage. Because the subject of schooling has such emotional content in the national debate over the future course of deaf education, we refrain from any claim based on our data that either the residential school or the public school has a clear advantage in fostering reading achievement. More of the students attending the public school in our study had handicaps, came from different ethnic backgrounds, and in some cases, started school later because they arrived from a foreign country. All of these characteristics complicate reading development under any circumstances. These observations notwith-

TABLE 10.2
Correlations of SAT–HI Reading Comprehension With Demographic Variables

Variable	N	SAT–HI Reading Comprehension
Deaf parents	98	.39**
Age of detection	91	– 27**
Tenure	98	.44**
Age of onset	98	.08
Handicaps	98	–.34**

Note. SAT–HI = Stanford Achievement Test–Hearing Impaired.
**$p < 0.01$.

standing, it is clear that the challenge of teaching deaf children to read is one shared by all schools.

STUDY 2: SPECIFIC LANGUAGE SKILLS AND READING ACHIEVEMENT

A central question of our study is whether and how ASL plays a role in reading development, beyond providing a linguistic and cognitive basis for the development of new language skills. To answer this question, we developed a battery of five tests in which specific ASL skills were tested. A total of 31 deaf children in four classrooms were given this battery of tests: two fourth–fifth grade (n – 18) and two seventh–eighth grade classrooms (n = 13), one at each level at a residential and public school for participation in our language testing study. Each child was individually tested on the battery.

Three tests measuring general ASL competence were given: Two were previously developed by Supalla et al. (in press) and a third was developed by our group. The Verb Agreement Production test (Supalla et al., in press) asks the student to view action between two individuals and sign a response in which they inflect a signed verb that corresponds to the action. Their responses were also videotaped and then coded. The third test, Sentence Order Comprehension (Supalla et al., in press), presents students with signed sentences on videotape in which sentence order is manipulated. Students are then asked to point to a picture from a set of four that represents the meaning of the sentence. In the Imitation task, which we developed, students viewed a videotaped ASL sentence, signed by a native signer, and were asked to repeat the same sentence back to a video camera.

The 12 sentence items varied in complexity, with each item no longer than a single sentence. For scoring, semantic substitutions were accepted as correct,[6] but production errors or deletions in the signed response were coded as incorrect (see Mayberry & Fischer, 1989).

The remaining tests were based on a previous study of classroom practice in residential and public schools (Ramsey & Padden, 1998). In this study, we observed teachers—both deaf and hearing—using initialized signs and fingerspelled words at strategic points in classroom instruction about reading and writing. Initialized signs involve replacing the handshape of an ASL sign in order to create related vocabulary, for example, the ASL sign CLUSTER has many related initialized signs: GROUP, FAMILY, SOCIETY, DEPARTMENT, ASSOCIATION.[7] Sometimes teachers used initialized signs in place of ASL signs, but many times they were used in sequence with ASL signs in contrastive ways to highlight English vocabulary. In one example, while giving a spelling lesson, a deaf teacher used the ASL sign GARDEN, followed by an initialized counterpart, GARDEN, to emphasize that the children should write the word *garden*. Where initialized signs only represent one letter, usually the first letter of the English translation of the sign, fingerspelled words represent the entire sequence of letters that comprise the written word. When fingerspelling, signers execute in rapid sequence handshapes that correspond to each letter in the word. As with initialized signs, we saw teachers also use fingerspelled words in sequence with ASL signs and initialized signs. One teacher was explaining about volcanoes, during which she used an initialized sign, VOLCANO, and then immediately in sequence fingerspelled the word *volcano*.

Using examples of vocabulary we saw in our classroom study, we developed two tests that would evaluate how well students knew the association of these vocabulary items to their English counterparts and were able to write them in English. The Initialized Signs test involved 20 items on videotape, each featuring a native signer producing a sentence containing exactly one initialized sign. At the end of each sentence, the signer directed the student to "write [initialized sign]." The tester briefly paused the videotape as the student wrote a response, and then the next item was shown. For example, one sentence was as follows: BOY NOT FOLLOW RULE. NOW WRITE "RULE." Because this test yielded very few correctly spelled responses, we scored by a weaker standard in which the word did not need

---

[6]For example, a few students substituted Signing Exact English vocabulary, for example, BUS, for signs in the test sentences. They were accepted as correct if the meaning was the same or similar as the test vocabulary.

[7]The convention for representing ASL signs in English is to translate them using single word glosses in capital letters. Initialized signs are represented with a capitalized gloss as well, with the letter corresponding to the handshape of the sign underlined. Fingerspelled words are glossed with single letters joined by hyphens, for example, B-U-S, "bus."

TABLE 10 3
Correlations of SAT–HI Reading Comprehension With ASL Tests

Test	N	SAT–HI Reading Comprehension
Verb agreement	22	.51*
Imitation	23	46*
Sentence order	24	.76**

Note SAT–HI = Stanford Achievement Test–Hearing Impaired.
*$p < 0.05$ **$p < 0.01$.

to be spelled correctly but needed to be recognizable as the target word by three naive independent readers.[8]

On the Fingerspelling task, students watched a sentence on videotape containing one fingerspelled word and were asked a question to aid their recall of the fingerspelled word. In one example, students were shown the signed sentence (translated in English), "The girl needs *ice* for her drink." Following the sentence, the signer on videotape asked "What did the girl need?" We scored according to an exact written replication of the fingerspelled word; that is, the response had to be correctly spelled.

Beginning first with our three tests of ASL ability, we found all to correlate with the student's score on the SAT–R. Interestingly, the relation held for deaf children of hearing parents who would be expected as a group to have less experience with ASL. Of the three tasks, the Sentence Order Comprehension seemed to be the easiest, with students scoring on the average 80% correct. In this task, students were asked to recognize the agent of the signed sentence and select the picture that corresponded to the identity of the agent. The Imitation task was the most difficult, with the average score at 45% correct. The task measures the ability to comprehend, recall, and reproduce sentences in ASL, all of which would appear to draw from not only linguistic ability but memory as well. The Verb Agreement Production measures ability to produce correct ASL verb inflections and does not require recall. Students scored on the average 70% correct (Table 10.3).

To evaluate the possibility that the relation between the ASL and reading tests was a measure of general test-taking skill rather than a relation between two language skills, we examined the students' SAT–M scores to see if this

---

[8]We recruited undergraduate hearing students from a child development class to read each misspelled attempt. If three students independently agreed on what the intended word was, and if it matched the test item, we scored it as correct.

too had a relation to performance on ASL tests. As it turned out, SAT–M did not correlate with either the Imitation or Verb Agreement Production tests but it correlated with the Sentence Order Comprehension, a task that, for most of our students, was easy to complete. We are not confident that this latter task produces enough variation in scores to observe relations with other skills. Last, the SAT–M also correlated with SAT–R, most likely because this test involves some reading of math problems (Table 10.4).

For students with less skill in ASL, the Fingerspelling task was very difficult to complete. Some struggled with even three- or four-letter words like *wax* or *bark*, reporting instead a collection of letters that did not appear in the word. Others were able to write some of the letters of the word but could not retain their correct order. When we compared test scores, we found that performing well on the task correlated with performance on the SAT–R *and* our ASL tasks (Table 10.5). It is perhaps not surprising that there is a relation between fingerspelling and reading if fingerspelling

TABLE 10 4
Correlations of SAT–Math Computation Wtih Language Tests

Test	N	SAT–HI Math Comprehension
Verb Agreement	16	30
Imitation	18	.18
Sentence order	18	.62*
SAT–HI reading	73	.75**

Note SAT–HI = Stanford Achievement Test–Hearing Impaired
**$p < 0.05$. **$p < 0.01$

TABLE 10.5
Correlations of Fingerspelling Test With Language Tests

Test	N	Fingerspelling
Verb Agreement	25	.71**
Imitation	26	.87**
Sentence order	25	.64**
SAT–HI reading	22	.43*

Note SAT–HI = Stanford Achievement Test–Hearing Impaired.
**$p < 0.05$. **$p < 0 01$

is seen as a code for print, but it is also interesting that strong ASL skills also play a role (Table 10.5).

A different pattern was found for the Initialized Signs test (Table 10.6). There was no relation between having deaf parents and the student's score on the Initialized Signs test. However, this skill and fingerspelling are highly correlated, which suggests that they are related to each other. Additionally, scores on the Initialized Signs task correlated highly with the ASL measures. This suggests that, as hypothesized, this group of tasks is interrelated. Because initialized signs represent only one alphabetic letter, typically the first letter of the word, the task requires students to know how to spell the rest of the translation without any further clue. As might be expected, students who had better reading ability performed better on this task.

The composite portrait offered by the relation between language skills and reading ability is an intricate one, worth elaborating at some length here. We have demonstrated that there is a relation between certain tests of ASL ability and reading achievement and that this is not a spurious one based on general test-taking skill. Additionally, we found a modest relation between reading skills and what we call *associative skills,* or being able to recognize and translate initialized signs and understanding fingerspelled words, then writing them down. Because associative skills and ASL skills are strongly related, we believe that these special skills that involve both ASL and representations of English are good sites for further research into reading ability in signing children.

So far we have demonstrated only that there are relations, not whether early acquisition of fingerspelling or initialized signs promotes reading development. It is entirely possible that development of reading skill leads to skill in fingerspelling comprehension and translating initialized signs. Hirsh-Pasek & Treiman (1982) advanced this view. From studies of young deaf children, some as young as 3 years old, it is clear they can recognize

TABLE 10.6
Correlations of Initialized Signs Test and Language Tests

Test	N	Initialized Signs Test
Verb Agreement	23	.76**
Imitation	25	74**
Sentence order	24	.71**
SAT–HI reading	21	.80**

Note SAT–HI = Stanford Achievement Test–Hearing Impaired.
**$p < 0.05$. **$p < 0.01$.

fingerspelled words without knowing their counterparts in print (Kelly, 1995; Padden, 1991; Padden & LeMaster, 1985). Indeed, there can be a long dissociation between the two skills until the child begins to learn to read: In some cases, these young children are surprised to discover that fingerspelled words have counterparts in print. These studies suggest that although fingerspelling, reading, and writing are related by virtue of their coding of the alphabetic system, the timetable for development in each may be very different and uncoordinated until later in life. Of special interest is how and where the systems converge to produce a coordinated set of knowledge about English in print. Our fingerspelling task was not solely a recognition task in which children were simply asked to report the meaning of the word, but it required students to write the words in English. This skill may take place later, when students are able to bring all three skills—fingerspelling, reading, and written spelling—to bear on the task. Again, it is interesting to see that when these skills are marshalled to complete the Fingerspelling task, the student is more likely to have very good ASL skills as well, supporting our claim that the successful deaf signing reader is one who can draw from several composite skills.

STUDY 3: MODES OF READING INSTRUCTION

In this study, our goal was to observe more closely instructional practices of teachers involving print, and to study observable reading processes in individual deaf students. For the first part of the study, involving instructional practices, four classrooms were videotaped three times in one academic year, once each in the fall, winter, and spring. Two classrooms were at the elementary level, one at each school setting, and the remaining two were at the middle school level, also one at each school setting. Each visit yielded 1 week of videotaped classroom activity. For the second part of the study, each student participating in the classrooms was videotaped while reading a story aloud. From these observations, we aimed to learn more about institutional influences on reading behaviors.

Reading Processes

A task was devised in which a member of our research staff asked each student in the classroom study to "read aloud" or sign from a book selected as being at or slightly above their reading level (we used their teachers' judgments). If students wanted assistance with individual print words, it was given. Although we do not assume that this task for deaf children is identical to reading aloud for hearing children, nor that it is an easy one to do, the children generally complied because reading aloud in signs is a common task in both school settings. The transcribed signed reading aloud was compared to the target story and coded for miscues. Conventional miscue categories were used, including omissions, substitutions, self-corrections, and observation of sentence boundaries. We also noted finger-spelling and mouthing, as well as use of initialized signs and classifier signs while reading aloud.

We found that students had widely varying reading aloud behaviors, and some could not retell with comprehension after reading aloud a story. Aside from the general difficulty many had, at least two major patterns of reading behavior could be observed in students, one characterized by "attacking and analyzing words," and another, by "seeking meaning." The differences are best exemplified by comparing the performance of two fourth-grade students, Billy and Roy,[9] who are native signers. Billy has a deaf mother and a hearing father, and Roy has two deaf parents. Billy has always attended a public school; Roy attended a public school briefly but is currently a student at the residential school.

Billy is not an exceptional reader: He scored in the 56th percentile on the SAT–R of deaf readers his age. When Billy read aloud, his attention was focused on individual words. To Billy, reading meant mapping individual signs onto print words or morphemes. This strategy led to many miscues, most of which resulted in sentences that did not make sense within the meaning of the story. For example, in an illustrated story about baseball, he signed "flying mammal" in response to the print word *bat*, and "swim" in response to *swing*. In the former he was prompted with the correct sign BASEBALL BAT. However, Billy's confusion persisted, and in the next occurrence of *bat*, he fingerspelled the word, suggesting that he did not have a sense of the word or the story. On the latter, he hesitated as he made the miscue, rechecked the print, did not self-correct, and signed "SWIM" again. Billy was unable to respond to the text as he read, did not indicate dialogue or represent character shifts, and failed to observe sentence boundaries or punctuation marks. Billy attempted to represent each English morpheme with a sign. He also made fluent and frequent use of SEE (Signing Exact English)[10] lexicon, including pronouns and copulas (HE, SHE, IS), although he used very few content signs from the SEE lexicon. He mapped ASL signs onto print words, but all were uninflected, and he did not use classifier predicates. As he struggled to decode every word, his pace of reading slowed.

---

[9]The names we use are pseudonyms.

[10]Billy's teacher employed a version of a pedagogical tool used by some educators to represent English vocabulary, called Signing Exact English (Gustason et al., 1980) and more commonly known by its acronym, SEE. This pedagogical tool offers a vocabulary book of devised initialized signs to be used in place of ASL vocabulary.

At the end of the reading aloud task, Billy was asked to retell the story. Not only did his retell fail to relate the print story, it did not stand alone as a meaningful story. Rather, Billy signed a series of marginally related ideas, strung together with THEN. We know that Billy's difficulty with the written narrative is not because he lacks language or narrative skills, because in another task not discussed at length here, students were asked to retell from a video cartoon. On this signed task, Billy performed well. Billy's difficulty is because he does not comprehend written text very well and cannot use his decoding attempts to build up a narrative.

Our second reader, Roy, is a fifth grader who attended a public school Total Communication program for deaf students through first grade, then transferred to a residential school, where he lives in the dorm. Roughly comparable to Billy, he is in the 58th percentile of deaf readers his age according to his SAT–R score. But in contrast to Billy, Roy's attention during reading was focused on seeking meaning in the text. Like other meaning-seeking readers in our sample, Roy scanned each page of text before he began reading. Between signed utterances, he kept his gaze on the page much longer than Billy, suggesting that he was reading beyond individual words. He observed sentence boundaries and other punctuation marks, represented character shifts as characters spoke, and consistently recognized and self-corrected his miscues.

Roy matched individual signs to words in print selectively. Sometimes he signed a one-to-one match, with one ASL sign for an English word; but often he translated in which the match was not exact. For example, an illustrated story about a dispute between the Sun and the Wind had this sentence "They saw flowers opening and birds flying." Billy signed "THEY SEE FLOWER OPEN BLOOM AND BIRD FLY-WITH-WINGS CL: trace path birds flying around." Just as Billy's dominant strategy was to force an exact match between parts of words and signs, Roy's dominant strategy was to look at sentences or even larger text structures and seek coherent meaning in them. Roy devoted much less attention to representing individual English words in signs, and used SEE lexicon sparingly, alternating with fingerspelling (e.g., once he signed THE, but the rest of the time he fingerspelled it).

We view these differences as artifacts of experience and pedagogy. Billy and Roy's reading scores are not significantly different, yet their reading strategies are distinct. Billy's interpretive skills are very limited; he must first demonstrate word comprehension before he can complete text comprehension. Roy is allowed latitude in adding and expanding on the meaning of the text he is reading. He not only has to recognize (not necessarily decode) words in a sentence, but also comprehend their meaning in terms of the narrative. In essence, the two school settings offer different hypotheses of reading development: the public school, that decoding individual words and building vocabulary from word recognition underlies reading development, and the residential school that word comprehension derives from understanding the text as a whole. The more top-down mode of the latter approach follows from the school's commitment to bilingual education, in which students are routinely taught to compare meaning in ASL and English. The more bottom-up mode of the public school derives from the school's interest in monitoring vocabulary development in English. The literature in deaf education is represented by both points of view, and as our encounters with the two school settings demonstrate, schools are still struggling to evaluate which best aids reading development.

We are not prepared at this time to argue that one or the other approach to reading behavior leads to superior results. Instead our point here is that children do not happen into one or the other type of reading behavior, but are guided into doing so by specific pedagogical approaches. Schools' choices of pedagogy are not incidental, but drawn from their ideas about the nature of reading in deaf children, whether it is fundamentally an English decoding skill or an associative skill between languages. At the residential school that Roy attends, the curriculum emphasizes bilingual approaches, and the types of top-down activities that Roy uses are specifically taught to him.

Instructional Practices

We found further contrasts between the two school settings when we studied teachers' methods of talking about English print. This component of our investigation was drawn from videotaping five classrooms at two school settings, comprising a total of 90 hours of videotape. Seven teachers were featured, with two classrooms sharing team teachers. Each teacher was videotaped individually three times in an academic year, one week each in the fall, winter, and spring. Three of the 7 are public school teachers and the remaining 4, residential school teachers. Three are native signers, 1 at the public school district, and 2 from the residential school. Three of the teachers are deaf, 1 at the public school and 2 at the residential school (Table 10.7).

From these data, we took a sampling of six 15-minute segments featuring each teacher, with a total of 42 segments across all teachers. Because on our first pass, we noticed a differential use of fingerspelling and initialized signs across teachers, we started first with a simple frequency count. Each fingerspelled word and each initialized sign used by the teacher was transcribed for the duration of the sampled segment. Comparing average occurrence of fingerspelled words and initialized signs across samples for each teacher, we found first that deaf teachers in either setting finger-

TABLE 10.7
Distribution of Teachers Across School Setting

Teacher Group (N = 7)	Native Language	
	English	ASL
Residential school		
Deaf	0	2
Hearing	2	0
Public school		
Deaf	1	0
Hearing	1	1

spelled more than twice as often as hearing teachers. Deaf teachers finger-spelled an average of 176 words (including repetitions of the same word) in our sample and hearing teachers fingerspelled an average of 75 words. The deaf teacher at the public school accounted for more instances of fingerspelling than her other two hearing colleagues at the same setting combined. But school setting was influential: Residential school teachers fingerspelled an average of 152 words compared to the public school teachers' average of 74 words. Within the residential school group of teach-ers, although one deaf teacher had a very large number of instances of fingerspelling, there was little difference between the second deaf teacher and the two hearing teachers. In sum, fingerspelling is used more by deaf teachers but also more by teachers who work in the residential school.

When we were counting the number of instances of fingerspelled words, we noticed that some of the teachers repeatedly fingerspelled the same word in short intervals, and further, they typically combined fingerspelled words with ASL signs and at times, initialized signs in what appeared to us to be a process of stringing together similar types drawn from different systems. When we transcribed these chained sequences, they first appeared to be repetitions, but they were actually variations on a theme: finger-spelling, print, and signing all linked together to suggest equivalence and commonality. One teacher, for example, in a lesson about volcanoes, fingerspelled the word *volcano*, then pointed to the same word written in chalk on the blackboard, then used an initialized sign VOLCANO, all in rapid sequence, one after the other. These "chaining" structures immedi-ately struck us as places where associations could be cultivated between signs and printed words. As with fingerspelling, this technique was used selectively; some teachers favored it far more than others. Deaf teachers used an average of 30 instances of chaining across their samples whereas

TABLE 10.8
Mean Number of Language Structures by Teacher Group

| Teacher Group (N = 7) | Language Forms | |
	Fingerspelling	Chained
Residential school		
Deaf	176	230
Hearing	275	5.5
School setting		
Deaf	152	21.5
Hearing	74	8.7

hearing teachers used chaining a low average of 5.5 times. Residential school teachers used chaining an average of 21.5 times and public school district teachers an average of 8.7 times (Table 10.8).

Why are fingerspelling and chaining structures more prominent among deaf teachers? We can think of two answers. First, the structures are amply present in everyday ASL. Deaf adults use fingerspelling in the natural course of signing, with each other and with children. Fingerspelling is not only a frequently used system, found in signers of all ages, social classes, and ethnicities, but is fully integrated in ASL grammar (Padden, 1998). Likewise, chaining structures are frequent. In routine everyday ASL, signs are followed by fingerspelled words, for example, TRASH-CAN T-R-A-S-H; or in classifier signs and signs: ROUND-OBJECT P-L-A-T-E. Kelly (1995) described "sandwiches," or structures where repetitions of the same form appear with an intervening contrasting form, such as a fingerspelled word inserted between two repetitions of a sign with related meaning. Kelly found that these structures are pervasive in the early language environments of deaf families with young deaf children.

Second, it may be that redundancies in sign structures are necessary where visual information is rapid and vulnerable. As deaf people accustomed to the requirements of visible language and the demands of signing in visual environments, these teachers repeated words, phrases, and sentences as a means of making their signing clear and accessible to their students. What we see being used in the classroom is an elaborate and purposeful extension of routine structures in ASL, to include not only signs and fingerspelled words but also initialized signs and even written words on the blackboard. Hearing teachers, on the other hand, repeat vocabulary less often, and seem not to be aware of chaining structures, unless as we have found, they teach in a residential school.

ASSOCIATION AND REPRESENTATION

We return to what we believe is the most interesting question of this inquiry: Why is there a relation between specific sets of ASL abilities and reading ability given that the two systems have little in common? The relation holds even for deaf children of hearing parents who acquire ASL skills at school, although it is more prominent in native signers. This question, it should be noted, is not the same as asking whether ASL is *necessary* for reading and writing development in deaf children. Deaf children who grow up with oral deaf parents who do not sign are reported to succeed at reading (de Villiers, Bibeau, Ramos, & Gatty, 1993), demonstrating at the very least that there must be more than one possible route to reading development in the deaf child. We leave the question of which reading strategies are effective or efficient for a fuller discussion; the question of how specific ASL structures come to have a relation to reading and writing skill is worth asking. We have always understood learning to read as a task of linking two related systems, one a representation of the other. But what is revealed by the case of signing children is that unusual, even unexpected, relations can be cultivated, it appears, by systematic exposure to systems of meaning.

Our argument is a variation on those offered by a number of individuals in which the analytical capabilities of human beings are influenced by the presence of written literacy in the culture. Goody (1987), Donald (1991), and Olson (1994) made claims that the pervasive presence of an alphabetic system in a culture drives the possibility that individuals will discover analysis by phoneme, to appreciate that words have smaller units beyond the level of the syllable. The presence of alphabetic literacy in all facets of everyday life, they argued, has accelerated the transition from illiteracy to literacy in an individual's life to a matter of a few years, somewhere between the second and third years of life to the fifth or sixth. To reach every aspect of the child's life, societal resources are fully deployed, from the spread of book technology to the daily presence of adults who themselves are skilled readers and trained to guide the child into life as a reader. Olson (1994) specifically further argued that phonological awareness is an unusual cognitive skill that is promoted and cultivated by the massive presence of alphabetic literacy in the early lives of children growing up in literate environments. Exposure to rhyming games and songs that are characteristic of early schooling serves as a precursor to developing reading skill.

Signing deaf children are also surrounded with alphabetic literacy, but oral games and songs are not directly available to them; instead, their parents and teachers offer other language games, some explicit but others inexplicit. A comparatively massive opportunity for young native signers may be the system of fingerspelling where, at a young age, deaf children practice not just the skill of fingerspelling but also learning regular orthographic sequences that characterize words. They also practice using a common morphological form in ASL, the initialized sign whereby the handshape of the sign is usually marked, drawing not from the phonemic inventory of ASL signs but from the alphabetic inventory of fingerspelled letters. When these children come to school, particularly those schools that are committed to signed language as a basis of instruction, these sign language games are not only continued but explicitly highlighted as a form of English language instruction.

We reiterate that there is nothing natural about reading. For all children, an association must be made. It may seem that associating "like" systems, an oral language and an alphabetic system based on the language, is easier than associating unlike systems, but the matter of what is alike and what is not alike has a surprising range. Take, for example, Read's (1975) discovery of young hearing children's "creative spellings." Not only did the children spontaneously create their own spellings, they did so using an unexpected analysis: Instead of linking sounds of a spoken word with letters of the same word in print, the children were linking the *names* of the letters of the alphabet with letters of a word in print. The invented spelling RID does not refer to *rid* but to *ride*, in which the letter *I* is represented according to its name. Invented spellings such as these are short-lived bursts of creativity that last only until the weight of cultural convention forces them to be replaced. Eventually children switch to spelling by phonemic analysis. But the first inventions are entirely reasonable; they just are not conventional.

In our earlier work (Padden, 1993), we found that when deaf children invented their spellings, they made different associations, not by the names of letters but by the visual characteristic of the written characters themselves. They were not linking spoken words with print words but alphabetic letters to print words. In other words, they were forming links from within the system itself, creating novel ways of developing orthographic competence. In a short time, they managed to capture orthographic regularities, from constraints on doubled letters to characteristics of letter clusters in English written text. For example, the spelling attempts contained possible doubled consonants and avoided impossible doubling, such as -*hh*- or -*ww*-. Despite this novel nonphonemic approach, many of them went on to become adequate spellers. In fact, one characteristic of average deaf readers is that they tend to be better spellers than they are readers (Dodd, 1980; Hanson, 1986). Very possibly, a more visual analysis of orthography is superior to a sound-based one if spelling ability is the goal.

What we find in our data is a continuation of our earlier discovery: Deaf children seek links between accessible systems, not between words they cannot hear or speak but between signs that have some tangible link to English print, in this case, fingerspelling and initialized signs. Furthermore, there is evidence from our studies that these links are not entirely fruitless: The better readers in our sample were better at recognizing fingerspelled words and writing them down in print. They were also better at recognizing that initialized signs had a link, although small and tenuous, to words in print. These links are not easy to make, and again, there is nothing natural about them, but they are cultivated from consistent and, we would argue, massive exposure organized and orchestrated by one's culture. Deaf children who grow up with ASL are exposed not only to early language experience, which undoubtedly contributes to reading success, but they also grow up learning strategies for linking systems, in this case, ASL and written English.

Because we suspect we cannot leave this issue without a few parting comments, we return briefly to the question of whether we have evidence that knowledge of ASL is necessary for acquisition of reading ability in young deaf children. This is an issue fraught with distractions of all kinds. If evaluating optimality were the only aim, then by the same token, we could argue that hearing children should pursue the strategy of deaf children when learning to spell; that is, they should learn to spell visually, not auditorily. Without trying to be facetious, it underscores a point about the nature of reading and writing: It is a language skill that is always learned under limited circumstances. Chinese-speaking children learn to read not by associating elements of Chinese to an alphabetic system but to an ideographic script. English-speaking children learn to associate sounds of English, not via fingerspelled handshapes but via English written text. Signing deaf children, we are starting to learn, form associations that have yet to be described in the reading literature. Unfortunately, some of the reading literature on deaf children is wistful and hopeful that somehow optimal strategies based on those used by hearing children can be adapted for use with deaf children. What this literature ignores is a fundamental principle about learning to read and write that we are starting to discover must also hold for deaf children: That it is not merely a linguistic or cognitive achievement (although it undoubtedly is) but it is a social achievement of marshalling cultural resources to instruct the younger members of the group (Duranti & Ochs, 1986; Heath, 1983). Viewing signing deaf children as cultural beings has always been controversial, but it is probably the best strategy for mapping out the nature of reading development in this population.

If we pursue the trajectory of reading development in the deaf population further, we are likely to encounter interesting twists. At least one will be the discovery that signing deaf adults who are skilled readers can perform phonological analysis on written English words even though they do not hear and do not speak intelligibly. It may be argued, and some have already, that any capable mastery of an alphabetic system must at some point appreciate its underlying phonological system (Hanson, 1989; Hanson, Liberman, & Shankweiler, 1984). Evidence from skilled deaf adult readers suggests strongly that this is so. But it is unclear at what point deaf readers master this ability. Some research suggests they do not do so initially (Schaper & Reitsma, 1993; Waters & Doehring, 1990), so the ability must have developed at a later point. Possibly, signing deaf children begin with associating elements of ASL to print, and then over time convert this knowledge to knowledge about the oral aspects of print. However the trajectory is to be represented, a description of reading ability in young deaf children will necessarily chronicle transitions through reading development, in which composite skills such as fingerspelling, morphological analysis, and phonological analysis converge to create the deaf reader. The picture that is beginning to emerge is one of a remarkably different route, one that draws from an assortment of cultural and individual capabilities. The portrait of the successful deaf reader must indeed be a unique one.

As we conclude, we offer the following summary points. First, we find a strong correlation between deaf children of deaf parents and comparatively higher reading achievement scores. This relation may be due to background characteristics shared by deaf children of deaf parents, which include early first language exposure and the fact that most are White, are introduced to school earlier, have less likelihood of handicaps, and have longer experience at school. All these characteristics play a role in reading and school achievement. Deaf children of hearing parents who share these characteristics also are more likely to have higher reading scores when compared to other deaf children less advantaged in these ways.

Second, our findings show that skill in fingerspelling interacts with reading achievement. We do not know whether skill in fingerspelling makes reading development possible, or if good reading skill leads children to fingerspell more and recognize fingerspelled words better. Delving deeper into this question requires a more refined set of tests, which our next project will develop. We also find that good readers can report English translations for initialized signs. Again, we do not know what role initialized signs may play for bilingual deaf children. It is possible that initialized signs may provide an initial push to beginning readers by helping them recall the first letter of English words, but they still must learn to complete the full English word. Most interesting, we find that skill in both fingerspelling and writing down English translations of initialized signs strongly correlates with ASL competence.

Third, our findings are limited to the question of reading development in severely to profoundly deaf children who use signed language in everyday contexts. Our observations of reading instruction suggest that families and institutions play a role in cultivating certain skills as means of acquiring competence in reading. We expect that deaf children in general have multiple routes to reading ability and that we have identified only a subset of these possible routes. A complete study of reading development in the entire population of deaf and hard-of-hearing students will likely identify several subgroups, each with a different array of language skills.

Fourth, different school settings organize reading instruction differently. We find from comparing reading and re-tell abilities of deaf children who are matched in family background that they may have very different reading strategies depending on which school they attend. One school we studied emphasizes translation ability whereas the other emphasizes decoding skills.

Finally, from our early analyses of teacher language in the classroom, we find again that school settings play a role. Residential school settings seem to engender more fingerspelling and more chaining structures, which we see to be predominant in classes involving literacy education. On the other hand, deaf teachers regardless of school setting are more likely to fingerspell and are more likely to use chaining structures. We do not argue here that fingerspelling and chaining are sufficient techniques for teaching reading, but that they stand out as two of the more noticeable examples of differences among teachers across classrooms. The profile of the skilled signing deaf reader suggests that these techniques may play a role in cultivating the abilities they share.

REFERENCES

Adams, M. (1990). *Beginning to read* Cambridge, MA: MIT Press.

Arnold, P., & Mason, J. (1992). Reading abilities and speech intelligibility of integrated hearing-impaired children. *Educational Research, 34,* 67–71.

Campbell, R (1992). Speech in the head? Rhyme skill, reading, and immediate memory in the deaf. In D. Reisberg (Ed.), *Auditory imagery* (pp. 73–93) Hillsdale, NJ· Lawrence Erlbaum Associates.

Conrad, R. (1979). *The deaf schoolchild.* London: Harper & Row.

de Villiers, J., Bibeau, L., Ramos, E., & Gatty, J. (1993) Gestural communication in oral deaf mother-child pairs: Language with a helping hand? *Applied Psycholinguistics, 14,* 319–347.

Dodd, B. (1980). The spelling abilities of profoundly pre-lingually deaf children In U. Frith (Ed.), *Cognitive processes in spelling* (pp. 423–440). London: Academic Press.

Donald, M. (1991). *Origins of the modern mind* Cambridge, MA: Harvard University Press.

Duranti, A., & Ochs, E. (1986). Literacy instruction in a Samoan village. In B. Schieffelin & P. Gilmore (Eds.), *The acquisition of literacy Ethnographic perspectives* (pp. 213–232). New York: Academic Press.

Goody, J. (1987). *Domestication of the savage mind.* Cambridge, MA: Cambridge University Press.

Gustason, G., Pfetzing, D., & Zawolkow, E. (1980). *Signing exact English.* Los Alamitos, CA: Modern Signs Press.

Hanson, V. (1986). Access to spoken language and the acquisition of orthographic structure: Evidence from deaf readers. *The Quarterly Journal of Experimental Psychology, 38A,* 193–212.

Hanson, V. (1989). Phonology and reading: Evidence from profoundly deaf readers. In D. Shankweiler & I. Liberman (Eds.), *Phonology and reading disability: Solving the reading puzzle* (pp. 69–89). Ann Arbor: University of Michigan Press.

Hanson, V., Liberman, I., & Shankweiler, D. (1984). Linguistic coding by deaf children in relation to beginning reading success. *Journal of Experimental Child Psychology, 37*, 378–393.

Hayes, P., & Arnold, P. (1992). Is hearing-impaired children's reading delayed or different? *Journal of Research in Reading, 15*, 104–116.

Heath, S. (1983). *Ways with words Language, work and life in communities and classrooms.* Cambridge, MA: Cambridge University Press.

Hirsh-Pasek, L., & Treiman, R. (1982). Recoding in silent reading: Can the deaf child translate print into a more manageable form? *The Volta Review, 84*, 71–82.

Holt, J. (1994). Classroom attributes and achievement test scores for deaf and hard of hearing students. *American Annals of the Deaf, 139*, 430–437.

Holt, J., & Hotto, S. (1994). *Demographic aspects of hearing impairment: Questions and answers.* Washington, DC: Gallaudet University, Center for Assessment and Demographic Studies.

Karchmer, M., Milone, A., & Wolk, S. (1979). Educational significance of hearing loss at three levels of severity. *American Annals of the Deaf, 124*, 97–109.

Kelly, A. (1995). Fingerspelling interaction: A set of deaf parents and their deaf daughter. In C. Lucas (Ed.), *Sociolinguistics in deaf communities* (pp. 62–73). Washington, DC: Gallaudet University Press.

Kuntze, M. (1994, October). Developing students' literary skills in ASL. In B. Snider (Ed.), *Post Milan ASL and English literacy: Issues, trends, and research* (pp. 267–281). Washington, DC: Gallaudet University.

Liberman, I., Shankweiler, D., Liberman, A., Fowler, C., & Fischer, F. (1977). Phonetic segmentation and recoding in the beginning reader. In A. Reber & D. Scarborough (Eds.), *Toward a psychology of reading* (pp. 207–225). Hillsdale, NJ: Lawrence Erlbaum Associates.

Mayberry, R. (1989, April). *Deaf children's reading comprehension in relation to sign language structure and input* Paper presented at the Society for Research in Child Development. Kansas City, Kansas.

Mayberry, R., & Fischer, S. (1989). Looking through phonological shape to sentence meaning: The bottleneck of non-native sign language processing. *Memory & Cognition, 17*, 740–754.

Mertens, D. (1990). A conceptual model for academic achievement: Deaf student outcomes. In D. Moores & K. Meadow-Orlans (Eds.), *Educational and developmental aspects of deafness* (pp. 25–72). Washington, DC: Gallaudet University Press.

Moores, D., & C. Sweet. (1990). Factors predictive of school achievement. In D. Moores & K. Meadow-Orlans (Eds.), *Educational and developmental aspects of deafness* (pp. 154–201). Washington, DC: Gallaudet University Press.

Olson, D. (1994). Where redescriptions come from. *Behavioral and Brain Sciences, 17*, 725–726.

Padden, C. (1991). The acquisition of fingerspelling by deaf children. In P. Siple & S. Fischer (Eds.), *Theoretical issues in sign language research. Vol 2: Psychology* (pp. 191–210). Chicago: University of Chicago Press.

Padden, C. (1993). Lessons to be learned from young deaf orthographers. *Linguistics and Education, 5*(1), 71–86.

Padden, C. (1998). The ASL lexicon. *International Review of Sign Linguistics, 1*, 33–51.

Padden, C., & LeMaster, B. (1985). An alphabet on hand: The acquisition of fingerspelling in deaf children. *Sign Language Studies, 47*, 161–172.

Paul, P., Bernhardt, E., & Gramly, C. (1992). Use of ASL in teaching reading and writing to students: An interactive theoretical perspective. *Conference Proceedings Bilingual considerations in the education of deaf students, ASL and English* (pp. 75–105). Washington, DC: Gallaudet University.

Prinz, P., & Strong, M. (1998). American Sign Language (ASL) proficiency and English literacy within a bilingual deaf education model. *Topics in Language Disorders, 4,* 47–60.

Ramsey, C. (1997). *Deaf children in public schools.* Washington, DC: Gallaudet University Press.

Ramsey, C., & Padden, C. (1998). Natives & newcomers. Literacy education for deaf children. *Anthropology and Education Quarterly, 29,* 5–24.

Read, C. (1975). *Children's categorization of speech sounds in English.* Urbana, IL: National Council of Teachers of English.

Schaper, M., & Reitsma, P. (1993). The use of speech-based recoding in reading by prelingually deaf children. *American Annals of the Deaf, 138,* 46–54.

Singleton, J., Supalla, S., Litchfield, S., & Schley, S. (1998). From sign to word: Considering modality constraints in ASL/English bilingual education. *Topics in Language Disorders, 4,* 16–29.

Supalla, T., Singleton, J., Newport, E., Supalla, S., Coulter, G., & Metlay, D. (in press). *Test battery for American Sign Language morphology and syntax.* San Diego, CA: Dawn Sign Press.

Waters, G., & Doehring, D. (1990). Reading acquisition in congenitally deaf children who communicate orally: Insights from an analysis of component reading, language and memory skills. In T. Carr & B. Levy (Eds.), *Reading and its development Component skills approaches* (pp. 323–373). New York: Academic Press.

Chapter 11

Creating an Involvement-Focused Style in Book Reading With Deaf and Hard of Hearing Students: The Visual Way[1]

Susan M. Mather
André Thibeault
Gallaudet University

In this study, we examined the strategies used by five teachers when they read a book to their deaf students. For example, when reading to the children, did they follow the book word for word? Or, did they reconstruct the story when they read the book? The observed teachers were equally divided between hearing and deaf users of Manually Coded English (MCE) and American Sign Language (ASL). They were asked to read the picture book *Five Chinese Brothers* (Bishop & Wiese, 1965) to their classes. There were five research goals for our project: (a) to transcribe five videotaped reading activities; (b) to identify and analyze what interpersonal involvement strategies teachers used for first-person discourse when reading; (c) to examine how closely the teachers followed the use of first-person discourse in the book; (d) to determine how often the teachers translated from third-person discourse to first-person discourse in the book; and (e) to analyze the factors that influence the quality and quantity of constructed dialouge, specifically, the teachers's own dependence on visual and/or auditory stimuli and the instructional mode of communication (MCE or ASL) that the teacher used. Before describing our research project, we discuss differences in spoken and written discourse, and more specifically, how episodes of dialogue are reported in these two types of discourse.

---

[1]This study is part of a 3-year research grant from the Office of Special Education and Rehabilitative Services under the U.S. Department of Education.

Following this discussion, we explain how constructed dialogue is expressed in ASL.

Tannen (1985) noted that differences between spoken and written discourse have been accounted for under two hypotheses: one dealing with contextualization and another dealing with cohesion in the discourse. Under the contextualization hypothesis, spoken discourse is seen as highly context bound; the discourse refers to the context of immediate surroundings, visible to both speaker and hearer who are copresent in time and space (e.g., *Take a good look at this*; p. 128). A spoken discourse can be minimally explicit because members of the audience can always ask for clarification on the spot if they do not understand a point. Also, if participants in spoken discourse happen to share similar social backgrounds and assumptions about the world, then their discourse may rely significantly on this shared experience, further reducing the need for explicitness in the discourse.

Written discourse, however, is seen as more decontextualized. In writing, immediate context is absent; writers and readers are separated in time, place, and space. The reader cannot ask for clarification when confused. The writer must, therefore, anticipate all possible confusion and preclude it by filling in necessary details, or as many details as possible; for instance, explaining the steps of a logical argument. Furthermore, writers and readers may share minimal social context. The writer can make only a few assumptions about shared attitudes and beliefs.

When speaking, cohesion is created when the speaker uses the following features: pitch, tone of voice, speed, and expression (both vocal and facial). These nonverbal and paralinguistic features reflect what the speaker's attitude toward the message is, or what Labov (1972) called "evaluation" in narrative. Evaluation establishes cohesion by showing relations among ideas, highlighting relative importance, and providing certain information (foreground or background). In writing, by contrast, these nonverbal and paralinguistic features are lost; they cannot be captured on paper. Writing, however, can create involvement by use of capitalization, underlining, italics, and exclamation points (Tannen 1988). Writing, although it relies on lexicalization, can help create discourse as if it were face-to-face interaction by adding certain comments to written dialogue.

Despite these marked differences in modes, Tannen (1988) found that ordinary conversation and literary discourse share the same linguistic features used to create interpersonal involvement. She identified certain features and divided them into two categories of patterns of language. One category consists of features that are used to sweep the audience along with their rhythm, sound, and shape. Another category includes those features that require audience participation in order to make sense, such as imagery, detail, and dialogue.

CONSTRUCTED DIALOGUE IN SPOKEN LANGUAGE

Tannen (1986) argued that "the term *reported speech* is a misnomer. The examination of the lines of dialogue represented in storytelling or conversation, and the power of human memory, indicate that most of those lines were probably not actually spoken" (p. 1). She suggested the term *reported speech* should be called *constructed dialogue*. She found that reported speech is not actually a verbatim report of words as they were spoken, but rather a reconstruction in which remembered dialogue is transformed by the teller's personal experience and storytelling prowess. She contended that this helps to create interpersonal involvement between speaker or writer and audience. To create interpersonal involvement in constructed dialogue, the narrator or author uses first-person discourse as in face-to-face dialogue.

For example, in a pilot study comparing how Brazilian and American speakers told the story of Little Red Riding Hood, Ott (1983) found that Brazilian speakers used far more constructed dialogue than the American speakers (cited in Tannen, 1989). The American in the study used six such instances, all formulaic for this fairy tale:

"Grandma, what a big nose you have."
"All the better to smell you, my dear."
"Grandma, what big ears you have."
"All the better it is to hear you, my dear."
"Grandma, what a big mouth and big teeth you have."
"All the better to eat you with, my dear."

The Brazilian, however, used 43! His version of the fairy tale represented almost all action in dialogue. In part through dialogue, he made the familiar story into an original drama through the creation of scenes. For example, he started the story in the following way:

One time on a beautiful afternoon, in her city, her mother called her and said:
"Little Red Riding Hood, come here."
"What is it, mother? I am playing with my dolls, can I continue?"

The speaker first set the scene in a particular place (a city), at a particular time of day (afternoon), with particular weather (beautiful). He then depicted action between characters, including dramatic conflict: The mother summoned her daughter to do a task for her; the daughter was engaged in a particular activity—playing with dolls—which she was reluctant to interrupt.

Long segments in this account are composed only of dialogue. For example, when the little girl is accosted by the wolf on her way to her grandmother's house:

> "Little Red Riding Hood, Little Red Riding Hood."
> And Little Red Riding Hood stopped and looked: "Who is there?"
> "Ah, who is talking here is the spirit of the forest."
> "Spirit? But I don't know you."
> "No, but I am invisible, you can't see me."
> [Imitating child's voice] "But what do you want?"
> "Where are you going, Little Red Riding Hood?"
> "Ah, I'm going to my granny's house."
> "What are you going to do there, Little Red Riding Hood?"
> "Ah, I am going to take some sweets that my mother prepared for her."
> "Ah, very good . . . the sweets are delicious, they are, they are, they are, they are . . ." [Licking his lips]
> "Do you want one?"
> "No, no, no, no. [Accelerated] Spirits don't eat. Okay, okay. Then, now, yes, yes, you are going to take it to your granny. . . . remember me to her, okay?"
> "Okay, bye."

Through constructed dialogue and other features, this Brazilian speaker created a vivid new story out of the familiar fairy tale.

Chafe (1982), Ochs (1979), Schiffrin (1981), and Tannen (1982, 1985, 1986) observed that narration is more graphic when the narrator uses speech in the form of a first-person discourse (usually called *direct quotation*, or *direct speech*, or *constructed dialogue*) instead of a third-person discourse (*indirect quotation* or *indirect speech*). The following are examples of first- and second-person pronouns used in reference to third persons from the book, *The Five Chinese Brothers* (see arrow markers and underlining added for emphasis):

> On the morning of the execution, the Second Chinese brother said to the judge:
> → "Your Honor, will you allow me to go and bid my mother good-bye?"
> "It is only fair," said the judge (p. 29).

In these utterances, the author is not using *you* (and *your*) to refer to the reader, or *me* (and *my*) to refer to herself. Instead, by using direct quotation, *I* and *you* become, alternately, the Second Chinese Brother and the Judge.

Schiffrin (1981) found that regardless of using the past tense in indirect speech, people used present tense in the constructed dialogue of their stories, even though the story had clearly already happened. The use of the present tense is often referred to as the *historical-present tense.* She noted that using historical present is a way to create involvement. Examples of historical-present tense (see marked arrows) are as follows (underlining added for emphasis):

> On the morning of the execution, the Second Chinese brother said to the judge:
>
> → "Your Honor, <u>will</u> you allow me to go and bid my mother good-bye?"
> → "It <u>is</u> only fair," said the judge.

The writers could have chosen to use indirect quotation and past and subjunctive tenses had they desired a less involved style, for example:

> On the morning of the execution, the Second Chinese brother spoke to the judge and asked him if he could be allowed to go and bid his mother good-bye.

The authors took advantage of the option to create a more graphic or involved style by using first- and/or second-person pronouns and historical-present tense in the writing.

CONSTRUCTED DIALOGUE
IN AMERICAN SIGN LANGUAGE

Several studies claim that constructed dialogue in American Sign Language does exist but in a different form from spoken language. Liddell (1980), Padden (1986, 1990), Meier (1990), Engberg-Pedersen (1992), Lillo-Martin (1992), Mather (1990), and Winston (1991, 1992) referred to role playing or role shifting as conveying a character's thoughts, words, and actions. In the present study, we found that the signers who want to create an imaginary dialogue between two characters would employ three devices. The devices of role shifting are the use of (a) eye-gaze signals, (b) surrogate space, and (c) head- or shoulder-tilt markers as counterparts to the way a speaking narrator would use shifts in tone of voice, pitch, speed, and expression (both vocal and facial) to represent a fictitious dialogue between two people.

Eye-Gaze Signals

Mather (1987) found that there are three types of eye-gaze signals that a signer can employ; two with groups and one with individuals. When talking to a group, a signer employs *group-indicating gaze* by looking at the group in a smooth arch-like fashion from right to left or vice versa. If a person in the group wants the signer to relinquish his turn, the speaker acknowledges this person by gazing back at him or her. The eye signal (*individual gaze*) lets the group know that the signer is now talking with one particular person. These two signals inform the group that the signer is talking either with one person or with the whole group.

The third type is *audience gaze*, which is a bit different from group-indicating gaze. To let the entire audience know that the signer is talking to them, the signer gazes directly toward a midpoint in the audience (instead of a smooth arch-like gaze). The signer can alternate between audience gaze and group-indicating gaze. Each type has its own signals, depending on when the signer wants to talk with people and to whom. For example, if the signer wants to talk with a specific group in the audience, he gives a group-indicating eye signal. In doing so, the signer thrusts his head forward (lower) and gazes in a smooth arch-like fashion over the particular group. If he wants to talk with the larger group (audience), he leans his head back a bit and returns his gaze to a midpoint in the audience. For example, this might happen if the speaker wishes to have a group of people stop talking or approach the stage.

Any signing storyteller would use these eye gaze-signals in everyday conversations and for fictitious conversations as well. These eye-gaze signals can be used to communicate with a surrogate person or surrogate audience, or even with a specific surrogate group within the surrogate audience as well (Mather, 1997).

In the present study as well as in other observed events, we found that teachers and others (e.g., interpreters or sign language students) would give confusing eye signals. For example, a teacher gazed mistakenly at the audience at the same time as he signed to the surrogate person. This confused the audience as to whether he was communicating with them directly or with the surrogate person, as he gave two different signals (gazing at the audience while signing in the surrogate space). Thus, we found that it is essential that a narrator keep the two spaces separate, one with the audience and another with the surrogate person (see Fig. 11.1).

Surrogate Space

Due to the nature of visual communication, we know that the narrator cannot turn and face the wall to sign; otherwise, the audience would not be able to see him signing. This is a situation that does not arise for hearing

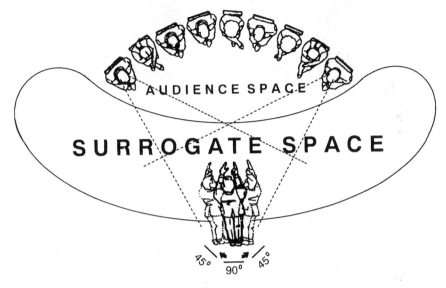

FIG. 11.1.

narrators. Regardless of whether the narrator gazes at them or not, the hearing audience can imagine the scene with or without their eyes closed from hearing the narrator's constructed dialogue.

Liddell (1995) observed that a signer will associate with an imaginary person and interact with him as though he is in the signer's environment. The signer can even indicate the imaginary person's height by looking up at a taller person or down at a shorter person. He describes the imaginary person as a "surrogate" person. The person is in the signer's immediate environment, which is known as *surrogate space*. In this case, the signer is not talking with a real person but rather with a surrogate person.

To convey a clear and imaginary dialogue visually in the surrogate space, there are a few things that the signing narrator has to determine before he can set up space boundaries: (a) How big is the audience? (b) How far should the signer be from the audience? (c) How many characters does the signer plan to include in the story? (d) Is there a limit to the available space in which the signer can create two or more imaginary talkers? (e) Can the audience see the signer clearly when he assumes a role and talks with another imaginary character?

First, the signer's eye gaze to an imaginary addressee must be out of the audience boundaries, either to the right or left of the audience or above or below it. It is important to note that it is not required that the signer be out of the audience boundaries in both dimensions. It is possible, but rare, for a signer using the vertical dimension (as for a child–adult discourse) in front of the audience to look above it and below it to indicate

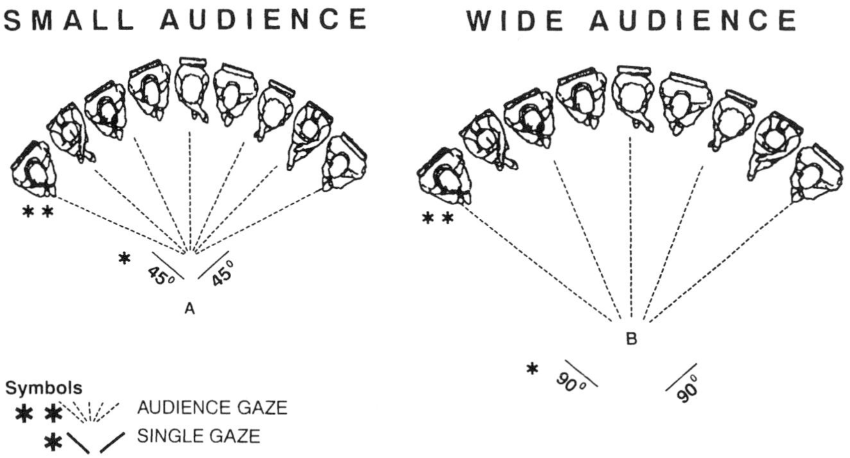

SMALL AUDIENCE   WIDE AUDIENCE

Symbols
✱ ✱ ＼｜／ AUDIENCE GAZE
✱ ＼ ／ SINGLE GAZE

FIG. 11.2.

the separation between the actual audience and imaginary entities as long as the signer avoids eye contact or gaze with the audience. In doing this, the narrator would adjust his body position by shuffling a bit, to make sure everyone in the audience could clearly see him signing. The signer must know the space boundaries. The deaf actors at the National Theatre of the Deaf were taught that they must turn at an angle somewhere between 45° and 90° from center (personal communication with E. Blue, 1997). We have observed many times that a teacher, a deaf parent, or a deaf adult would steer a deaf child to make sure the audience could clearly see him signing before he could assume the role of first-person narrator.

The size of the surrogate space depends on the size of the audience—the larger the audience, the less surrogate space or vice versa is needed, as long as the narrator keeps the boundary between the audience space and surrogate space separate. So he would continue to verify that the audience could see him clearly when he begins a constructed dialogue. He would shift his body to an angle around 45° from center, depending the size of the audience and their visual access to the narrator's signing (see Fig. 11.2a). If the audience is wider, the narrator may have to move back further into an angle that is 90° from center (see Fig. 11.2b).

Head- or Shoulder-Tilt Markers

Lentz (1986) found that signers can assume two roles by shifting their body to indicate that they are changing from the first character to another, so as to form a dialogue between two imaginary characters. Bahan (1996) and others mentioned that people do tilt their head or shoulder when they take up the roles of others.

After making many observations in different settings (e.g., formal presentations and meetings) and of videotapes of various deaf narrators, we found that the narrator often tilts his head or shoulder down to the side facing the audience rather than to the space where the audience is not. If the audience is on the left side, the narrator would tilt that way first. It does not matter where the audience is; the narrator often tilts toward it, usually on the right side first.

In doing this, the narrator will give a signal to the audience first by mentioning whose role he is taking (e.g.,"ME MOTHER"). Then, he slowly shifts away from the audience and tilts his shoulder (or head) to the right to indicate that he is taking the role of Character A as the current speaker and talking with the surrogate addressee, Character B.[2] Next, he would take the role of Character B by shifting and tilting his shoulder back to the left side, then talking with Character A, who becomes the surrogate addressee. That would place Character A on the right side and Character B on the left throughout the book reading. These right and left shoulder-tilt markers parallel English speakers who use first-person pronouns (I) vocally by shifting their vocal tone to reflect two people in their imaginary dialogue during a book reading. Thus, the narrator would continue to have dual roles by establishing a right tilt marker for Character A and a left tilt marker for Character B.

In summary, our previous findings and observations showed that taking up a role is not as simple as one might think, because one has several devices to align: eye gaze, use of space, and head or shoulder tilt. The narrator also has to make sure that the audience can see him. At the same time, he must keep the two spaces separate in order not to confuse talking with the audience with handling a constructed dialogue, by using the two tilt markers (one for right and another for left) for two characters. He must also be consistent with these devices.

We spoke with one of the teachers who was part of this study about handling these devices. She admitted that she had trouble handling them when she tried to use constructed dialogue. Her remark was not surprising because we had the opportunity to use those findings to teach sign language students and found that they had problems similar to four teachers in this study. (We discuss this in detail later.)

Our sign language students had trouble trying to remember how to use the devices correctly, even confusing which way they should tilt their heads.

---

[2]The signer may talk about himself or take the role of one of his friends as Character B. He would let his audience know in the first place that he is talking about himself or his friend.

Interpreters also made similar mistakes. We could see the audience's re-
action when an interpreter (or even a signing presenter) gave one or two
confusing signals. Two very common remarks were: "I MISS WHAT IN-
TERPRETER (or SPEAKER) SAY ABOUT WHO SAY WHAT?" or "I LIKE
THAT INTERPRETER BETTER THAN OTHER BECAUSE I CAN FOL-
LOW WHAT EACH PERSON SAY" (referring to a speaker's narration
about the conversation between him and another person).

Visual Involvement-Focused Style

According to Tannen (1989) and Schiffrin (1981), speakers often use
first-person discourse, historical-present tense, or voice quality to identify
which character the narrator is assuming as a way of creating interpersonal
involvement. To create his story—an involvement-focused style in the visual
way—the signing narrator creates first-person discourse by shifting and
taking dual roles in the surrogate space. Thus, every dialogue has a signer
(or a speaker) and an addressee as listener. There is not an exclusive role
for each, but rather each participant has a dual role, as speaker and as
addressee. As we have shown, role shifting is not as simple as a body shift.
It involves three complicated devices: the use of specific eye-gaze signals,
the establishment and creation of a surrogate space, and head- or
shoulder-tilt markers.

Thus, we call the storytelling used by the deaf community *visual involvement-focused storytelling* as opposed to *auditory involvement-focused storytelling.*
Both can use constructed dialogue (first-person discourse), however, the
narrator for the deaf audience must avoid eye contact with the audience
to allow them to visualize an imaginary dialogue without having to figure
out if the narrator is addressing them or portraying the characters in the
story. The hearing audience and narrator do not have to worry about eye
contact because they use auditory cues to portray the imaginary dialogue.
In other words, members of the deaf community adapt first-person dialogue
from printed or spoken dialogue into a "visual way" of book reading. Thus,
we call that strategy a visual involvement-focused style. Hearing narrators
similarly adapt the written first-person dialogue by using voice quality,
pitch, intonation, and paralinguistic features as Tannen and others noted.
Because they employ auditory features to create the involvement, we call
this an auditory involvement-focused style.

RESEARCH PROCEDURES

What follows are the general procedures we used in this study for book
reading, videotaping, interviewing, transcribing, and data analysis, in addition to a description of the settings and participants in the study.

Background of Teachers, Schools, and Style of Book Reading

Different approaches are used by teachers of varying backgrounds and styles. The observed teachers were divided between hearing and deaf users of ASL[3] and hearing and deaf users of MCE[4] (see Table 11.1).

Residential School Setting. The residential school in this study had two teachers (one hearing and one deaf) who used ASL with their students. One of the teachers, who was deaf, was also a noted storyteller. Her videotapes of stories are marketed and sold nationwide by a company that specializes in videotapes and books of signed stories in ASL. She had a group of 6 students who ranged in age from 6 to 8 years. Her style of book reading was to read the whole book first and retell the story in ASL without the English text.

The other teacher was hearing and a well-known person in the community for her involvement with people who were deaf and hard of hearing. She also was a certified sign language interpreter. She had a group of 6 students who were 4 to 6 years old. Her style of reading was somewhat different from the first teacher. She read each page first before she retold the story.

Public School Setting. The public school in the study had two self-contained classrooms of students who were deaf. A hearing individual was strongly recommended as one of the best teachers. She could switch from

---

[3]There are two instructional modes of communication that are often used with a student who is deaf: ASL and MCE. The following is a brief (and by no means complete) description of them, with an emphasis on those features that are most different, because preliminary findings indicate that these differences may influence how a teacher reads with students. ASL is a visual-spatial language, which has three components: manual, nonmanual, and spatial. The manual information is the part of the language that is made with the hand or hands (signs and fingerspelling). Nonmanual information includes motions of the head and body as well as facial expressions, which can be used to provide linguistic (e.g., nonmanual question markers) and nonlinguistic information that is carried on the face (Davies, 1983; Liddell, 1980; Mather, 1991; Valli & Lucas, 1995). ASL uses the hands, the whole face (including mouthing) and body, and the positioning of the body and its parts in space to encode both linguistic and nonlinguistic messages.

[4]MCE is a general cover term for a number of varying codes that are dependent on both ASL and English. These codes were invented by groups of educators for the purpose of helping students with hearing impairments learn English. These systems are generally composed of a basic core of manual signals borrowed from ASL, to which are added a number of invented affixes used to show English tense markers, plurals, and so forth. The signs are used in English word order and are generally accompanied by voicing. Because the focus is primarily on the speech signal, this communicative event has been described by some researchers as sign-supported speech (Johnson, Liddell, & Erting, 1989).

TABLE 11 1
Background of Study Participants

Teacher	Language Use	Auditory Status	Students	Schools
1	ASL	Deaf	Age: 6 to 8 How many. 6, Deaf	Residential
2	ASL	Hearing	Age. 4 to 6 How many: 5, Deaf	Residential
3	ASL/MCE	Hearing	Age 3 to 5, How many: 6, Deaf	Self-contained
4	MCE	Deaf	Age: 5 to 7 How many: 12, Deaf and Hearing	Mainstreamed
5	MCE	Hearing	Age: 3 to 5 How many: 13, Deaf and Hearing	Mainstreamed

Note. ASL = American Sign Language MCE = Manually Coded English.

ASL to MCE effectively and effortlessly. She was also a certified sign language interpreter. She used both ASL and MCE with her group of 6 students who were 3 to 5 years old. This teacher's storytelling method was similar to that of the second teacher who read each page first before she retold the story. There were several incidents in which the students interrupted her storytelling and forced the teacher to reread the page or repeat the story line. This affected the style of her storytelling and is discussed in the results section.

Private Day School Setting. The third school was a private day school and was considered a mainstreamed program. It was an interesting school for two reasons: (a) instruction was visually oriented, and (b) students with normal hearing were reverse mainstreamed from public schools to the private school for various reasons. Some students who had normal hearing were sent by their school districts because they benefited from visually centered activities. These included, for example, students who could hear but could not talk, or students who could not absorb information auditorily, resulting in dependence on visual channels. Also included were students with normal hearing whose parents were deaf and used sign language at home, as well as students who were siblings of deaf students. Both teachers from this school used MCE. One teacher, who was hard of hearing, had a group of 22 students (combined deaf, hard of hearing, and hearing) aged 5 to 7 years old. Another teacher, who was hearing, had a group of 13 students (also deaf, hard of hearing, and hearing) aged 3 to 5 years old. Both teachers were similar in their story reading styles. They read and signed almost every line instead of reading the whole passage and signing afterward. Both consulted their teacher's aide who was fluent in ASL and a skilled storyteller. Unlike them, the first three teachers did not seek consultation for telling the story.

Book Selection.   The following criteria were developed for selection of the book. It had to have two types of discourse—first-person discourse (direct speech)—and third-person discourse (indirect speech) so that effects of involvement style could be observed. It also had to be generally popular to encourage a successful book-reading event for everyone. Based on these criteria, *Five Chinese Brothers* (Bishop & Wiese, 1965) was chosen for this study.

Book Reading Procedures.   Five teachers (3 hearing and 2 deaf) were asked to read the picture book *Five Chinese Brothers* with their classes. The book was given to them 1 week prior to data collection to ensure familiarity. They were also told about the purpose of the study—that we were studying how to create interpersonal involvement in book reading and that they were encouraged to try to create interpersonal involvement as much as they could.

Data Collection and Transcription

Videotaping Procedures.   Because the teachers were the primary focus of this investigation, a full-screen view of head and upper torso was essential. One camera was therefore used to obtain a full-screen frontal view of the teacher's head and upper torso. This camera was set up at the students' eye level, to help determine whether and when the teacher was looking at the students. It was also crucial to this project to examine the students' responses to the teacher. Because the analysis would be both quantitative and qualitative for each child, it was essential that every child's face and body be visible. At the same time, the picture included at least a partial view of the teacher to enable accurate analysis of the interaction between teacher and child. Therefore, two camcorders focusing on the students from both sides of the teacher ensured that all of the students' faces were visible on one screen or the other.

Transcription Procedures.   Information was transcribed about the teacher's use of linguistic features and use of involvement strategies in reading. Both authors are fluent in ASL and members of the deaf community. We first worked separately on each tape and then worked together as a team on each tape. In total, this study involved transcription and analysis of five videotaped reading activities by teachers.

The transcription procedures for each tape had two steps. First, English glosses for the signs and some contextual notes were recorded. This provided a general idea of what had transpired in the session. Second, nonmanual information and more elaborate contextual notes were also coded, and a translation was provided. The nonmanual information was transcribed first to ensure an accurate English translation. Then we narrowed down more specific devices and transcribed them to note whether the teachers used them during their constructed dialogue for the purpose of this study. This second pass through the videotape was also used to make any necessary corrections to the glosses from the first step.

Interviewing Procedures. Interviews were conducted with 5 teachers and their supervisors and 30 members of the deaf community. The main purpose of doing interviews with teachers was to find out what they thought and to collect remarks that might help us describe or identify problems or strategies during our data analysis. The more effective strategies we could identify the better, because we hoped ultimately to make recommendations based on these teachers'experiences for those who want to learn how to use an effective visual involvement-focused style in reading with deaf and hard of hearing students.

The first author, who was also principal investigator, had the opportunity to interview the 5 teachers before and after the book-reading activity. Before they started, the teachers were able to share their perspectives about the book selected for this project, their reading styles, and their definitions of involvement in reading. After their storytelling, they were asked follow-up questions, such as what they thought about their strategies, what they found difficult, what they would do if they could start again, and what they would do if they did not have to follow the school's policy of deaf education. Most of their remarks are included in the results section.

Both authors had the opportunity to ask at least 30 participants to view these 5 teachers' storytelling. These participants shared their perspectives about the storytelling and whether they could follow the stories and what they liked best about them. All of their remarks are also found in the results section.

Data Analysis Procedures: Constructed Dialogue
During Book Reading

When we began our data analysis, we viewed as many videotapes[5] as we could find on the Gallaudet University campus. We also had the opportu-

---

[5]The videotapes that we used are ASL Storytimes, Volumes 1 to 8 from Gallaudet University Department of ASL, Linguistics, and Interpretation.

nity to observe many actual events with and without interpreters, both on and off the Gallaudet campus, such as National Association of the Deaf conventions (1994 and 1996) and special deaf organizations. We also observed many classrooms other than those of the 5 teachers in this study and watched parents who shared in book reading with their children. These observations helped us determine what "devices" members of the deaf community use to create visual involvement-focused storytelling strategies. We also tested the findings and applied these to our sign language students who shared their perspectives.

These observations and interviews helped us narrow down four analysis procedures. First, we analyzed teachers' storytelling on the videotapes to determine whether they used first-person dialogue by looking at their specific devices. These specific devices, already described, included the direction of eye gaze, use of surrogate space, and shoulder or head tilting, all intended to indicate whether a teacher had taken on the role of a first-person character engaging in a surrogate dialogue. The devices were also clearly identified as instances of a visual involvement-focused dialogue. First-person discourse in signing was considered and counted as an instance only when the signer used these specific devices.

Second, we examined the data to determine how closely the teachers followed the use of first-person discourse in the text. For example, we counted all instances of first-person discourse in the text. All phrases in quotes were considered to be instances of first-person discourse, provided it was understood that the quoted element had been spoken. For example, the sentence "The Chinese brother said, 'Will you allow me . . .' " or " 'It is only fair,' said the judge" was considered an instance, but in the sentence "The first Chinese Brother made great movements with his arms and that meant 'Come back!' " Neither the 'come back' nor the mention of the gesture was counted as an instance. In total, there were 19 instances of first-person dialogue in the text.

Third, we compared these 19 textual first-person dialogue instances (direct quotation) with the teachers' storytelling on the videotapes. We found that there were discrepancies between the number of instances in the text and the number of instances the teachers used. These discrepancies can be explained, in part, by the following: (a) the teachers expanded on the existing direct dialogue in the text, and (b) the teachers added completely new dialogue.

Not only did teachers expand or add completely new dialogue, some switched from textual third-person discourse (indirect quotation) into the first-person constructed discourse. Thus, fourth, and last, we then set out to determine how often the teachers' use of first-person constructed discourse was a conversion from third-person discourse in the text. Because almost any sentence in the text could be made into some form of first-person constructed dialogue, we based our analysis on the teachers' use of first-person constructued dialogue alone, not on the number of instances in the text. Heightened use of the first person identified in this analysis can be explained by the following: (c) the teachers switched from textual third-person discourse (indirect quotation) into first-person constructed discourse; and (d) the teachers converted communicative actions in the text into a form of first-person constructed discourse.

Now we discuss in detail each of the four phenomena just listed. Each includes an example of a textual excerpt and a teacher's use of first-person constructed dialogue.

1. Expansion of an Existing Dialogue. Sometimes the teacher expanded on the first-person discourse in the text. Each turn of dialogue that was added to the existing exchange was considered an instance of dialogue expansion. In the following example, there is an exchange of five turns between a little boy and the first Chinese Brother (see Example 1: 1–5) in the printed text (Bishop & Wiese, 1965, p. 7). This constructed dialogue was expanded by the teacher to include two more turns (see Example 2: 6–7) to the first five textual turns:

Example 1
1. One day, as he was leaving the market place, a little boy stopped him and asked him if he could go fishing with him.
2. "No, it could not be done," said the first Chinese Brother.
3. But the little boy begged and begged and finally the First Chinese Brother consented.
4. "Under one condition," said he, "and that is that you shall obey me promptly."
5. "Yes, yes," the little boy promised.

One of the teachers followed these five turns exactly during storytelling and added two more. The book did not mention when and where they would meet to go fishing after the boy promised with a "Yes." So the teacher took up the role of the Chinese Brother and informed the little boy (by gazing down) that they would meet next morning by the ocean (see the marked arrow 6). Then the teacher shifted back from the role of the Chinese brother to the role of the little boy who responded with an enthusiastic look of acknowledgment, "YES," three times (see the second marked arrow 7). This created a nice closing, with an acknowledgment between the boy and the First Chinese Brother that they agreed to meet at the ocean in the morning.

Example 2

Gaze: -- gaze down

Body: --- shoulder tilt to left

→ 6.   #OK MEET TOMORROW MORNING GO-to WATER
       OCEAN++ THAT-ONE
       "Ok, we'll meet tomorrow morning by the ocean."
       (Shifting from the Chinese Brother's role to the role of the little
       boy)

Gaze: -----gaze up (with an enthusiastic-look)

Body: -----shoulder tilt to right

→ 7.   YES YES YES
       "Yes, yes, yes."

The two additional lines (Examples 6 and 7) in the signed constructed dialogue were counted as two instances of expansion of that existing dialogue.

2. Creation of a Completely New Dialogue. Some added lines of dialogue were not an expansion of existing dialogue because they had no textual counterpart. They were instances of completely new dialogue. The book scene below (Example 3) shifts straight from the boy being drowned to the arrest of the brother. There is no mention of the first Chinese brother informing the people what happened. In the storytelling (Example 4), the teacher took the role of the Chinese brother and informed the villagers that he told the boy to come and the boy refused. This was a completely new, added element to the story.

Example 3

All of a sudden the sea forced its way out of his
[first Chinese Brother's] mouth, went back to its bed . . .
and the little boy disappeared. When the First Chinese
Brother returned to the village, alone, he was arrested,
put in prison, tried, and condemned to have his head cut off. (p. 20)

Example 4

Gaze: --- gaze at the actual audience

Body: -- face the audience
       BROTHER 1CL-WALK TO VILLAGE

Gaze: (shifting)—gaze down at the surrogate audience in the surrogate
       space

Body: -- shoulder tilt at left
                I-INFORM-YOU 'WELL' I TELL YOU BOY COME=+++
GAZE: gaze at the actual audience
BODY: -----face the audience
                HE REFUSE "WELL."
                The brother walked back to the village and informed the people,
                I told the boy to come back in but he refused.

**3. Switch From Third-Person Discourse (Indirect Quotation) in the Text Into
Constructed First-Person Discourse.** Traditionally, indirect speech is viewed
as a third person relaying what was said, as in Example 5.

Example 5
A little boy stopped him and asked him if he could go fishing with him
(p. 7).

The implication is that he actually said, "Can I go fishing with you?" It
does not necessarily imply that he said those words exactly, but it indicates
that some words to that effect were spoken. It is a speech-based statement
in third-person form. This type of indirect talk typically takes advantage
of *ask, say, inform,* and so forth, to introduce the statement. The text had
a few examples of this type of indirect speech, and those instances in this
study were often converted by the teacher into first-person constructed
dialogue. In doing this, the teacher shifted her eye gaze away from the
class into the surrogate space and then tilted her shoulder to the right
side and took the role of the little boy gazing up at the Chinese brother
(see Example 6).

Example 6
Gaze: -----gaze-audience (shifting)-----gaze up at the surrogate Brother
Body: ------face the audience -------------------- shoulder-tilt at right
                LITTLE BOY STOP   ASK   MIND CAN GO FISHING WITH YOU
                (The little boy stopped and asked, do you mind if I go fishing
                with you?)

When the teacher got to the indirect discourse, she shifted into the
role of the boy, thus turning the indirect textual discourse into direct
constructed discourse.

**4. Conversion of a Textual Communicative Action Into a Form of First-Person
Speech.** Other parts of the text were also converted to constructed first-
person dialogue, but they did not fit exactly into the traditional description
of indirect speech. The common property of these parts of the text was

an implication of communication. Actions such as begging, deciding, and smiling can have an intention and a particular meaning behind them and can therefore be deciphered into speech. There are certain verbs that are communicative in nature and can imply that speech has taken place (see the marked arrow in Example 7).

Example 7
> A little boy stopped him and asked him if he could go fishing with him.
> No, it could not be done, said the first Chinese Brother.
→ But the little boy begged and begged. (p. 7)

What the little boy said is not made explicit, but the action of begging implies that he could have said something. Begging, in most cases, is a verbal activity. Some of the teachers completed and added the third phrase, "Please can I . . ." after the word *beg*, as in Example 8. This is speech implied by the descriptive verb *to beg*.

Example 8
Gaze: -------------------------- gaze up
Body: -------------------- shoulder-tilt on the right side
       PLEASE CAN ME GO WITH YOU PLEASE
       The boy insisted, "Please can I go with you, please . . ."

We see here that the verb *beg*, which in the book is a third-person descriptive verb, had been added with the direct quotation, "Please can I go with you, please?" converted into first-person discourse; and this plausible conversation fits with the word *beg*.

Some of the actions described in the text did not have any implied speech behind them, but they functioned as communicative actions that were sometimes converted into a form of first-person speech (see the marked arrow in Example 9).

Example 9
→ But the second Chinese Brother got up and smiled.
   He was the one with the iron neck and they simply
   could not cut his head off. Everybody was angry
   and they decided that he should be drowned. (p. 26)

The brother's smile communicates to the crowd that he is still alive and well. This passage was sometimes decoded as a smile plus the first-person speech, "I'm fine!" or "I'm still alive!" The smile is a communicative action that implies those things. It does not necessarily mean that those things were said, but it has a communicative intention that could have been expressed through those words. The smile itself was sometimes used in first-person discourse, and further speech was added to it, as in Example 10.

Example 10
Gaze: ---------- at actual audience (shifting)—at the imaginary audience
Head: --------------at the audience (shifting)—above the actual audience
BUT SECOND CHINESE BROTHER GET-UP SMILE HELLO ME #OK:
But the Second Chinese Brother got up and said (smiling), "Hello I am okay"

The communicative intention behind the smile is translated into an actual first-person quote. He greets the audience and says that he is okay.

Another phrase considered to be implied speech was "They decided." The verb *decide* does not always indicate a verbal activity; it can be a private, mental activity. But when a decision is made by a group, that implies that some discussion has led to the decision, as in Example 11 from the text. The crowd has just failed to execute the Chinese brother for the fourth time:

Example 11
       Everybody was getting more and more angry every minute and they
→   all decided to smother him.

Compare this with the retelling by one of the teachers in Example 12.

Example 12
Gaze: ----------------------------gaze up at the imaginary Chinese brother
Body: --- rotate and tilt to left
(2h) CL: 4-LOOK-AT: "crowd of people look at the second brother"
MUST 'WELL' SOMETHING PUNISH AGAIN MUST
"We must do something and must punish him again"

The signer in this case took up the role of the crowd using group-indicating gaze and discussed what they should do about the Chinese Brother after their second attempt to execute him failed, followed by a first-person interpretation of the resolution they came to.

RESULTS

Two analyses were conducted for each teacher. First, a comparison of the 19 instances of textual direct dialogue to the number of instances of teachers' constructed direct dialogue was made. This includes number of instances of existing textual discourse being expanded into completely new constructed dialogue not in the book, as well as the number of instances of teachers' switching from textual indirect dialogue and communicative actions into constructed direct dialogue.

The results of the first analysis are displayed in Fig. 11.3. Note that some teachers would delete textual discourse instances and some would expand on the existing dialogue instances, adding completely new instances not in the book. As shown in Fig. 11.3, Teacher 1 followed the textual direct quotations 19 out of 19 times, expanding 11 times on the existing dialogue instances, and creating two completely new dialogue instances. Teacher 2 reduced the textual direct dialogue instances from 19 to 10 and expanded the existing direct dialogue instances five times. Teacher 3 reduced the textual instances from 19 to 14 and expanded twice and created only one new dialogue instance. Teacher 4 followed the textual direct quotations 19 out of 19 times and expanded on the existing quotations one time. Teacher 5 reduced the textual direct instances from 19 to 14 times and did not expand or create any new instances.

The results of the second analysis, shown in Fig. 11.4, investigated whether teachers would switch from textual third-person discourse or communicative actions into constructed first-person dialogue or add an utterance to complete the dialogue (e.g., "The little boy begged and begged").

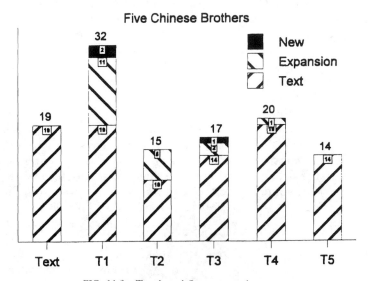

FIG. 11.3. Text-based first-person discourse.

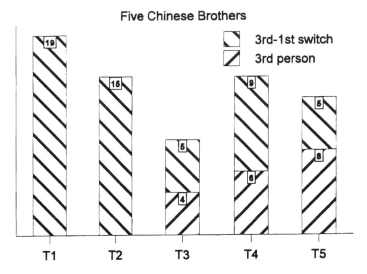

FIG 11.4. Text-based third-person discourse

Teacher 1 switched from textual third-person dialogue instances into first-person constructed dialogue instances 19 times. Teacher 2 reconstructed 15 third-person phrases into first-person discourse. Teacher 3 had five instances of this switch and four instances of indirect discourse that she left in third-person discourse. Teacher 4 had nine instances of the switch and six instances of indirect discourse. Teacher 5 had five instances of this switch and eight instances of third-person discourse.

We examined further why four teachers were not consistently using first-person discourse. We were able to pinpoint three main distractions that caused them to miscue the use of specific devices. These distractions were (a) gazing back to the book for the next story line, (b) dealing with a student's interruption, and (c) answering or clarifying students' questions. Sometimes they would switch from the use of visual involvement-focused dialogue to auditory involvement-focused dialogue during the middle of their constructed dialogue. It could be that they were not aware of this transition.

Teacher 1 did not have any of these problems. This may have something to do with her book-reading style. During the interview, she reported her strong belief that one should get the feeling of a story first by reading a book beforehand and then telling it all the way through without the book. That way, she said, one would be able to focus on storytelling in signing. Thus, she was consistent with the full use of visual involvement-focused style storytelling.

Teacher 2 had two kinds of pauses that might interrupt her storytelling flow. The first kind of pause was used to ask students questions about the story (e.g., *What do you think will happen next?*). When asked her why she employed this strategy, she reported that checking out with her students would help her know if the students could follow her story. The second kind of pause was to interrupt her storytelling and ask her students to stop talking. We decided to examine further why her students would talk. We found that they were trying to figure out what the teacher had said such as, "WHO SAID THAT?" or "I THOUGHT THE CHINESE BROTHER SAID THAT NOT THE JUDGE?"

Discussing among themselves and trying to repair a teacher's miscue are very common among hearing, minority students in White classrooms, as well as among deaf students (Johnson & Erting, 1989; Mather, 1987). It appears that Teacher 2 misinterpreted her students' behavior and thought they were chatting. She did not realize that her students were trying to repair her miscue. Also, her students would ask her a question after they failed to repair her miscue during their discussion. She would then nod her head and smile and continue her book reading without answering their question.

Kluwin (1981), Dillon (1982), Wood, Wood, Griffiths, and Howarth (1986), Mather (1987, 1989), and Rodda and Grove (1987) found similar problems among teachers. Ewoldt and Saulnier (1992) pointed out in their 5-year study of literacy that teachers often miscued their signing as well as failed to detect students' questions by either giving a wrong answer or discarding their question as off the point. They strongly suggested that teachers should try to figure out why students asked those questions, especially when teachers already "mentioned" them during their book reading.

During the interview, Teacher 2 was asked if she had any problems telling a story. She admitted that she had trouble trying to remember the places for surrogate characters (even though she could remember the dialogue lines) at the same time as trying to juggle several devices. That, she felt, really interrupted her thought process. However, in spite of some problems, Teacher 2 still was able to use visual involvement-focused story-telling fully (30 constructed dialogue instances out of 19 textual first-person discourse instances). If it were not for her miscues, her scores would have been much higher.

As for Teacher 3, we were able to identify two problems causing her to miscue or delete some story lines. First, she had to pause in her storytelling to answer a student's question and once in a while she also had to ask a particular student who "talked" to himself to pay attention. We noticed that she would switch from first-person speech into third-person discourse in the middle of her imaginary dialogue either after answering a question or after going back to the book to read it again. For example, when she took up the role of a first-person character (e.g., the role of the Chinese Brother), she began her first-person dialogue line in surrogate space and realized that a student was not paying attention or was asking a question. She would pause in the middle of her line and deal with the student. After handling the student, she would turn her gaze back to the book. That was when she switched from the original first-person dialogue to third-person dialogue. It appeared that printed English in the book might have influenced her thought process. The other miscue she made was after she had paused to deal with a student and went back to continue her imaginary dialogue, and she made a mistake on one of her cues by gazing up instead of gazing down.

During the interview she mentioned that she followed the story and used ASL principles as much as she could; however, she admitted that she had ambiguous feelings about using MCE and following the story word for word with her students, as required by her school policy. She would use ASL if there were no hard of hearing students in her class. Another possible problem that caused her to confuse her devices was switching between using visual involvement-focused dialogue and auditory involvement-focused dialogue. Evidence of this was when she switched styles. At first, she would follow the textual first-person discourse in surrogate space and then shift slowly into the audience space. One of her students would reply, "YES, MY BROTHER . . ." or "I CAN HOLD WATER." She corrected him and told him that the story was about the Chinese Brother. Unlike Teacher 2, who failed to detect the students' questions or discussion, Teacher 3 had excellent signing receptive skills and was able to handle or clarify her students' question-like statements or comments. However, she apparently did not realize how auditory involvement-focused dialogue can confuse her students.

Teachers 4 and 5 both said during the interview that they strongly believed they should follow the storybook, word for word. However, this study showed that both of them did not follow the story exactly, especially Teacher 4, who made a drastic change in her storytelling (29 out of 19). The change was so dramatic that Teacher 5 came to Teacher 4 right after her storytelling and asked her why she did not follow the story. Her reply was, "I CAN'T HELP BUT I FEEL SO INVOLVED WITH THIS STORY THAT I FORGOT THAT I WAS SUPPOSED TO FOLLOW WORD FOR WORD. I AM SORRY."

The principal investigator had the opportunity to ask Teacher 4 why she shifted from the use of MCE to ASL. The teacher admitted that she found herself using ASL more and more over the years because she felt intuitively ("INSIDE HER") that using ASL made more sense to her. Also, she said she noticed that her students seemed to be drawn into her storytelling more when she used ASL.

For Teacher 5, the main problem was with the use of spaces for different characters. She did not keep the spaces separate: She read the book (or faced the audience) and signed simultaneously, regardless of whether the dialogue was direct or indirect. She even used both spaces (the book and the audience) for surrogate space as well. This explains why she had many miscues in her use of devices and her total number of instances of first-person dialogue was not as high as others. This does not mean that she and others were poor storytellers. They may simply be unaware of a deaf audience's sensitivity to eye contact.

IMPLICATIONS AND DISCUSSION

This study shows that regardless of hearing status and language use, one should keep the two different styles of involvement-focused storytelling separate; that is, a visual involvement-focused style and an auditory involvement-focused style. For example, the book authors used the involvement-focused style by using a first-person quotation such as "The first Chinese Brother said, 'Your Honor, will you allow me to go and bid my mother good-bye?' " (p. 22). The reader recognizes that the story is about two characters who engage in an imaginary dialogue rather than between the reader and the author, in spite of the fact that the author uses English first- and second-person pronouns (*I, You, My,* and *Your*) in the story.

Hearing students have a similar experience when they listen to a teacher's storytelling and know that their teacher is not referring to herself as *I* and to the hearing students as *You.* They have the advantage of not needing to use their eyes to watch the teacher relate an imaginary dialogue. As for the deaf audience, the teacher has to avoid eye contact with them and employ a different strategy—visual involvement. For example, in any signed language, one will use the sign "YOU" by pointing one's finger at that person, indicating "YOU." Thus, when one uses the sign "YOU" at an audience of deaf students, they will think the teacher is referring to them as "YOU." So the members of the deaf community adapted and employed a different strategy that would not create this continued eye contact between a narrator and the audience. They created two separate spaces, audience space and surrogate space. In order to use surrogate space, one has to mark it with eye gaze (to indicate the height of a person) and then use the right-tilt marker for the first person and the left-tilt marker for the second person (so the audience knows who said what to whom. The teacher is freed from eye contact with her deaf students and uses the sign, "YOU" to refer to the surrogate person, thus maintaining the spaces separately. This is one of the primary visual involvement strategies in book reading.

One must not only know the difference between auditory involvement strategies and visual involvement strategies in storytelling, one must also manage the consistent devices that keep the two spaces—audience and surrogate—separate, by knowing when to give a signal before one can shift eye gaze from the audience to the surrogate and vice versa, and by maintaining the same location via tilt markers (e.g., right for the first surrogate character and left for the second surrogate character) within the surrogate space. These devices for creating visual involvement-focused dialogue during storytelling are a constant challenge for anyone who learns a signed language as their second language, as well as those who must manage student behavior during storytelling.

In summary, Teacher 1 was the only teacher who created many more dialogue instances (three times more) than appeared in the text and more than any of the other teachers. She also was the only one with a consistent use of first-person discourse, including the correct devices (e.g., eye gaze, tilt markers, and space). Thus, we predicted that it would be far easier to follow Teacher 1's storytelling because she used correct first-person discourse in a visual way more consistently than any other teacher. When we asked informants, both hearing and deaf students and staff with excellent receptive signing skills, to watch her and other teachers' storytelling on videotapes, they all said that they could follow her story and felt drawn into the tale and involved with her ever engaging dialogue. She was much like the Brazilian storyteller who used the high involvement style by creating more constructed dialogue turns (Ott, 1979). This might explain why there were no interruptions from her students, who seemed to be mesmerized by her storytelling. Thus, she was able to tell the story straight through without ever having to reread the story or handle her students at all.

This could mean two things for students. First, the strategy of creating high-involvement in storytelling visually helps involve students in the reading activity by drawing students into imagining the scene in which characters have a lively face-to-face conversation. It will delight students, as images help create a scene visually. In turn, they can imagine what things or people look like. A direct dialogue helps create a scene visually by demonstrating what people say and look like (instead of sound like). Thus, the representation of the visual scene and direct speech are considered essential to the accurate representation of characters and their worlds. Davidson, Lia, and Troyer (1988) suggested that the more the adult involves the child in the reading activity, the more the child benefits.

The second impact is when a teacher misses one of the devices for first-person discourse or switches from the visual involvement-focused dialogue to the auditory one, or vice versa. This miscue could interrupt students' thought flow, forcing them to try to clarify the teacher's confusing signal(s) by either figuring this out in their heads or discussing the miscue with one of their peers. They might not be able to sit back and enjoy the story in a leisurely fashion without having to figure out constantly what the teacher means. In addition, if students cannot follow their teachers' storytelling, they may be prevented from being able to read the book on their own.

Krashen (personal communication, 1996), who is noted for his theory of second language acquisition, agreed that reading books can and does help English as second language students acquire written English literacy without having to acquire spoken English. Something we need to examine further is to what extent deaf students can acquire written English via books.

Regardless of their language use or hearing status, teachers and parents should be able to create a sense of involvement by using visual and correct devices; otherwise, teachers' storytelling will be senseless or confusing and will prevent students from being able to understand and read books on their own.

This study strongly suggests that sign language and deaf education programs should develop courses that will teach parents and students how to use direct-dialogue devices for creating a visual effect of first-person discourse and to be aware of the difference between the auditory involvement-focused style and the visual involvement-focused style in storytelling. That way, they can keep those styles separate, one for hearing audiences and the other for deaf audiences. No matter how much they want to use the same strategy for hearing students, they still cannot avoid the issue of eye contact. It is essential that all teachers, parents, and interpreters of the deaf be aware of this issue.

ACKNOWLEDGMENTS

The authors thank Robert C. Johnson and Connie Gartner for proofreading this chapter; Arika Okrent for her wonderful and invaluable assistance and comments with this project including editing consultation; Scott Liddell for his helpful comments; Charles Robinson for his art work; and Jill Morford, Charlene Chamberlain, and Rachel Mayberry for their support in this project.

REFERENCES

Bahan, B. (1996). *Non-manual realization of agreement in American Sign Language* Unpublished doctoral dissertation, Boston University, MA.

Bishop, C. H., & Wiese, K. (1965). *The five Chinese brothers.* New York: Coward-McCann.

Chafe, W. (1982). Integration and involvement in speaking, writing, and oral literature. In F. O. Roy (Series Ed.) & D. Tannen (Vol. Ed.), *Spoken and written language: Exploring orality and literacy* (pp. 35–53). Norwood, NJ: Ablex.

Davidson, J. L., Lia, D., & Troyer, C. R. (1988). Emerging literacy: What we know should determine what we do. In J. L. Davidson (Ed.), *Counterpoint and beyond: A response to becoming a nation of readers* (pp. 17–26). Urbana, IL: National Council of Teachers of English.

Davies, S. (1983). The tongue is quicker than the eye: Nonmanual behaviors in ASL. In W. Stokoe & V. Volterra (Eds.), *Proceedings of the International Symposium on Sign Language Research* (pp. 185–193). Silver Spring, MD: Linstok Press.

Dillon, J. T. (1982). The effect of questions in education and other enterprises. *Journal of Curriculum Studies, 14,* 127–165.

Engberg-Pedersen, E. (1992, July). *Speech reports, reported thought, and other kinds of reports.* Paper presented at Theoretical Issues in Sign Language Research IV, San Diego, California.

Ewoldt, C., & Saulnier, A. (1992). *Engaging in literacy: A longitudinal study with three to seven year old deaf participants* (Report by the Center for Studies in Education and Human Development). Washington, DC: Gallaudet University.

Johnson, R., & Erting, C. (1989). Ethnicity and socialization in a classroom for deaf children. In C. Lucas (Ed.), *The sociolinguistics of the deaf community* (pp. 41–83). New York: Academic Press.

Johnson, R. E., Liddell, S. K., & Erting, C. J. (1989). *Unlocking the curriculum Principles for achieving access in deaf education* (Working Paper No. 89-3). Washington, DC: Gallaudet University, Gallaudet Research Institue.

Kluwin, T. (1981). The grammaticality of manual representations of English in classroom setting. *American Annals of the Deaf, 126,* 417–421.

Labov, W. (1972). The transformation of experience in narrative syntax. In W. Labov (Ed.), *Language in the inner city* (pp. 354–396). Philadelphia: University of Pennsylvania Press.

Lentz, E. M. (1986). Strategies for teaching verbs and role shifting. In C. Padden (Ed.), *Proceedings of the 4th international symposium on sign language research and teaching* (pp. 58–59). Silver Spring, MD: NAD.

Liddell, S. (1980). *American Sign Language syntax.* The Hague: Mouton.

Liddell, S. (1995). Real, surrogate, and token space: Grammatical consequences in ASL. In K. Emmorey & J. Reilly (Eds.), *Language, gesture, and space* (pp. 19–41). Hillsdale, NJ: Lawrence Erlbaum Associates.

Lillo-Martin, D. (1992, July). *The point of view predicate in American Sign Language.* Paper presented at Theoretical Issues in Sign Language Research IV, San Diego, California.

Mather, S. M. (1987). Eye gaze and communication in a deaf classroom. *Sign Language Studies, 54,* 11–30.

Mather, S. M. (1989). Visually oriented teaching strategies with deaf preschool children. In C. Lucas (Ed.), *Sociolinguistics of the deaf community* (pp. 165–187). New York: Academic Press.

Mather, S. M. (1990). Home and classroom communication. In D. F. Moores & K. P. Meadow-Orlans (Eds.), *Educational and developmental aspects of deafness* (pp. 232–254). Washington, DC: Gallaudet University Press.

Mather, S. M. (1991). *The discourse marker OH in typed telephone conversations among deaf typists.* Unpublished doctoral dissertation, Georgetown University, Washington, DC.

Mather, S. M. (1997). Initiation in visually constructed dialogue: Reading books with three-to eight-year-old students who are deaf and hard of hearing. In C. Lucas (Ed.), *Multicultural aspects of sociolinguistics in deaf communities* (pp. 109–131). Washington, DC: Gallaudet University Press.

Meier, R. (1990). Person deixis in American Sign Language. In S. Fischer & P. Siple (Eds.), *Theoretical issues in sign language research* (Vol. 1, pp. 165–190). Chicago: University of Chicago Press.

Ochs, E. (1979). Planned and unplanned discourse. In T. Givón (Ed.), *Syntax and semantics: Discourse and syntax* (pp. 51–80). New York: Academic Press.

Ott, M. M. B. (1983). *Orality and literacy in Brazilian and American storytelling: A comparative study* Unpublished manuscript, Georgetown University.

Padden, C. (1986). Verbs and role-shifting in American Sign Language. In C. Padden (Ed.), *Proceedings of the 4th international symposium on sign language research and teaching* (pp. 44–57). Silver Spring, MD: NAD.

Padden, C. (1990). The relation between space and grammar in ASL verb morphology. In C. Lucas (Ed.), *Sign language research theoretical issues* (pp. 118–132). Washington, DC: Gallaudet University Press.

Rodda, M., & Grove, C. (1987) *Language, cognition, and deafness.* Hillsdale, NJ: Lawrence Erlbaum Associates.

Schiffrin, D. (1981). Tense variation in narrative. *Language, 57,* 45–62.

Tannen, D. (1982). Oral and literate strategies in spoken and written narratives. *Language, 58,* 1–21.

Tannen, D. (1985). Relative focus on involvement in oral and written discourse. In D. R. Olson, N. Torrance, & A. Hildyard (Eds.), *Literacy, language, and learning: The nature and consequences of reading and writing* (pp. 124–147). Cambridge, England: Cambridge University Press.

Tannen, D. (1986). Introducing constructed dialogue in Greek and American conversational and literary narrative. In F. Coulmas (Ed.), *Direct and indirect speech* (pp. 311–332). Berlin, Germany: Mouton.

Tannen, D. (1988). Hearing voices in conversation, fiction, and mixed genres. In D. Tannen (Ed.), *Linguistics in context: Connecting observation and understanding* (pp. 89–113). Norwood, NJ: Ablex.

Tannen, D. (1989). *Talking voices: Repetition, dialogue, and imagery in conversational discourse.* Cambridge, England: Cambridge University Press.

Valli, C., & Lucas, C. (1995) *Linguistics of American Sign Language: An introduction* (2nd ed.). Washington, DC: Gallaudet University Press.

Winston, E. A. (1991). Spatial referencing and cohesion in an American Sign Language text. *Sign Language Studies, 73,* 397–410.

Winston, E. A. (1992). Space and involvement in an American Sign Language lecture. In J. Plant-Moeller (Ed.), *Expanding horizons: Proceedings of the 12th national convention of the registry of interpreters for the deaf* (pp. 93–105). Silver Spring, MD: RID Publications.

Wood, D. J., Wood, H., Griffiths, A., & Howarth, I. (1986). *Teaching and talking with deaf children.* New York: Wiley.

Chapter 12

Theorizing About the Relation Between American Sign Language and Reading

Charlene Chamberlain
Rachel I. Mayberry
McGill University

One of the oldest questions in the history of deaf education is whether and how signed language knowledge will affect the learning of spoken and written language. For at least 200 years, deaf education in North America has been fraught with the so-called oral–manual controversy (Moores, 1996). At the heart of this controversy is the question of what is the best way to teach deaf children to read and write and thus acquire the language of society. However, the "best way" is elusive. The ebb and flow of educational practice for most of this century, and much of the last, brought into vogue first one method (sign only), then the other (oral only), then a combination of the two, then back again to the first. All of this effort notwithstanding, deaf students on average still read at about a fourth-grade level when they leave high school (Allen & Schoem, 1997; Holt, Traxler, & Allen, 1997). This level is about the same as Pintner and his colleagues found in the early part of this century when deaf students' reading skills were first tested (Pintner, 1916, 1927; Reamer, 1921).

The purpose of this chapter is to reexamine the question of, and speculate about, the relation between skill in American Sign Language (ASL) and reading. The chapters in the second half of this book focus on the reading skills of deaf children who use signed language as a primary language. Thus, we have three main goals for this chapter. The first goal is to situate these chapters in a historical context of previous research on the relationship between signed language and reading. The literature reviewed is by no means exhaustive but is intended instead to be illustrative. The point is to show that signed language skills have often played an important role in the examination of reading skills in deaf students and to explain how the present chapters are the next step in the historical conceptualization of the question. The second goal is to provide a theoretical framework for the present chapters, based on a current theory of the reading process developed for hearing readers, and to examine how signed languages may fit with it. We propose that the "simple view of reading" (Hoover & Gough, 1990) provides a useful framework for investigating important issues in the course of reading developmental in deaf children. The third goal is to point out areas in need of further research and to propose alternative research designs and methodologies that can help address these areas of research need.

SIGNED LANGUAGE AND READING: THE RESEARCH EVOLUTION

A review of past research shows that signed language, or "manual communication" as it was sometimes called, was often included in research designs as a grouping variable but not tested explicitly. The studies reported in the chapters of this book represent the next step in this research evolution because the significance of signed language was recognized and explicitly measured. Before discussing recent research, however, we describe early research that did not directly measure ASL skill.

Classroom Language: Manual Versus Oral Versus Combined

One of the first researchers to adapt language and cognitive measures used with hearing children for use with deaf children was Pintner and his colleagues (Pintner, 1916, 1927; Pintner & Paterson, 1917, 1918; Reamer, 1921). In what was the better part of three decades of research, Pintner and his colleagues carried out some of the largest existing studies of deaf students' reading and language skills, testing several thousand deaf students. Pintner's studies have only been surpassed in size by the Stanford Achievement Test norming projects that began in the late 1960s.

Pintner first began his work with deaf students by testing their cognitive skills. However, he soon realized the importance of investigating their language abilities, due to what he observed to be the deaf children's limited language, which he defined as knowledge of written English. Interestingly, Pintner (1916) presaged the current educational trend of bilingual education for deaf children by making the point that "the acquisition of language by a deaf child is somewhat analogous to the acquisition of a foreign language by a hearing child. If the data were at hand, it would be interesting to compare the rate of acquisition of language by the deaf with the rate of acquisition of a foreign language by a hearing child not living in the country in which the foreign language is spoken" (p. 425).

In two detailed studies examining reading comprehension skills (although they were referred to simply as "language abilities" in these studies), Pintner and Paterson (1917, 1918) tested a total of 1,235 deaf students, 9 to 20 years old. The measure used in the first study was the Trabue Language Scale (Pintner, 1916). In the second study, the measure was the Woodworth and Well's Directions Test (Pintner & Paterson, 1917). The Trabue scale is what is now referred to as a cloze test, where a child is given written sentences with words missing and must fill in the blanks. The Directions test was essentially a sentence comprehension task. For example, the student read a sentence like, "Cross out the g in tiger" and needed to follow the written direction. In both studies, the authors compared the performance of students from oral classes with students from "manual" classes. No explicit measure of signed language competence was included in either study.

The findings were similar for both studies. On the Trabue Language Scale, the oral student group had higher median scores than the manual students with grade equivalents of approximately 4.5 and 3.5, respectively (Pintner, 1916). No tests of statistical significance were provided, however. It is important to note that doing so would have required calculation of statistics by hand, because there were no calculators or computers at the time. Pintner's explanation for this apparent difference in performance was that the "brighter" students were chosen for oral work. However, it is important to note that this was also at a time when technology was not available to test hearing. It is more likely that the hearing levels of the oral students were higher than the manual students and they were perhaps better readers for that reason. Degree of hearing loss plays a large role in reading success because it is a causal factor in the acquisition of spoken language (Allen & Schoem, 1997; Conrad, 1979). However, it is impossible to know if this difference was statistically significant, which makes the finding difficult to interpret. On the Directions Test, the oral students apparently performed at higher levels than the manual students, but this was not until after age 14 (Pintner & Paterson, 1917).

Reamer (1921), a student of Pintner's, expanded this work to include a more extensive battery of cognitive tests and eight educational tests, including four measures of reading comprehension and writing skills. Reading comprehension was measured by the Trabue Scale, a vocabulary measure, a silent reading comprehension measure, and a grammar and punctuation test. Reamer tested a total of 2,172 students, aged 8 to 21, at 26 schools for the deaf. Her experimental design again included a comparison of oral and manual students with the addition of "combined" students, that is, those students exposed to both spoken and signed languages.

In contrast to Pintner's earlier finding, Reamer (1921) instead found no apparent difference in performance between the "pure oral" and "pure manual" students on either of the cognitive or reading comprehension (educational) measures. In fact, she stated that "in psychological terminology we see no indication of additional transfer from speech and lip-reading to reading and writing English, over and above any transfer that may exist from signing and fingerspelling to these subjects of instruction" (p. 101).

In 1927, Pintner and Paterson published a replication of Reamer's (1921) study using the same test batteries with 4,452 deaf students, aged 12 to 25. These students were from 41 schools for the deaf, including 13 day schools and 28 residential schools. The design of this study was nearly identical to the Reamer study. Interestingly, their findings were similar to their previous findings and in contrast to Reamer's findings. They found that the oral students apparently performed at higher levels than the manual and combined students on the educational test battery, including the tests of reading comprehension. Because both studies included students from what would appear to be nearly every deaf school in the United States, it is likely that many of the same students were tested in both studies.

Even in these very early studies of deaf students' reading skills, a speculative link between signed language and reading is evident. This link was made through the grouping of students vis-à-vis the modality of instruction coupled with testing of reading and other educational skills. Skills in signed language were not explicitly tested, and there is no indication that these researchers suspected that deaf children from deaf families would perform any differently compared to deaf children from hearing families. This insight would come much later. In the ensuing decades, the wave of educational practice changed from various approaches—oral, manual, or combined—to one approach, oral only (Moores, 1996). This change effectively washed away any notion that signed language skills would have any bearing on reading development or on the educational progress of deaf children.

In an early and often cited study, Pugh (1946) provided indirect, yet positive, evidence of a relation between signed language and reading. She tested the reading abilities of deaf students and one of the comparisons she made was between students from day and residential schools. Although there was no explicit mention of signed language skills, there is nonetheless an indirect link to signed language. Even though the prevailing method of classroom instruction was oral-only by the mid 1940s, most deaf parents sent their deaf children to residential schools rather than to day schools. So, although classroom instruction would have been oral-only, the language outside the classroom would have been signed language in the dorms and playgrounds. Indeed, Pugh found an apparent difference in performance between the day and residential students. The residential students outperformed the day school students (particularly at older ages) on two standardized reading tests.

Deaf Families Versus Hearing Families

A more direct approach to investigating the possible link between signed language and reading was forming in the late 1950s. Anecdotal reports were beginning to surface from teachers of deaf children who noticed that those from deaf families seemed to do better than those from hearing families on reading and writing and overall in academic achievement (Stuckless & Birch, 1966). Several studies around this time investigated the educational achievement of deaf students and included a comparison between deaf children from deaf families and deaf children from hearing families. But deaf children from deaf families constitute less than 10% of the deaf population, and this occasionally led to small sample sizes that would make it difficult to find statistically significant differences. Nevertheless, the majority of these studies found positive effects of signed language exposure on reading skills and academic performance. Signed language skills were not explicitly tested in any way, however. It is important to remember that, by this time, all schools had oral-only instruction (Moores, 1996). So the comparison of deaf of deaf and deaf of hearing meant comparing those students who were exposed to signed language at home with those who were not; all the students in the sample had oral-only language of instruction at school.

One of these small sample size studies was conducted by Goetzinger and Rousey (1959). These researchers tested a total of 101 deaf students ranging in age from 14 to 21. All but 3 of the students were from residential schools and 10 students came from deaf families. In one of the several comparisons made in this study, Goetzinger and Rousey compared a group of 8 deaf of deaf and 8 deaf of hearing on a standardized reading test, matching the groups on IQ, age, and years in school. The findings showed no significant differences between these two groups of students; both groups were reading at approximately the fourth-grade level (Goetzinger & Rousey, 1959). These researchers concluded that these results provided evidence that early use of signed language did not lead to enhanced reading achievement as measured by this test. But this conclusion was inadequate: Conclusive evidence cannot be argued with a negative finding from such a small sample size. Finding no difference between groups is not proof that differences do not exist (Cozby, 1985). Conclusive evidence that no differences exist would require several well-designed studies with adequate sample sizes, all showing no difference.

In contrast to Goetzinger and Rousey (1959), however, several other studies with much larger sample sizes did find a positive relation between native signed language skills and academic achievement, including reading comprehension. For example, Vernon and Koh (1970) reviewed a decade of studies that investigated the deaf family versus hearing family comparison; they also conducted a large study of their own. The findings of all the reviewed studies showed that deaf children with deaf parents performed better on tests of reading and academic achievement than the oral-only students, those with hearing families (Vernon & Koh, 1970).

In one particularly large study, Stuckless and Birch (1966) tested 105 deaf students with deaf parents and 337 deaf students with hearing parents. The students were tested with a battery of tests of speech skills, reading comprehension, speechreading, written language, and psychosocial adjustment. From this sample of 442 students, 38 pairs of deaf of deaf and deaf of hearing, matched on IQ, sex, hearing levels, and number of years in school, were selected for further comparison. The average age of both groups was 14. The results showed that the deaf of deaf students performed at significantly higher levels on three of the five measures: reading comprehension, written language, and speech reading. There were no differences between the groups on the remaining two measures—speech and psychosocial adjustment (Stuckless & Birch, 1966). The authors also reported that, despite the fact that the deaf of deaf performed at higher levels than the deaf of hearing students, both groups were reading at less than a fourth-grade level (Stuckless & Birch, 1966).

Vernon and Koh (1970) also tested a large sample of 269 deaf students ranging in age from 11 to 20. The test battery was similar to that used by Stuckless and Birch (1966) and included measures of reading, writing, speech skills, and psychological adjustment. Another similar design feature was that the authors matched 32 pairs of deaf of deaf and deaf of hearing students from the larger sample, controlling for age, sex, and IQ. Their findings were consistent with the previous studies; the deaf of deaf students scored at significantly higher levels on all measures of reading and writing achievement than the deaf of hearing, and there were no differences on any of the speech measures (Vernon & Koh, 1970). When the sample was broken down by age group, the deaf of deaf scored almost 1.5 years ahead of the deaf of hearing at each age on academic achievement measures. Although the reading levels of these students did not match appropriate grade levels for hearing students of the same age, the deaf of deaf group achieved a ninth-grade level by age 18 to 20, and the deaf of hearing group achieved a fifth-grade level. These authors concluded that early exposure to signed language facilitated academic achievement and linguistic development and therefore should be encouraged.

To summarize, this brief overview of several decades of research revealed that most studies showed a positive effect of signed language on reading and academic achievement. However, none of these studies actually measured signed language skills. Instead, the research strategy was to make knowledge of signed language a dichotomous, independent factor. The researchers assumed that the students they tested either did or did not have knowledge of signed language. This judgment was based on either the hearing status of the students' parents or the locus of their schooling. This classification was then used as a grouping variable: plus or minus knowledge of sign language. It would be easy to dismiss these early studies as being inadequate for not including any direct measures of deaf students' signed language skill, but precisely what skills would these investigators have assessed? Scientific analysis of the linguistic structure of signed languages is recent. Stokoe's pioneering description of ASL lexical structure did not appear until 1965 (Stokoe, Casterline, & Cronebeg, 1965). Linguistic, developmental, and psycholinguistic investigations of signed languages only became commonplace a decade or so later (e.g., Klima & Bellugi, 1979). Without the appropriate linguistic insights and tools, ASL skills could not be measured, in the same way that statistics could not be computed without calculators by Pintner and his colleagues in the earliest of studies.

Measures of ASL Emerge

The next step in the research evolution investigating signed language skills and reading began to take place in the early 1980s. A revolution in deaf education was taking place during the 1970s, as Moores (1996) described. This revolution entailed the return to a combined approach—speech and sign, for classroom instruction from an oral-only approach. The combined approach was actually the prevailing methodology in North America during the late 19th and early 20th centuries (Reamer, 1921). Two important factors led to this switch: the general dissatisfaction with the outcome of the oral-only approach (Mayberry, 1992; Moores & Sweet, 1990) and the cumulative findings of the research studies summarized earlier, namely, a positive effect of signed language knowledge on reading comprehension and academic achievement (Israelite, Ewoldt, & Hoffmeister, 1992). What this meant for investigating the relation between signed language skills and reading was that many deaf children were now exposed to some form of signed system in the classroom. These signed systems were seldom, if ever, a natural signed language such as ASL (Hoffmeister, chap. 9, this volume). Nonetheless, researchers recognized the importance of actually measuring signed language knowledge in some way rather than just using signed language as an independent grouping factor in experimental design.

Dissatisfaction with the oral-only approach for the development of reading skills came from the continued low levels of reading achievement of deaf and hard of hearing students compared to their age-matched, hearing peers. In the 1970s, the median grade-level reading of deaf students was at only about a third-grade level by the time they left high school (Allen, 1986; Trybus & Karchmer, 1977). This meant there had been no change in median reading levels since 1916. In light of these findings, two large federally funded projects were initiated, one in Canada and one in the United States, to investigate the predictive factors of reading skills in deaf and hard of hearing students. The Canadian project was conducted by researchers at McGill University (Donin, Doehring, & Browns, 1991; Mayberry, 1989; Mayberry & Chamberlain, 1994; Mayberry, Chamberlain, Waters, & Doehring, 1999; Mayberry & Waters, 1991; Waters & Doehring, 1990) and the U.S. project was conducted by researchers at the Central Institute for the Deaf (Geers & Moog, 1989) and Gallaudet University (Moores et al., 1987; Moores & Sweet, 1990).

Both the Canadian and U.S. projects had two separate streams. One stream investigated predictive factors in reading skills for oral-only students and another stream investigated the predictive factors for total communication or combined students. Of interest here are the studies examining the reading skills of total communication students, one conducted by Mayberry (1989; Mayberry & Chamberlain, 1994; Mayberry et al., 1999) and one conducted by Moores and his colleagues (Moores et al., 1987; Moores & Sweet, 1990). These were the first studies to include explicit measures of signed language skill in their research designs.

The design of the Gallaudet study (Moores et al., 1987; Moores & Sweet, 1990) was similar to the studies discussed in the previous section in that knowledge of signed language was used as a grouping variable. The research design was a departure from those of previous studies because there was no direct statistical comparison of the students from deaf families and students from hearing families. Instead, the purpose of the study was to investigate the predictive factors for literacy skills separately for the students in the these two groups. Moores et al. (1987) investigated the possible links between ASL and reading by testing 65 students with deaf parents and 65 students with hearing parents, ranging in age from 16 to 18. Both groups had the same average hearing loss, more than 100 dB in both ears. A total of 38 measures was used: 7 dependent (or criterion) measures of reading and 31 independent (or predicator) measures. The predictor variables included measures of academic achievement, English grammar and structure, communicative fluency, verbal and performance IQ, speech production, and hearing levels (Moores et al., 1987). The reading measures used were relatively standard for this population: the Stanford Reading Comprehension subtest, the comprehension subtest of the Peabody Individual Achievement Test, Gates-MacGinitie Reading Speed and Accuracy subtests, a cloze procedure, and a narrative comprehension and retelling test.

Of particular interest for our discussion here are the signed language tests. As Moores et al. (1987) reported, there were no reliable and valid measures of ASL vocabulary and grammar available at the time. So they used the Linguistic Proficiency Interview (LPI), which had previously been shown to be a reliable measure of second language proficiency (p. 57). The LPI is an interview format measure conducted by native language users. Interviewers are trained to rank the interviewee's proficiency on a 5-point scale from 0 (*no skill*) to 4 (*fluent skills*). Students in both groups were given the LPI in three modes: ASL, English-based signing, and oral English. The ASL scale did not capture much variability among the students from the deaf parent group: 53 of these 65 students scored at ceiling (4.0), with an overall average rating of 3.79. The overall average score of the hearing parent group was 3.31, but the authors did not report how many were at ceiling. Both groups had similar scores on the English-based signing measure, 2.97 for the deaf parent group and 2.85 for the hearing parent group. The oral language measure showed the widest range of scores for both groups—0 to 4—with the average for the deaf parent group being 1.3 and the average for the hearing parent group being 1.52. The Stanford Reading Comprehension grade-level scores were about sixth grade for the deaf parent group and about fifth grade for the hearing parent group.

A correlation analysis between the reading measures and the language proficiency measures showed the following findings. There were strong positive correlations between reading and other measures of English language knowledge. It is important to note that these tests were mostly administered in the read and written mode so that a strong correlation would be expected. Correlations between scores on the English-based sign and oral LPI with reading scores were moderate for both groups, between $r = .30$ to .42 (p .103). By contrast, the ASL measure showed no significant correlation with reading scores for either group (Moores & Sweet, 1990).

Moores et al. (1987) provided two possible explanations for the lack of correlation. The first was the independence of the two languages. Because ASL and English are completely different languages, a correlation between the two would not necessarily be expected. However, as we explain later, there is no evidence for this hypothesis. The other reason Moores et al. gave was the small range of scores on the ASL measure, particularly for the deaf parent group. Because the majority of these students scored at ceiling on the ASL LPI, which was a global 5-point scale to begin with, it would be difficult to find a correlation due to the lack of variation in scores.

In contrast to the lack of correlation of this large-scale study, Mayberry and her colleagues (1989; 1994; 1999) did find a positive correlation between a standardized reading test and comprehension of ASL. The purpose of this study was to see if reading comprehension skill varied as a function of amount and type of signed input (deaf family vs. hearing family). The main hypothesis guiding the research was that the quality and quantity of overall linguistic input that the deaf student receives is an important factor in reading development because it may be a causal factor in the development of signed language.

To examine this hypothesis, Mayberry and her colleagues (1989, 1994, 1999) conducted a cross-sectional, developmental study by testing 48 children in three age groups (7–9, 10–12, and 13–15 years) with equal numbers. Half the children at each age level were from hearing families where little if any signed language was used, and half the children were from deaf families where they were exposed to signed language from birth. The two groups were matched on age, sex, hearing loss, and nonverbal IQ at each age level. Most of the students attended day schools where the language of classroom instruction was some version of Manually Coded English (MCE), accompanied by spoken English, that is, "Total Communication." A few students from deaf families attended a residential school where the language of classroom instruction was also MCE and spoken English.

ASL comprehension was measured at the narrative and sentence level. Stories were created that used a traditional story grammar; two stories were given in sign. Each story was followed by a set of comprehension questions. Each question probed a different aspect of story grammar. In addition, some of the questions required understanding of information explicitly given in the story, whereas other questions required understanding of implicit information. Two different ASL stories were counterbalanced across the children so that half the children saw one ASL story and half saw another ASL story. The comprehension questions were given immediately after the story. The children responded in sign and their responses were videotaped and transcribed.

The second ASL measure used was the Sentence Span Test first devised by Daneman and Carpenter (1980). The task is a combination comprehension and working memory measure originally designed to measure ease of sentence comprehension. There were two parts to the task. First, the child was given a sentence and asked to say whether it was true or false. Next, the child was asked to remember the final sign of the sentence. After seeing each subsequent sentence and saying whether it was true or false, the child gave the final signs of the preceding sentences. The score for the task represented the number of sentences for which the child could remember the final signs. The sentence span task uses a dual task paradigm to measure the amount of mental effort required to comprehend sentences. The easier it is for a child to comprehend a sentence, the more spare mental capacity he or she has to remember the final signs of the previously comprehended sentences. The task is akin to reading text where previously comprehended information must be kept in memory to be linked with current sentences, except as Waters and Caplan (1996) pointed out, the to-be-remembered item is not related to the next sentence as it would be in reading.

Reading comprehension was measured in two ways. The first measure was comprehension of a written short story with the same story structure and types of questions as the two ASL stories. The children read the story and the questions but gave their answers in sign. The second measure was the reading comprehension subtest of the Stanford Achievement Test.

When Mayberry et al. (1989, 1994, 1999) analyzed the children's performance on the ASL comprehension task, they found that the children from deaf families outperformed those from hearing families on the ASL story measure at all age levels. Moreover, the magnitude of the difference increased with age. The same was true for performance on the ASL sentence span measure. On the reading story measure, the children from deaf families outperformed those from hearing families except at the youngest age, where there was no difference, as Fig. 12.1 shows. On the reading comprehension subtest of the Stanford, the children from deaf families outscored those from hearing families at all ages.

With respect to the question of whether knowledge of ASL is related to reading comprehension, Mayberry et al. (1989, 1994, 1999) conducted a series of correlations. There were strong positive correlations between the ASL comprehension measures and the reading measures. Comprehension of the ASL stories correlated with reading story comprehension, $r =$ .63, and with performance on the Stanford, $r = .69$. Performance on the ASL sentence span measure correlated with story reading comprehension, $r = .49$, and with the Stanford at $r = .49$. The latter correlation is similar to that found for hearing students' performance on measures of reading achievement and experimental measures of simultaneous reading comprehension and working memory, around $r = .41$ (Daneman & Merikle, 1996).

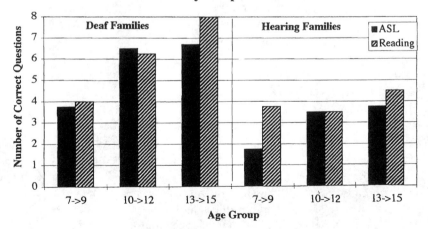

FIG. 12.1   Students' comprehension of stories given in either ASL or print, grouped by age level and ASL input (deaf or hearing families).

The Moores et al. (1987) and Mayberry et al. (1989, 1994, 1999) studies represent the first attempts to include explicit measures of signed language skill in investigating reading development of deaf children. However, there are more differences than similarities between these two studies. Mayberry's et al. (1989, 1994, 1999) study was developmental in design and examined reading comprehension as a function of amount and kind of linguistic input. The Moores et al. (1987) study investigated the correlates of reading comprehension in 16- to 18-year-olds, primarily examining variables of English language knowledge. Even though both studies measured signed language skills, the findings were different: Mayberry et al. found several positive correlations between ASL and reading skills but Moores et al. did not. This discrepancy is most likely due to the global nature of the LPI measure leading to an insensitivity to variability in signed language skill.

The research investigating reading skills of deaf students over the course of this century evolved in a logical pattern, beginning broadly with researchers using knowledge of signed language as a grouping variable to more narrowly focusing on knowledge of sign skill itself. This pattern involved a complex interplay between factors related to the classroom and home language environments and reading development. Signed language skills, although only explicitly measured within the last few years, have in fact been taken into consideration in reading research with deaf children historically. Not all researchers, however, concluded that signed language knowledge was helpful to reading development, particularly in the earliest studies. Yet, on the whole, the findings were mostly positive and rarely negative: Exposure to and knowledge of ASL was associated with higher performance on reading measures. The next step in this research evolution is represented by the chapters in the second half of this book. These studies are characterized by more refined measurement of ASL knowledge. The reason for this refinement was the accumulating understanding of the linguistic structure, acquisition, and processing of languages perceived by eye.

SIGNED LANGUAGE AND READING:
THE CURRENT PERSPECTIVE

The next step in examining the relation between ASL and reading is represented by the chapters in the second half of this book. All these studies are characterized by more refined measurement of ASL knowledge. This refinement is now possible due to the accumulating understanding of the structure of ASL, its acquisition, and its processing. Each study found a positive correlation between knowledge of ASL and reading skill. We now compare these studies and in doing so demonstrate the robustness of the findings.

The Strong and Prinz Study

Strong and Prinz (chap. 8, this volume; 1997) measured students' variability in ASL skill several ways. First, they tested 155 students who represented a wide age range, (8–15 years); 40 students had deaf mothers. The inclusion of students with deaf mothers ensured that a proportion of the students tested had native-like skill in ASL. The inclusion of these students provides a crucial test of the hypothesis that ASL development is related to reading, because these students would be expected to have developed ASL in a normal fashion—they presumably learned ASL from birth at home. The inclusion of native ASL learners also provides a means of replicating previous findings that native ASL learners outperform nonnatives on tests of academic achievement.

Second, Strong and Prinz (chap. 8, this volume; 1997) measured ASL skill with six tests, two production tasks and four comprehension tasks. One production and one comprehension task focused on a particular ASL structure—classifier constructions—whereas the other tasks encompassed multiple ASL structures at the sentence and narrative levels, as in telling and comprehending a story and comprehending calendar and map directions given in ASL. These researchers used a standardized test to measure reading, the Woodcock Johnson Test Battery, which assesses reading at the levels of single vocabulary items, sentences, and paragraphs. They also included three writing measures designed to measure vocabulary, syntax, and narration skills.

The relation between ASL knowledge and reading (and writing) was ascertained by computing correlations and statistical tests of differences. Before doing so, all the ASL tests were converted to a single composite score and all the reading and writing tests to another composite score. The correlation between the ASL composite score and the literacy composite score was $r = .58$ for the entire sample. When the correlations were broken down by age, they remained high and significant for students between the ages of 8 and 11 but not those between the ages of 12 and 15. Strong and Prinz (1997) attributed this to a lack of variability on the ASL measures for the oldest students. The difference tests showed that the students with deaf mothers outperformed those with hearing mothers, thus replicating the long line of research studies previously described.

The Hoffmeister Study

Hoffmeister (chap. 9, this volume) measured students' variability in ASL development in a fashion similar to Strong and Prinz (chap. 8, this volume; 1997). First, he tested 50 students who ranged in age from 8 to 16; 14 of the students had deaf parents. The inclusion of students with deaf parents, as in the previous study, provided an important control. This ensured that some students acquired ASL in a normal fashion, from birth at home. Hoffmeister's design included students from both residential and day schools because he had observed differences in the ASL environments of these two types of schools.

Second, Hoffmeister (chap. 9, this volume) measured ASL skills with three word knowledge tasks: ASL synonyms, antonyms, and plurals–quantifiers. He also measured MCE knowledge by testing recognition of complex English syntactic structures given in MCE. Reading skill was measured with the reading comprehension subtest of the Stanford. When he removed the effects of age by computing a partial correlation, he found that the students' performance on the ASL measures was positively correlated with their reading scores at levels of $r = .51$ to $.53$. Their performance on the MCE measure was also correlated with reading scores at a level of $r = .38$.

Linking his study with previous research, Hoffmeister (chap. 9, this volume) performed statistical difference tests that showed that the students with deaf parents outperformed the other students on all the measures: reading comprehension, ASL, and MCE. His findings, like those of Prinz and Strong (chap. 8, this volume; 1997), show that students' level of ASL development is related to their linguistic backgrounds and to their reading skills. The finding was demonstrated two ways in these two studies: Performance on ASL measures correlated with reading performance and the performance of students who acquired ASL in a normal fashion, from birth at home, was measurably higher than students whose linguistic histories were more variable.

The Padden and Ramsey Study

The approaches Padden and Ramsey (chap. 10, this volume) took to measuring ASL development among deaf students were both similar to and different from those of the previous studies. Padden and Ramsey selected important factors that characterized the student bodies at the two schools they studied, one residential and one day school. They observed that more students attending the residential school had deaf parents as compared to the day school. Also, more students attending the day school had other handicaps in addition to deafness compared to the residential school. There were also pedagogical differences between the educational settings: The educational approach at the residential school was more ASL based in comparison to the day school.

Using a database of 98 students whose grades ranged from elementary to middle school, Padden and Ramsey found, first, that four background factors were significantly associated with performance on the reading comprehension subtest of the Stanford. Having deaf parents correlated positively with reading scores; this finding replicated the findings of the previous studies. Having other handicaps and an older age of hearing-loss detection were negatively correlated with reading scores. The fourth background factor, which was positively correlated with reading scores, was the length of time at school. These findings are an important signed language counterpart to previous research with orally trained deaf students. Background factors such as degree of hearing loss, age of detection, family support, and additional handicaps have all been found to be associated with spoken language development in deaf students (Conrad, 1979; Geers & Moog, 1989).

Second, Padden and Ramsey measured students' ASL skill by testing 31 students from four classes: two fourth-grade classes (around 9 years of age) and two seventh-grade classes (around 11 years of age); one class at each grade was at the residential school and the other at the day school. They measured ASL skill with a set of five tasks: sentence order, verb agreement, sentence imitation, fingerspelling in sentences, and initialized signs in sentences. They measured reading skill with the reading comprehension subtest of the Stanford. Performing a series of correlations, they found that performance on the ASL measures was positively correlated with reading scores at levels of $r = .43$ to $.80$. However, the possible confound of age was not removed from these correlations. This important control is needed to ensure that the correlation between reading and ASL is not due to improvement on both tasks as a result of getting older.

These studies, in tandem with the earlier research described previously, demonstrate that ASL development is related to the reading skills of deaf students for whom signed language is a primary language. The findings show repeatedly that the direction of ASL and reading development are the same: Increases in ASL skills co-occur with increases in reading development, as shown in Table 12.1.

ASL Measures: Structures and Psycholinguistic Tasks

The studies included in this book assessed students' knowledge of different ASL linguistic structures with a wide array of psycholinguistic tasks. It is instructive to consider the variety of structures and tasks used in these studies. Doing so demonstrates that the similar findings across these studies are neither spurious nor narrow in scope but rather are robust and highly generalizable.

ASL Structures. The ASL structures assessed in these studies are best characterized by the fact that they do not overlap with written English and are not a part of the canonical structure of English-based sign, such as MCE. The fact that these studies assessed knowledge of ASL structures is very important. As Hoffmeister (chap. 9, this volume) explained, an im-

TABLE 12.1
Correlations Between ASL and Reading Measures: Summary of Research Studies

Research Study	ASL Measure	Reading Measure	Age	N	r
Moores et al (1987, 1990)	Language proficiency interview	Composite of five standardized tests	16–18	130	*ns*
Mayberry et al. (1989, 1994, 1999)	Story comprehension	Story comprehension	7–15	48	.63
	Story comprehension	Stanford			.69
	Sentence span	Story comprehension			.49
Strong and Prinz (1997, this volume)	Composite of 6 comprehension and production tasks	Composite of 6 reading and writing tests	8–15	155	.58
Hoffmeister (this volume)	Synonyms	Stanford	8–16	50	.51
	Antonyms	Stanford			.51
	Plurals-quantifiers	Stanford			.53
Padden and Ramsey (this volume)	Sentence order	Stanford	9–15	31	.76
	Verb agreement	Stanford			.51
	Sentence imitation	Stanford			46
	Fingerspelled words in sentences	Stanford			.43
	Initialized signs in sentences	Stanford			.80

Note. ASL = American Sign Language.

236

portant educational concern has been the proposition that ASL knowledge would impede reading development in deaf students because ASL and written English are two different languages; hence, students would experience linguistic interference from their primary language in learning to read a second language. Note that this hypothesis predicts a negative correlation between ASL and reading development. As Table 12.1 shows, all the findings are in the opposite direction: ASL and reading development are positively correlated.

What ASL structures were measured that led to these findings? Hoffmeister (chap. 9, this volume) examined understanding of synonyms and antonyms not found in English or MCE. Knowledge of such ASL structures would reflect students' development of the ASL lexical-semantic system. The same is true of the ASL plural and quantifier markers he examined. Padden and Ramsey (chap. 10, this volume) examined understanding of sign order in ASL sentences and ASL verb agreement. Knowledge of these ASL structures would reflect students' development of the ASL morphosyntactic system. Both the Padden and Ramsey (chap. 10, this volume) and Strong and Prinz (chap. 8, this volume; 1997) studies examined understanding of ASL classifier structures. Knowledge of classifiers would reflect the students' development of complex predicate structures in ASL. The same is true of the understanding of ASL calendar and spatial–mapping constructions that Strong and Prinz (1997) also assessed.

Psycholinguistic Tasks. Next we ask what the tasks used in these studies tell us about ASL development and its relation to reading. It is noteworthy that the tasks used in these studies vary with respect to the underlying psycholinguistic processes required of the students to perform them. The fact that the correlations were similar in magnitude across this wide array of tasks again underscores the reliability of these findings.

The experimental tasks encompassed both comprehension and production of specific ASL structures, as well as ASL at the word, clause, sentence, and narrative levels separately in some studies and altogether in other studies. For example, Hoffmeister (chap. 9, this volume) primarily used picture-identification tasks. Here, comprehension was tapped without recourse to linguistic production and with minimal reliance on memory. Rather, the student needed only to recognize word meanings. Strong and Prinz (chap. 8, this volume; 1997) used both the simple task of picture identification and the more complex task of answering questions about an ASL story and producing a narrative in sign.

Padden and Ramsey's (chap. 10, this volume) tasks tap an especially wide variety of psycholinguistic processes. Some of their tasks used simple picture identification whereas other tasks required in-depth sentence processing in addition to analysis of surface form and linguistic rules linking

ASL and English. The sentence-imitation task required multiple psycholinguistic processes including sentence comprehension, memory, and reconstruction. Their sentence tasks requiring identification of fingerspelled
words and initialized signs within ASL sentences probably represent the
most difficult of all the tasks used in these studies.

What was required in the initialized signs task? Here, the ASL sentence
had to be comprehended and, in addition, its lexical surface form had to
be retained in memory. Next, the lexical item containing a handshape
representative of a particular relation between written English and MCE
(and ASL) had to be identified. Padden and Ramsey (chap. 10, this volume)
noted that this was a particularly difficult task for the students. This type
of task represents a dual task paradigm commonly used in reading research,
as previously explained. The task requires the ability to comprehend the
sentence and simultaneously focus on sophisticated knowledge of ASL
sublexical formation rules and their relation to written English word forms
for a small subset of the ASL lexicon.

Finally, Padden and Ramsey's (chap. 10, this volume) ASL sentence task
requiring identification of fingerspelled words given within signed sentences is akin to a cloze procedure. Fingerspelling recognition within sentence contexts presumably reflects the ability to use linguisitic context to
help predict fingerspelled words. No doubt this task tapped both knowledge
of fingerspelled and English word forms as well as the degree to which
ASL sentences are understood. This type of task may be akin to a dual
task paradigm because it requires sentence comprehension in addition to
subsequent lexical selection and memory based on both the surface form
of the comprehended sentence and rules relating signed and spoken language via fingerspelling.

Hence, we see that these studies assessed a wide array of ASL linguistic
structures tapping a wide array of psycholinguistic and cognitive processes.
Despite this diversity, the resulting correlations are similar in magnitude
and in the same direction, as Table 12.1 shows. Simple psycholinguistic
tasks involving simple ASL structures yielded correlations similar to very
complex tasks involving whole sentences or entire narratives. The similar
results across these tasks and studies shows that the findings are reliable.
ASL development is associated with reading development in students for
whom signed language is a primary language.

The nature of correlation is such that we do not know from these studies
what factor is causing this relationship. Both ASL knowledge and reading
skill increase in the same positive direction. The correlation is both significant and consistent in magnitude across four independent studies using
different ASL linguistic structures and a variety of psycholinguistic tasks.
This leads to the next important research question and concerns the nature
of the relation between ASL and reading. It is improbable that ASL de-

velopment alone is responsible for the development of reading in deaf students. We assume this because spoken language development alone is insufficient for the development of reading in children who hear normally, as many researchers and educators have long pointed out. With few exceptions, children must be taught to read. In the following section, we consider the possible relation between ASL and reading development from a theoretical perspective.

MODELS AND MEASURES OF READING DEVELOPMENT

With the ample demonstration of a strong and positive correlation between ASL knowledge and reading measures provided by the chapters in this book, our task is now to try to explain how this is possible. The case of a deaf child whose primary language is ASL and who is learning to read English is a form of bilingualism for which there is no parallel. These deaf children use a language that has no written form.[1] This fact alone is not unique; there are many languages in the world that do not have a written form. But when deaf children enter school, they need to learn to read and write a language that they cannot hear and do not know well, if at all. This unique aspect differentiates deaf children from hearing bilingual children on two fronts.

Many children arrive at school without any literacy skills in their first language and need to learn to read and write in a second language, for example, English children in French immersion in Canada and Spanish speaking children in the United States. Typically, however, the young English-speaking child learning to read and write in French and the young Spanish-speaking child learning to read and write in English both have auditory access to the language they are trying to learn to read. This is not the case for the deaf child. A second barrier to learning in general, and learning to read in particular, is that many deaf children often do not come to school with a complete and fluent first language with which to learn a second. As Morford and Mayberry (chap. 7, this volume) discuss, the unique circumstances of signed language acquisition of most deaf children, that is, not from birth and not from native adult users of the language, have many consequences for general language development (Mayberry, 1994; Mayberry & Eichen, 1991). These consequences have

---

[1]We acknowledge that there are a number of writing systems for signed languages (for a review, see Miller, 1994). But the point here is that there is no universally accepted orthography that is used in classrooms or home environments analagous to written English, French, Spanish, and so forth.

been shown to apply to learning a second language as well as a first (May-berry, 1993; Mayberry & Lock, 1998).

With this unique picture of the average deaf signing child who is faced with the task of learning to read, the question becomes whether there are any models of reading development that can accommodate this novel situation. The short answer, we believe, is no. What we need is a model of reading development that will specifically address the unique and com-plex situation of the deaf signing child learning to read. Why is having a specific model necessary? At the risk of venturing into the acrimonious debate about reading instruction, we believe that having a specific model of how deaf signing children learn to read can both guide future research and allow us to develop more appropriate methods of instruction. How, then, can we begin the process of developing a specific model?

The Linguistic Interdependence Theory

The first step is to find a model of the reading process that can provide a starting point to investigate the unique situation of the deaf signing child learning to read. The Linguistic Interdependence Theory (e.g., Cummins, 1989; Cummins, 1991; Cummins & Swain, 1986) was proposed as a model for the bilingual education—ASL and written English—of deaf students (e.g., Hoffmeister, chap. 9, this volume; Strong & Prinz, chap. 8, this volume). The basic tenet of this theory is referred to as the common underlying proficiency (CUP) model of bilingual proficiency (Cummins & Swain, 1986). This is the concept that "the literacy-related aspects of a bilingual's proficiency in L1 and L2 are common or interdependent across languages" (p. 82). The primary implication of this concept is that expe-rience, at home or in the general community, with either language will lead to increased competence underlying both languages (p. 82). As Cum-mins and Swain argued, this increased competence transfers between lan-guages.

The CUP model of bilingualism is in contrast to the separate underlying proficiency model (SUP), which is based on the concept that first and second language proficiency are completely separate. The primary implication of this model would be that experience with a first language does not transfer or enhance the second language (p. 81). In other words, if a student is weak in the second language, then what is needed is more second language, not more first language. Even though the SUP model has much intuitive strength, as Cummins and Swain (1986) stated, there is little empirical support for it. Instead, Cummins and his colleagues (Cummins, 1989, 1991; Cummins & Swain, 1986) reviewed ample evidence showing that there is indeed an interdependence, or common underlying proficiency, between first and second language for hearing bilingual readers.

The direct applicability of this model to deaf signing readers has been a matter of debate, however. Mayer and Wells (1996) provided a thorough and strong critique of the use of the model for this population. The main thrust of their critique is that reading cannot be learned directly through the use of ASL without any intermediate link because of the "nonequivalence" between ASL and English. That is, they stressed the fact that there is no written form of ASL and deaf children generally lack access to oral English. Because of this nonequivalence, Mayer and Wells argued that the Linguistic Interdependence Theory cannot be applied to the situation of deaf signing children learning to read.

However, the strong and positive correlations between reading and ASL reported in the chapters of this book unquestionably provide beginning empirical support for the Linguistic Interdependence Theory of bilingual education and can be interpreted from that framework. Yet, there are still large gaps in our knowledge base about the exact process of the acquisition of reading skills in deaf signers that need to be worked out. This kind of question might best be answered by structured equation modeling or path analysis because there may not be a direct causal relation between ASL knowledge and reading but rather a facilitating effect. In the meantime, we next describe an alternative model of reading, the "simple view," that we believe can be used as a starting point. The simple view of reading provides an explanation for the successful reading of some deaf signing children and explains why so many deaf students have reading difficulty as well.

The Simple View of Reading

A conceptualization of the reading development process that we think can provide a basis for developing a model of reading for deaf signing children is referred to as the simple view of reading (Hoover & Gough, 1990; Juel, 1988; Juel, Griffith, & Gough, 1986; Tunmer & Hoover, 1992). This model was validated and further supported by Carver (1998). Although the simple view was tested on data from hearing bilingual beginning readers, it is not specifically a model of bilingual reading. Nevertheless, it provides a straightforward and yet complete view of the reading development process. Moreover, given the complex circumstances of signed language development for deaf children, the simpler the reading model, the easier it will be to develop explanations and testable hypotheses in future research.

The basic tenet of the simple view is that reading comprehension is made up of just two components: decoding and linguistic comprehension. Hoover and Gough (1990) explained that the simple view of reading is in contrast to a long history in experimental psychology of the notion that reading is complex. As they described, many of the higher mental operations ascribed to the complex view of reading—such as problem solving, reasoning, thinking, evaluating, or conceptual understanding—can be accomplished by people who cannot read. These activities are certainly a part of linguistic comprehension, and are indeed complex, but they are not specific to reading (p. 128). Characterizing reading from this perspective does not deny that reading is complex, rather the complexity is confined to just these two components: linguistic comprehension and decoding (p. 128).

Hoover and Gough (1990) provided the following definitions of these two components. Comprehension is "the ability to take lexical information (i.e., semantic information at the word level) and derive sentence and discourse interpretation" (p. 131). Linguistic comprehension measures must assess the ability to comprehend language, and this is often done with comprehension questions given after listening to a narrative. Reading comprehension, on the other hand, is essentially the same process and must be measured in the same way, only with print material instead of spoken language (p. 131). What separates linguistic comprehension from reading comprehension, then, is decoding, which these authors defined as "the ability to rapidly derive a representation from printed input that allows access to the appropriate entry in the mental lexicon, and thus, the retrieval of semantic information at the word level" (p. 130).

Two primary claims can be made from the simple view about successful reading comprehension as Hoover and Gough (1990) suggested. The first claim is that both components are equally important. Reading comprehension cannot be reduced to just decoding, because a full set of linguistic skills is necessary too. The second claim is that both components are necessary and that neither is sufficient alone. In other words, just knowing the language is insufficient for reading comprehension to develop; decoding ability is also required. Learning this aspect of reading is not natural and must be taught, as mentioned previously (p. 128).

Evidence for this view, as Hoover and Gough (1990) summarized, is research that demonstrates the separability of decoding and linguistic comprehension. For example, two extreme types of reading problems were described by Gough and Tunmer (1986). Dyslexic children have appropriate linguistic comprehension (listening skills) but impaired decoding abilities. In contrast, hyperlexic children have appropriate decoding or word recognition skills but impaired linguistic (listening) comprehension, although the incidence of hyperlexia is much lower than dyslexia in the hearing population.

Evidence also comes from correlation work investigating the relation between decoding and linguistic comprehension and the association of these two skills with reading comprehension. Hoover and Gough (1990) summarized these findings as follows. For beginning readers, decoding and linguistic comprehension are unrelated, but decoding has a much stronger association with reading comprehension than linguistic comprehension (p. 128). For later grades, decoding and linguistic comprehension are moderately correlated with each other, but linguistic comprehension has a much stronger association with reading comprehension than decoding (p. 129). Hoover and Gough also summarized the research findings using more complex designs than correlation, for instance, multiple regression and path analysis, which demonstrated a similar relation.

Whereas this evidence shows that decoding and linguistic comprehension are separable and significantly related to reading comprehension, it does not explain how. Hoover and Gough (1990) proposed that the two components are related to reading comprehension in a "multiplicative" relation, $R = D \times L$, where R stands for reading comprehension, D stands for decoding, and L stands for linguistic comprehension (p. 132). This type of relation is in contrast to an additive relation (e.g., $R = D + L$), which is informative and can account for a significant amount of variance but does not capture the conditional nature of the relation. As Tunmer and Hoover (1992) explained, "the effect of either skill on reading ability depends on the reader's level of competence in the other skill." (p. 179).

The multiplicative relation also explains the claim of necessity and nonsufficiency. In other words, because both components are necessary and neither is sufficient alone, reading skill will not progress if either skill is nil (Hoover & Gough, 1990, p. 132). A numerical example helps to illustrate this concept. Suppose skills in decoding and linguistic comprehension vary from 0 (*no skill*) to 1.0 (*perfect skill*). Then, if decoding skills are assessed at .5 and linguistic comprehension is assessed at 1.0, reading comprehension is only .5. Hence, reading comprehension is limited by the level of decoding skills. In the opposite scenario, if linguistic comprehension were assessed to be .5 and decoding skills assessed to be 1.0, reading comprehension would be limited by the level of linguistic comprehension.

The conditional nature of decoding and linguistic comprehension carries with it important implications for reading instruction and a definition of literacy, as Hoover and Gough (1990) explained. For reading instruction, the most important implication is that reading comprehension will not improve with instruction in only one area, that is, only decoding or only linguistic comprehension. Instruction is necessary in both components for reading comprehension to improve (p. 151). Hoover and Gough proposed that the definition of literacy implied by the simple view of reading (confined here to reading comprehension) is that literacy is the difference between linguistic comprehension and reading comprehension. More specifically, if there is no mismatch between what a person understands in face-to-face communication and what a person understands in written communication, then that person can be considered literate. If there is a mismatch between these two modes, then the person would be considered illiterate (p. 155).

THE SIMPLE VIEW OF READING
AND SIGNED LANGUAGE

How does the simple view of reading provide a framework for understanding the relation between signed language skills and reading skills for deaf readers? We propose that the simple view comes closer than any other model to explaining reading development in deaf children because of the strong role given to linguistic comprehension in reading comprehension. We next consider the linguistic comprehension component of the model in light of the ASL studies summarized here. Following this, we consider how the decoding component may apply to deaf students' reading development.

The Linguistic Comprehension Component

Leaving aside for the moment the unique bilingual situation of deaf children, we now ask whether the simple view of reading applies to students whose primary language is sign. The simple view of reading predicts that ASL comprehension will correlate with reading comprehension, although it is important to note that the Linguistic Interdependence Theory discussed earlier makes the same prediction. When researchers carefully measured the ASL skills of deaf students, they found positive correlations with reading comprehension as the model predicts. Moreover, when researchers carefully controlled for the factors associated with successful signed language acquisition in deaf students, positive correlations were again found with reading comprehension. Factors such as having early ASL input, an early age of detection of hearing loss, and multiple forms of ASL input outside the classroom all determine the age at which the deaf child acquires signed language and the richness of linguistic input the child receives throughout childhood. Previous research showed that these factors all significantly affect the long-range outcome of signed language acquisition (Mayberry, 1994; Mayberry & Eichen, 1991; Morford & Mayberry, chap. 7, this volume).

ASL and Spoken English Data. How do the ASL data fit the simple view of reading in comparison to spoken English data? In a study of 210 bilingual Spanish-English children, Hoover and Gough (1990) reported that the correlation between listening and reading comprehension in English was $r = .46$ for Grade 1 and $r = .71$, .80, and .87 for Grades 2, 3, and 4, respectively. Summarizing the findings from a number of other studies, these researchers reported that listening comprehension accounted for approximately 35% of the variance in reading comprehension in the early grades and 65% of the variance in the older grades.

Turning to the signed language data, the correlations between ASL and reading comprehension ranged from $r = .43$ to $.80$ with a mean of $.52$ (excluding the nonsignificant finding of Moores et al., 1987), as shown in Table 12.1.[2] ASL performance accounted for approximately 27% of the variance in the reading scores of the 274 deaf students tested in the studies summarized here.[3] Thus, ASL skills would appear to account for a similar amount of variance in these deaf students compared to hearing students, but only if we assume that the deaf students were beginning readers. Because the studies summarized here did not report reading levels and correlations between ASL skill as a function of reading level, it is impossible to interpret the comparison. Moreover, the comparison between hearing and deaf students is further confounded by differences in language measurement and student grouping. It is instructive to consider these differences.

Level of Comprehension Measures. Research testing the validity of the simple view of reading assessed reading and listening comprehension in hearing students with analogous comprehension measures, as in story comprehension. The majority of ASL studies summarized here used different measures of ASL and reading skills, as previously described. Mayberry et al. (1989; 1999) did use analogous measures in ASL and reading comprehension at both the sentence and story levels. The correlations between ASL story comprehension and the Stanford reading score and print story comprehension were appreciably higher ($r = .63$ and $.69$, respectively) than the correlations between ASL sentence span and the Stanford reading score and print story comprehension ($r = .49$ for both).

ASL Narrative Skills. Because the simple view of reading postulates that reading and language comprehension tap similar psycholinguistic and cognitive processes (beyond word recognition), it follows that ASL story comprehension should correlate better with reading comprehension than ASL sentence comprehension. Numerous complex skills underlie narrative comprehension on a face-to-face basis and the model postulates that these

---

[2]According to Padden and Ramsey (chap. 10, this volume), the two highest correlations are questionable. The ASL sentence-order task also correlated highly with the math computation subtest of the Stanford, whereas the other measures did not, suggesting that some skill other than a linguistic one is tapped by this task. The initialized signs (in sentences) task, with the highest correlation of .80, was noted by Padden and Ramsey to be extremely difficult for the students.

[3]Note that the Strong and Prinz (1997, chap. 8, this volume) correlation is based on composite scores for ASL and English that encompass both comprehension and production.

skills also underlie the comprehension of written text. This is not to say that the skills that underlie sentence comprehension on a face-to-face basis are unimportant to reading (e.g., lexical and morphosyntactic knowledge); obviously they are very important. Rather, many additional skills above and beyond sentence level skills are also required.

The Mather and Thibeault Study. Complex narrative skills that are not tapped in sentence comprehension are well illustrated by Mather and Thibeault (chap. 11, this volume), who describe some of the complex skills that underlie translation of ASL narratives from written stories. These skills include, among a host of others, the ability to distinguish reported speech from direct speech and who is speaking to whom about what happened when. Clearly, story comprehension entails a complex tapestry of psycho-linguistic and cognitive skills that extend well beyond the ability to decipher the structure of individual sentences. World knowledge, previous experience, reasoning skills, and linguistic expertise all interrelate in story comprehension. Mather and Thibeault demonstrate the enormity of the story comprehension and production tasks in sign as well as in written text. Their detailed descriptions of how teachers translate written stories into either ASL or MCE for their deaf students show how success or failure in doing so is contingent on knowledge of the relations between narrative and sentence structure as conveyed via grammatical structure and topographical space in ASL. A better understanding of narrative structure in ASL can potentially illuminate the reading difficulties of some deaf children. Indeed, some deaf children may have limited experience with discourse beyond a rudimentary level in any language as a consequence of impoverished opportunities for discourse exchanges with adults and peers; an inability to comprehend narration on a face-to-face basis may contribute significantly to their reading difficulties.

ASL Versus MCE Comprehension. In addition to the type of measurement used to assess language and reading comprehension, it is also important to consider the type of language used by the student in face-to-face communication. The studies summarized here all assessed ASL skills. This was essential, not only because this had never before been done, but also because ASL skill had been frequently hypothesized to impede reading development, as Hoffmeister (chap. 9, this volume) explained. The studies summarized here clearly demonstrate that this hypothesis is false. However, by exclusively measuring ASL skills, researchers risk underestimating the face-to-face language comprehension skills of many deaf students because their skill in English-based sign (as in MCE) or spoken English will be missed. Deaf students who have deaf parents or attend schools with ASL-based instructional practice would be expected to know ASL. Many other students without such linguistic experiences would not be expected to know ASL, because they are primarily exposed to some type of English-based sign along with spoken English and not ASL (although see Hoffmeister, chap. 9, this volume, for an alternative view on this question).

Two important issues arise when we apply the simple view of reading to deaf students with respect to the linguistic component of the model. First, let us assume that the most important aspect of the model's linguistic component is the overall sophistication of linguistic comprehension, not knowledge of particular syntactic structures in signed language. If this assumption were correct, it would mean that the degree to which deaf students can comprehend narration in sign should correlate best with their reading comprehension; the particular type of sign the deaf student comprehends would not be a factor.

There are two implications of this assumption. The first implication is that ASL and MCE comprehension should correlate equally well with reading comprehension among deaf students. The corollary implication is that the best linguistic correlate of deaf students' reading comprehension should be their ability to comprehend signed language on a face-to-face basis, regardless of sign type. For some students, this would require measurement of spoken language comprehension as well.

Preliminary evidence suggests that this assumption is correct, that the linguistic component of the simple view of reading model is blind to the particular type of sign that deaf students know. Of the studies summarized here, three measured MCE skill in addition to ASL. As Table 12.2 shows, the correlations between MCE skill and reading comprehension ranged from $r = .30$ to $.68$, with a mean of $r = .51$. For the 228 deaf students tested (98 of whom participated in the ASL studies), MCE skill accounted for 25% of the variance in reading skill. These findings are nearly identical to the ASL findings, as discussed earlier. Thus, there is evidence, albeit limited, that the particular type of sign the deaf student knows is irrelevant to the linguistic component of the simple view of reading. Rather, the sophistication of linguistic discourse may be crucial. More research is needed to investigate this controversial issue.

Inspection of the correlations between MCE skill and reading comprehension shown in Table 12.2 substantiates the necessity of assessing analogous levels in signed language and reading comprehension to apply the simple view of reading to the situation of deaf students. As was the case for the ASL measures, story-level MCE measures of comprehension correlated better with reading story comprehension and performance on the Stanford reading comprehension subtest than did measures of MCE at the sentence level or composite scores consisting of several tests.

TABLE 12 2
Correlations Between MCE and Reading Measures: Summary of Research Studies

Research Study	MCE Measure	Reading Measure	Age	N	r
Moores et al. (1987, 1990)	Language proficiency interview	Composite of five standardized tests	16–18	130	.30
Mayberry et al. (1989, 1994, 1999)	Story comprehension	Story comprehension	7–15	48	.67
	Story comprehension	Stanford			.68
Hoffmeister (this volume)	Sentence comprehension	Stanford	8–16	50	.38

Note MCE = Manually Coded English

Grouping Variables Required to Validate the Model. Finally, there are several differences between the studies of hearing students used to validate the simple view of reading and the studies of deaf students summarized here (which were not designed to test this specific model). Research with hearing students testing the simple view grouped students by age and reading grade level. Doing so led to the finding that listening and reading comprehension are more highly correlated in skilled readers than in beginning readers. This presumably reflects the contribution of decoding to beginning reading, as previously discussed. To ascertain whether the same differential relation holds between signed language comprehension and decoding skills for deaf readers, it would be necessary to group them by reading level and test their word-decoding skills as well, as we discuss later.

The studies summarized here tested the ASL and reading skills of deaf students who represented a wide range of ages, ASL skills, and presumably, reading levels. If the postulated relation between the two components of the simple view—linguistic comprehension and decoding—explain the reading skills of deaf students, then conflating beginning and skilled readers into a single group would have the effect of reducing the correlation between ASL and reading comprehension. This would especially be the case if the research sample included a disproportionate number of beginning as opposed to skilled readers. The limited research that grouped deaf students by reading level found few differences between skilled deaf and hearing readers (Yoshinaga-Itano, Snyder, & Mayberry, 1996). Testing this model will thus require researchers to group deaf students by reading level (and perhaps age as well) and measure signed language comprehension and word-decoding skills.

The Decoding Component

The simple view of reading entails a decoding component in addition to the linguistic component. Decoding is defined here as the ability to see a word in print, rapidly access the mental lexicon, and retrieve the appropriate meaning (Hoover & Gough, 1990, p. 130). This general definition and does not take into consideration the complexities of each of those subprocesses, but as a starting point it will suffice.

The Nature of Decoding for the Hearing Reader. Most research investigating decoding in deaf readers is modeled after research with hearing readers. For beginning hearing readers, it is generally acknowledged that access to the mental lexicon is through a phonological representation of the printed word (Adams, 1990). Phonological decoding is thought to be used by the beginning reader until the word has been read enough times for it to be recognized by sight (Ehri, 1992). Exactly how the phonological representation is accessed by beginning hearing readers is still a matter of debate. For example, it could be through knowledge of spelling–sound correspondence (e.g., Ehri, 1992), through rhyme or analogies (e.g., Goswami & Bryant, 1992), or through intrasyllabic information, onset and rimes (Treiman, 1992).

The main point here is that beginning hearing readers need a way to get from the printed word on the page to the meaning of the word already in their heads. Because the mental lexicon of hearing readers is the product of spoken language acquisition, it follows that their mental representation and access route of decoding are phonological in nature, namely, speech-sound based.

The Nature of Decoding for the Deaf Reader—Phonological Decoding. The bulk of research investigating the decoding skills of deaf readers has focused on whether or not they engage in phonological decoding (e.g., Campbell & Burden, 1995; Hanson, 1989, 1991; Hanson & Fowler, 1987; Waters & Doehring, 1990). Because of the central role phonological decoding plays for beginning hearing readers, it is often postulated to play the same central role for deaf readers. Leybaert (1993) provided an extensive review of studies investigating deaf readers' phonological decoding skills in working memory, reading (defined as word recognition), spelling, and explicit knowledge of phonological structure at the word level. Her review included studies of signers and nonsigners, skilled and beginning readers, and research conducted in North America and Europe. One of her conclusions was that, although there was evidence for phonological decoding in both signers and nonsigners, it varies widely. This variability was related to factors such as degree of hearing loss, age, reading level, and method of communication (p. 278). As Leybaert reported, these factors were not always controlled for in a systematic way in all studies.

It is outside the scope of this chapter to examine the studies of phonological decoding in deaf readers. However, it is important to acknowledge that deaf signing children may have access to phonological information from various avenues, such as in residual hearing, lipreading, or cued speech (Leybaert, 1993), which can also contribute to their decoding abilities. This would be in addition to their signed language knowledge, assuming that this knowledge is complete. Another possibility that has not been investigated is that deaf children who become skilled readers acquire knowledge of the phonological system represented by orthography as a consequence of reading. Hence, they would show evidence of using phonological decoding only after they become skilled readers but not when they are beginning readers.

Decoding and the Sign Lexicon. When decoding is defined as the skill of rapidly accessing the mental lexicon to retrieve meaning, it becomes clear that this process must be unique for deaf students, whose primary language is signed, in comparison to hearing students. Because the mental lexicon of these students consists of signs, their mental representations by logical extension would be sign based and not speech based (Mayberry, 1995), at least in the beginning stages of reading, although this view is controversial. Little is currently known about how beginning deaf readers whose primary language is signed decode printed words. Understanding how the beginning deaf reader does so is necessary if we are to apply the simple view or any other model of reading to deaf readers. Such information is also crucial to the task of teaching deaf students who sign to read well.

Research Controls. Before considering the research on decoding in deaf readers, it is helpful to consider what kind of research designs are required to apply the simple view of reading to deaf students with respect to the decoding component of the model. First, it would be necessary to investigate decoding skills in deaf children whose acquisition of signed language is native-like; that is, children who have acquired signed language from a very early age in rich linguistic environments. Doing so eliminates the confound of the deleterious effects of underdeveloped language skills on decoding skills. Hearing children come to the decoding task knowing literally thousands of words and having already acquired the bulk of the morphosyntactic rules of their native language. For this kind of research to succeed, it is important that the deaf students tested be in an analogous position to the hearing child with regard to signed language acquisition. Obviously, decoding skills are of no help to a child who has scant sign lexicon to which printed words can be linked. Finally, the question of how deaf students decode would be the same regardless of whether the child's primary exposure to sign has been in ASL or English-based sign such as MCE. Decoding skill concerns the level of printed word and the sublexical patterning of lexical units in the primary language, which would be highly overlapping in the case of ASL and MCE.

In addition to controlling for level of signed language acquisition, it would be necessary to investigate decoding skills in deaf children who are beginning readers as opposed to skilled ones. The role of decoding skills in reading changes with increased proficiency among hearing readers (e.g., Hoover & Gough, 1990). The decoding processes of deaf readers with respect to the nature of their lexical mental representations may undergo substantial change with increases in reading skill. This may be due to the possibility of multiple representations in decoding, as we describe next. Transformations in the decoding processes of deaf students can only be discovered if beginning and skilled deaf readers are grouped separately and then investigated. Finally, longitudinal research is required to thoroughly investigate this question. Tracking decoding skills from beginning through skilled reading is necessary if we are to discover possible sources of reading difficulty for deaf students.

The Nature of Decoding in the Deaf Reader. Little is known about whether and how deaf students use decoding strategies derived from mental representations of signed language. In considering this possibility, it is important to note that the term *decoding* is used broadly in the literature to refer to multiple functions during reading. Among others, some of the functions encompassed by the word *decoding* are (a) a prelexical link between the printed letters of a word and the word in the child's head (mental representation) that facilitates retrieval of word meaning (as in figuring out orthographic patterns in order to recognize words that the child already knows in sign or speech); (b) a postlexical, mental notepad to hold in mind meaning that has already been recognized in print (as in working memory); and (c) as a means to pronounce or express and hence keep in mind (overtly or covertly) an unknown word encountered in print until a meaning can be attached to the new word (as in novel word learning via reading).

Whereas the hearing reader is thought to accomplish all these functions during reading via a phonological code derived from speech, it is probable that the deaf reader whose primary language is signed uses different codes to perform each of these functions. Moreover, these multiple codes may change in functional importance as reading develops through increased linguistic knowledge and consolidation of that knowledge. In other words, multiple types of codes (representations) may be required for the deaf child to learn to read due to the multiple and complex relationships between written English and ASL. This possibility would help explain the contradictory findings in the literature with respect to how deaf readers who sign decode. Evidence has been found for phonological, sign-based, fingerspelling-based, and grapheme (visual-orthographic)-based decoding. We briefly focus next on the possibilities for sign- and fingerspelling-based decoding, because they are most closely associated with the child's knowledge of signed language.

Sign-Based Decoding. There is some evidence that skilled, adult deaf readers who sign use sign-based decoding in reading. In a series of carefully controlled studies, Treiman and Hirsh-Pasek (1983) found no evidence for articulatory (i.e., phonological) or fingerspelling codes in deaf adults' reading of words and sentences. They did find evidence for what they called sign-based recoding in most of the skilled deaf readers they tested. However, they further observed that the most highly skilled deaf readers all appeared to recognize words by sight and use no decoding. Their findings hint at the possibility that decoding strategies may change in deaf readers as reading skill increases, perhaps going from sign-based to sight reading.

Sign-based decoding would facilitate a postlexical, working memory function by providing a mental code to remember recognized word meanings (Mayberry, 1995). However, because there is very little representation of sign structure in English orthography, sign-based decoding could not fully serve the prelexical function of linking the orthographic patterns of printed words to the sign lexicon in the student's mind.

Fingerspelling-Based Decoding. Another proposed means of decoding for deaf students who sign lies in fingerspelling. Fingerspelling has long been proposed as a candidate for decoding due to its one-to-one relation with the letters of the alphabet. As Padden (1991) explained, fingerspelling is an important part of ASL. However, if we assume that the mental lexicon of the beginning deaf reader who signs is composed of signs, because this is the language form that the child knows, then fingerspelling cannot serve the same functions for the deaf reader that phonological decoding serves for the hearing reader. There is some overlap in the handshapes of many signs and many fingerspelled forms, as previously explained, but handshape is only one part of the sublexical structure of signs, as Marentette and Mayberry (chap. 5, this volume) describe.

There is some evidence that fingerspelling may play a role in the pronunciation–expressive function of decoding, as in being able to "name" unfamiliar word forms for which the student does not yet know the meaning. Hirsh-Pasek (1987) found that deaf students were more successful at learning unfamiliar printed words when they were encouraged to fingerspell them than when they read the words without fingerspelling them.

One study investigated the role of sign and fingerspelling in deaf beginning and skilled readers. Ross (1992) found evidence that beginning deaf readers discover and use rule-governed relations between orthographic patterning and the sublexical structure of sign but that more skilled readers do not use these links. Moreover, she found that fingerspelling was used by both beginning and more skilled readers to express words they did not know.

The ASL lexicon has multiple relations to the lexicon of written English, as is the case between any two languages. Some ASL signs have simple translation equivalents in written English, as in DOG → "dog".[4] Some ASL signs have simple translation equivalents that, in addition, contain handshapes corresponding to the initial letter of the written English word, as in COUSIN → "cousin." Here, the sign contains the "C" handshape of fingerspelling corresponding to the first letter of the written word (called *initialization*). However, many ASL signs and written English words have no direct relations but instead require multiple signs, words, or both to construct equivalent meanings across the two languages.

Ross (1992) investigated whether these relations predicted deaf signing students' word recognition. She developed four sets of written English words, each having a particular relation to ASL signs. One set consisted of English words with simple ASL translation equivalents; one consisted of words with initialized sign translation equivalents; and one set consisted of words with signs that were foils for the initialized signs (i.e., ASL signs with a handshape that is a fingerspelled letter but a different one from the initial letter of the written word, e.g., as in the sign INDIAN, which uses an "F" handshape). The last set consisted of words with indirect (i.e., multiple) sign translations.

Ross (1992) asked deaf students to complete two tasks. One task was lexical decision, where the student saw word-length stimuli on a computer screen; half the stimuli were English words and half were pseudowords; the student decided whether the stimulus was a real word or not. In a second, "naming–pronunciation" task, the student saw the stimulus words from the previous experiment on a computer screen and told the examiner what the word was via sign or fingerspelling (i.e., "pronounced it in sign").

---

[4]Capitalized words represent ASL signs and underlined letters represent the handshape parameter of these signs.

The decision of whether to sign or fingerspell any given stimulus was left to the student. Ross tested 30 deaf students whose primary language was signed and whose classroom instruction was in English-based sign within a Total Communication methodology. For her analyses, she grouped the students two ways, first by age (8–9, 10–11, and 12–14) and second by reading level (beginning readers, Grade 1.6 to 2.9; and more skilled readers, Grade 3.0 to 8.4).

The variety of responses the students gave on the naming–pronunciation task revealed the range of strategies deaf students devise to link written words with the signed language in their minds. In response to the written words, the students would often produce a single sign, an ASL classifier construction, or, in a few cases, a gesture. Other times the students produced sequences. They would first fingerspell and then sign a word or vice versa. They would produce a two-sign phrase or fingerspell the first letter of the written word and then produce a sign. A few students would speak the word and then fingerspell it.

In general, when the students produced signs or ASL classifier constructions for a stimulus word on the naming–pronunciation task, they had correctly recognized it on the previous lexical decision task. By contrast, when they fingerspelled a word, they typically had not recognized it on the previous task. In the latter case, they often also misspelled the word when fingerspelling it. The fingerspelling accuracy of the more skilled readers was much greater than the beginning ones. These findings provide preliminary evidence that fingerspelling plays a specific pronunciation–expressive function for deaf students for words they do not yet know and that this skill improves as a consequence of learning to read rather than vice versa.

Ross (1992) also found strong effects for the various sign–word relations that characterize the ASL and English lexicons. The two youngest groups (and the beginning readers) were more accurate at recognizing words with direct than indirect sign translations; the youngest students (and beginning readers) also recognized words with initialized signs most accurately and required more time to recognize the words with initialized sign foils. The more skilled readers recognized many more words and took less time to do so, and showed no initialized sign effects. In addition, the more skilled readers could more accurately tell the difference between "possible" nonwords from "impossible" nonwords. Clearly, the more skilled readers had developed decoding skills and an awareness of English orthographic patterns and how they fit with signs.

Ross's (1992) findings demonstrate that the beginning deaf reader whose primary language is signed actively seeks principled relations between the sublexical structure of the words of his or her primary language, signed language, and the written form of words on the page. By contrast, more skilled deaf readers have developed an ability to recognize printed words without direct links to their mental sign lexicon. Finally, Ross's findings show that decoding contributes to reading skill in deaf students who sign, as the simple view predicts. Missing from this study, however, is a simultaneous measure of narrative comprehension in signed language that is required to test the validity of the model for deaf readers.

Padden and Ramsey's (chap. 10, this volume) observations of teachers provides another source of evidence that multiple codes are required for the various functions of decoding by deaf readers. The deaf teachers they observed were much more likely than the hearing teachers to link words written on the blackboard with both sign and fingerspelling, going back and forth between these lexical representations, a procedure they called *chaining*. We suggest that this pedagogical procedure arises from the deaf teachers' intuitions about the complex relations of sign, fingerspelling, and print that need to be developed in the minds of deaf students if they are to become skilled readers. Much more observational and empirical work of this sort is required to understand and hence improve instruction in decoding for deaf students.

In sum, we attempted to relate the research on signed language and reading to a theoretical model—the simple view of reading. We propose that this model provides a useful framework for thinking about and discovering the complexities that underlie reading development in deaf children whose primary language is signed. The research studies included in this volume investigated the first component of the model—the relation between language comprehension and reading—but not the second component—decoding skills. Previous research has revealed intriguing possibilities as to how deaf children who sign might decode, but no research to date has tested both language comprehension and decoding skills simultaneously in deaf children. Doing so clearly requires that many variables be taken into consideration and controlled to investigate this unique form of bilingualism.

Adequate testing of the simple view requires that the signed language comprehension skills of deaf students be measured in the same fashion as their reading comprehension and that their decoding skills also be assessed. In addition, it is necessary that deaf students be grouped by reading level, beginning versus skilled, to determine whether the relation between linguistic comprehension and decoding is multiplicative in deaf students as their reading develops, as is the case for hearing readers. Finally, it is essential that deaf students whose knowledge of ASL is natively acquired be included in this research as linguistic controls, to understand what these factors and interrelations look like in deaf children whose signed language acquisition has been as normal as possible vis-à-vis hearing readers.

CONCLUSION

In this chapter, we showed that research studies that have taken into account the signed language skills of deaf students found positive effects of signed language knowledge on reading comprehension. We further explained how these historical, positive findings have been replicated and extended by the thoughtful and creative work of the four studies included in the present volume. We also developed a theoretical framework that applies to current research and provides a basis for future work. We think that the simple view of reading can provide that framework. Moreover, because the model emphasizes linguistic comprehension as well as decoding, it provides a clear explanation for the reading difficulties of many deaf students as well as the reading success of other deaf students.

We identified future research needs and clearly, there is much to be done. Some of the suggestions we made clarify the types of research designs and control variables that are necessary to best explore the unique form of bilingualism of deaf children. We have outlined two separate types of skills that must be addressed by reading research: decoding skills and face-to-face language comprehension. Finally, and perhaps most important, we proposed a way to conceptualize the role of signing in reading acquisition that can guide the discussion and interpretation of research, both past and future, of how reading is acquired through the eyes of deaf children who sign.

ACKNOWLEDGMENTS

Preparation of this chapter and some of the research reported here were supported by grants from the Natural Sciences and Engineering Research Council Canada (171239) and the Social Sciences and Humanities Research Council of Canada (410-98-0803) to R. Mayberry. We thank Jill Morford and Gloria Waters for helpful comments on earlier versions of this chapter.

REFERENCES

Adams, M. J. (1990). *Beginning to read: Thinking and learning about print.* Cambridge, MA: MIT Press.
Allen, T. E. (1986). Patterns of academic achievement among hearing impaired students: 1974 and 1983. In A. N. Schildroth & M. A. Karchmer (Eds.), *Deaf children in America* (pp. 161–206). San Diego, CA: College Hill Press.

Allen, T. E., & Schoem, S. R. (1997, May). *Educating deaf and hard-of-hearing youth: What works best?* Paper presented at the Combined Otolaryngological Spring Meetings of the American Academy of Otolaryngology, Scottsdale, AZ.

Campbell, R., & Burden, V. (1995). Pre-lingual deafness and literacy: A new look at old ideas. In B. D. Gelder & J. Morais (Eds.), *Speech and reading: A comparative approach* (pp. 109–123). East Sussex, England: Lawrence Erlbaum Associates.

Carver, R. P. (1998). Predicting reading level in grades 1 to 6 from listening level and decoding level: Testing theory relevant to the simple view of reading. *Reading and Writing: An Interdisciplinary Journal, 10,* 121–154.

Conrad, R. (1979). *The deaf school child* London: Harper & Row.

Cozby, P. C. (1985). *Methods in behavioral research* (3rd ed.). Palo Alto, CA: Mayfield.

Cummins, J. (1989). A theoretical framework for bilingual special education. *Exceptional Children, 56*(2), 111–119.

Cummins, J. (1991). Interdependence of first- and second-language proficiency in bilingual children. In E. Bialystok (Ed.), *Language processing bilingual children* (pp. 70–89). Cambridge, England: Cambridge University Press.

Cummins, J., & Swain, M. (1986). *Bilingualism in education: Aspects of theory, research and practice.* New York: Longman.

Daneman, M., & Carpenter, P. A. (1980). Individual differences in working memory and reading. *Journal of Verbal Learning and Verbal Behavior, 19,* 450–466.

Daneman, M., & Merikle, P. (1996). Working memory and language comprehension: A meta analysis. *Psychological Bulletin and Research, 3,* 422–433.

Donin, J., Doehring, D. G., & Browns, F. (1991). Text comprehension and reading achievement in orally educated hearing-impaired children. *Discourse Processes, 14,* 307–337.

Ehri, L. C. (1992). Reconceptualizing the development of sight word reading and its relationship to recoding. In P. B. Gough, L. C. Ehri, & R. Treiman (Eds.), *Reading acquisition* (pp. 107–143). Hillsdale, NJ: Lawrence Erlbaum Associates.

Geers, A., & Moog, J. (1989). Factors predictive of the development of literacy in profoundly hearing-impaired adolescence. *Volta Review, 91,* 69–86.

Goetzinger, C. P., & Rousey, C. L. (1959). Educational achievement of deaf children. *American Annals of the Deaf, 104,* 221–231.

Goswami, U., & Bryant, P. (1992). Rhyme, analogy, and children's reading. In P. B. Gough, L. C. Ehri, & R. Treiman (Eds.), *Reading acquisition* (pp. 49–64). Hillsdale, NJ: Lawrence Erlbaum Associates.

Gough, P. B., & Tunmer, W. E. (1986). Decoding, reading and reading disability. *Remedial and Special Education, 7,* 6–10.

Hanson, V. L. (1989). Phonology and reading: Evidence from profoundly deaf readers. In D. Shankweiler & I. Y. Liberman (Eds.), *Phonology and reading disability: Solving the reading puzzle* (pp. 69–89). Ann Arbor: The University of Michigan Press.

Hanson, V. L. (1991). Phonological processing without sound. In S. A. Brady & D. P. Shankweiler (Eds.), *Phonological processes in literacy: A tribute to Isabell Y. Liberman* (pp. 153–161). Hillsdale, NJ: Lawrence Erlbaum Associates.

Hanson, V. L., & Fowler, C. A. (1987). Phonological coding in word reading: Evidence from hearing and deaf readers. *Memory & Cognition, 15*(3), 199–207.

Hirsh-Pasek, K. (1987). The metalinguistics of fingerspelling: An alternative way to increase reading vocabulary in congenitally deaf readers. *Reading Research Quarterly, 22,* 455–474.

Holt, J. A., Traxler, C. B., & Allen, T. E. (1997). *Interpreting the scores. A user's guide to the 9th Edition Stanford Achievement Test for educators of deaf and hard-of-hearing students* (Tech. Rep. 97-1). Washington, DC: Gallaudet University, Gallaudet Research Institute.

Hoover, W. A., & Gough, P. B. (1990). The simple view of reading. *Reading and Writing. An Interdisciplinary Journal, 2,* 127–160.

Israelite, N., Ewoldt, C., & Hoffmeister, R. (1992). *Bilingual/bicultural education for deaf and hard-of-hearing students: A review of the literature of the effects of native sign language on majority language acquisition* Toronto: Ontario Ministry of Education.

Juel, C. (1988). Learning to read and write: A longitudinal study of 54 children from first through fourth grade. *Journal of Educational Psychology, 80,* 437–447.

Juel, C., Griffith, P. L , & Gough, P. B. (1986). Acquisition of literacy: A longitudinal study of children in first and second grade. *Journal of Educational Psychology, 78,* 243–255.

Klima, E. S., & Bellugi, U. (1979) *The signs of language.* Cambridge, MA: Harvard University Press.

Leybaert, J. (1993). Reading in the deaf. The roles of phonological codes. In M. Marschark & D. Clarke (Eds.), *Psychological perspectives in deafness* (pp. 269–309) Hillsdale, NJ. Lawrence Erlbaum Associates.

Mayberry, R. (1989, April). *Deaf children's reading comprehension in relation to sign language structure and input.* Paper presented at the Society for Research in Child Development, Kansas City.

Mayberry, R. I. (1992) The cognitive development of deaf children· Recent insights. In S. J. Segalowitz & I. Rapin (Eds.), *Handbook of neuropsychology, Vol. 7 Child neuropsychology* (pp. 51–68). New York: Elsevier.

Mayberry, R I. (1993) First-language acquisition after childhood differs from second-language acquisition: The case of American Sign Language. *Journal of Speech and Hearing Research, 36,* 1258–1270.

Mayberry, R. I. (1994). The importance of childhood to language acquisition: Evidence from American Sign Language. In J. C. Goodman & H. C. Nusbaum (Eds.), *The Development of Speech Perception* (pp. 60–89). Cambridge, MA· MIT Press.

Mayberry, R I (1995). Mental phonology and language comprehension, or what does that sign mistake mean? In K. Emmorey & J. S. Reilly (Eds.), *Language, gesture, and space* (pp. 355–370). Hillsdale, NJ: Lawrence Erlbaum Associates.

Mayberry, R. I., & Chamberlain, C. (1994, November). *How ya gonna read da language if ya dun speak it? Reading development in relation to sign language comprehension* Paper presented at the Boston University Conference on Language Development, Boston, MA.

Mayberry, R., Chamberlain, C., Waters, G., & Doehring, D. (1999). *Reading development in relation to signed language input and structure.* Manuscript in preparation.

Mayberry, R. I., & Eichen, E. B. (1991). The long-lasting advantage of learning sign language in childhood: Another look at the critical period for language acquisition. *Journal of Memory and Language, 30,* 486–512.

Mayberry, R. I., & Lock, E (1998, May). *Critical period effects on grammatical processing: Privileged status of the first language* Paper presented at the American Psychological Society Convention, Washington, DC.

Mayberry, R. I., & Waters, G. S. (1991). Children's memory for sign and fingerspelling in relation to production rate and sign language input. In P. Siple & S. Fischer (Eds), *Theoretical issues in sign language research* (Vol. 2: Psychology, pp. 211–229). Chicago: University of Chicago Press.

Mayer, C., & Wells, G. (1996). Can the linguistic interdependence theory support a bilingual-bicultural model of literacy education for deaf students? *Journal of Deaf Studies and Deaf Education, 1,* 93–107.

Miller, C. (1994) A note on notation. *SignPost, 7*(3), 191–202.

Moores, D F. (1996). *Educating the deaf: Psychology, principles, and practices* (4th ed) Boston, MA: Houghton Mifflin.

Moores, D. F., Kluwin, T N., Johnson, R., Cox, P., Blennerhasset, L., Kelly, L., Ewoldt, C., Sweet, C., & Fields, L. (1987). *Factors predictive of literacy in deaf adolescents* (Final Report to National Institute on Neurological and Communicative Disorders and Stroke Project No. NIH-NINCDS-83-19). Washington, DC· NIH.

Moores, D. F., & Sweet, C. (1990). Relationships of English grammar and communicative fluency to reading in deaf adolescents. *Exceptionality, 1,* 97–106.

Padden, C. (1991). The acquisition of fingerspelling by deaf children. In P. Siple & S. Fischer (Eds.), *Theoretical issues in sign language research* (Vol. 2: Psychology, pp. 191–210). Chicago: University of Chicago Press.

Pintner, R. (1916). A measurement of the language ability of deaf children. *Psychological Review, 23,* 413–436.

Pintner, R. (1927). The survey of schools for the deaf-V. *American Annals of the Deaf, 72,* 377–414.

Pintner, R., & Paterson, D. G. (1917). The ability of deaf and hearing children to follow printed directions. *American Annals of the Deaf, 62,* 449–472.

Pintner, R., & Paterson, D. G. (1918). The measurement of language ability and language progress of deaf children. *Volta Review, 20,* 755–765.

Pugh, G. S. (1946). Summaries from "Appraisal of the silent reading abilities of acoustically handicapped children." *American Annals of the Deaf, 91,* 331–349.

Reamer, J. C. (1921). Mental and educational measurements of the deaf. *Psychological Monographs, 132,* 1–129.

Ross, D. S. (1992). *Learning to read with sign language: How beginning deaf readers relate sign language to written words.* Unpublished master's thesis, McGill University, Montreal, Quebec.

Stokoe, W. C., Casterline, C., & Cronebeg, C. (1965). *A dictionary of American Sign Language* Washington, DC: Gallaudet College Press.

Strong, M., & Prinz, P. M. (1997). A study of the relationship between American Sign Language and English literacy. *Journal of Deaf Studies and Deaf Education, 2,* 37–46.

Stuckless, E. R., & Birch, J. W. (1966). The influence of early manual communication on the linguistic development of deaf children. *American Annals of the Deaf, 111,* 452–504.

Treiman, R. (1992). The role of intrasyllabic units in learning to read and spell. In P. B. Gough, L. C. Ehri, & R. Treiman (Eds.), *Reading acquisition* (pp. 65–106). Hillsdale, NJ: Lawrence Erlbaum Associates.

Treiman, R., & Hirsh-Pasek, K. (1983). Silent reading: Insights from second-generation deaf readers. *Cognitive Psychology, 15,* 39–65.

Trybus, R. J., & Karchmer, M. A. (1977). School achievement scores of hearing impaired children: National data on achievement status and growth patterns. *American Annals of the Deaf, 122,* 62–69.

Tunmer, W. E., & Hoover, W. A. (1992). Cognitive and linguistic factors in learning to read. In P. B. Gough, L. E. Ehri, & R. Treiman (Eds.), *Reading acquisition* (pp. 175–214). Hillsdale, NJ: Lawrence Erlbaum Associates.

Vernon, M., & Koh, S (1970) Early manual communication and deaf children's achievement. *American Annals of the Deaf, 115,* 527–536.

Waters, G., & Caplan, D. (1996). The capacity theory of sentence comprehension: A reply to Just and Carpenter. *Psychological Review, 103,* 761–772.

Waters, G. S., & Doehring, D. G. (1990). Reading acquisition in congenitally deaf children who communicate orally: Insights from an analysis of component reading, language and memory skills. In T. Carr & B. Levy (Eds.), *Reading and its development: Component skills approaches* (pp. 323–373). New York: Academic Press.

Yoshinaga-Itano, C., Snyder, L., & Mayberry, R. (1996). Can lexical/semantic skills differentiate deaf or hard-of-hearing readers and nonreaders? *Volta Review, 98,* 39–61.

Author Index

Subject Index

A

Adult-directed sign, 6-13, 30
Age of acquisition, 111-115, 122-125
  alphabetic literacy, 183
  and comprehension, 112
  in first vs. second language, 115
  and language processing, 113
  and phonological development, 123-125
  and production, 112
  and recall, 112
  and second language, 113
  and sentence shadowing, 112
Anatomical constraints on sign formation, 74
Articulators of sign
  distal, 65, 79
  dominance conditions, 72
  proximal, 79
  symmetry conditions, 83
  see also Phonological development
ASL, 191, 201, 202, 214
  acquisition related to MCE, 157
  amount of, 155
  antonyms, 152
  assessment of, 153
  complex narrative skills in, 246
  evaluation, 192
    cohesion, 192
  comprehension of, 149, 156
    ASL vs. MCE, 246-248
  deaf families vs. hearing families, 228
  delayed acquisition of, 112-113, 123

  and English bilingualism, 239
  exposure to, 150
  first vs. second language acquisition of, 115
  input, 146
  knowledge of and age, 154
  knowledge of and parental hearing status, 154
  and manual babble, 18-19
  and memory tasks, 152
  motherese, 6
  plurals, 152
  and positive correlation to reading, 233, 234, 235
  and reading, 145, 157, 158
    associative skills, 167, 176
  reading relation, 136-140, 165-187, 221-256
  related to MCE, 158
  and SAT-M, 174
  sentence structure and MCE, 159
  and spoken English data, 244
  synonyms, 152
ASL, measures of, 134
  classifier comprehension, 135
  classifiers production and comprehension, 233
  emergence of, 227-232
  Fingerspelling Task, 174, 175, 177, 235
  Imitation Task, 172, 174
  Initialized Signs Test, 173, 176, 235
  map direction production and comprehension, 233
  Vocabulary testing in ASL synonyms, antonyms, plurals, 234

269